Forbes®
GUIDE TO THE MARKETS
SECOND EDITION

Forbes®

GUIDE TO THE MARKETS

SECOND EDITION

Becoming a Savvy Investor

Marc M. Groz

WILEY

John Wiley & Sons, Inc.

Published by John Wiley & Sons, Inc., Hoboken, New Jersey.
Published simultaneously in Canada.

For general information on our other products and services or for technical support, please contact our Customer Care Department within the United States at (800) 762-2974, outside the United States at (317) 572-3993 or fax (317) 572-4002.

Wiley also publishes its books in a variety of electronic formats. Some content that appears in print may not be available in electronic books. For more information about Wiley products, visit our web site at www.wiley.com.

Library of Congress Cataloging-in-Publication Data
Groz, Marc M.
    Forbes guide to the markets : becoming a savvy investor / Marc M. Groz. — 2nd ed.
      p. cm.
    Includes index.
    ISBN 978-0-470-46338-3 (pbk.)
      1. Capital market.   2. Stock exchanges.   3. Mutual funds.   4. Bond market.   5. Over-the-counter markets.   I. Title.
  HG4523.G76 2009
  332.63′2—dc22

                                           2009007454

Printed in the United States of America
10 9 8 7 6 5 4 3 2 1

Contents

Acknowledgments

Many people helped in the creation of this new edition. First of all, I would like to thank my editors at Forbes (Vahan Janjigian and Barbara Strauch) and Wiley (Laura Walsh) for all their help and encouragement. I would also like to thank Anastasia Skoybedo and Chris Reich, my research interns at Topos, for their indefatigable fact-checking and service as "Emperor's Wardrobe Consultants" extraordinaire.

In the 10 years that have elapsed since the first edition of this book was published, many investment and other professionals have generously shared their knowledge, helping to shape this new edition. Special mention must go to: Ifty Ahmed, Reuven Brenner, Don Brownstein, Sanjeev Daga, Emanuel Derman, Asami Ishimaru, Tom Kyle, Jon Lukomnik, David McClean, Bill Overgard, Richard Rosenfeld, Jason Ruspini, Neil Strumingher, Michael Trenk, Jan van Eck, and Walt Weissman.

Extra special thanks goes to my wife, Robbin Juris, whose companionship is beyond measure. This book is dedicated first of all to her; it is also dedicated to my parents, who instilled in me a lifelong love of reading and writing; and, last but not least, it is dedicated to my boys: Gabriel, who was an infant during the writing of the first edition and is rapidly becoming an amazing young man; and Zachary, born three days after the attacks of September 11, 2001, an amazing kid without whom I might not be here at all.

Note to the Reader

The world of financial markets has its own special language. To help familiarize you with this language, we will highlight key financial market words and phrases in bold type, as they are discussed. Many of these terms are defined in the text, or in brief "side bar definitions" along the side of the page. For ease of reference, or to refresh your memory about what something means, the glossary at the end of the book contains all of the definitions provided in the text.

About the Author

Marc Groz is a leading authority on financial markets. He has developed investment strategies for two top-ranked investment funds and served as chief risk officer for two multi-billion dollar hedge funds. He is managing member of Topos, an asset manager and risk advisory firm.

Marc's views on the markets have been quoted by *The Financial Times*, *The Wall Street Journal*, *Barrons*, *Risk*, Reuters, TheStreet.com, MarketWatch.com, Forbes.com, *Business Week*, and *The New York Times*. He has appeared on CNBC, Fox Business News, Bloomberg (radio and TV), and BBC-TV Worldwide.

He has lectured widely to diverse audiences, ranging from his students at New York University to members of the International Association of Financial Engineers. He has moderated panel discussions on financial innovation with Yale University professor Robert Shiller and regulatory reform with Connecticut Attorney General Richard Blumenthal.

Marc's interest in how things really work spans decades. After achieving Honors in the Westinghouse (Intel) Science Talent Search, Marc was accepted at the age of sixteen by Harvard, M.I.T., and Columbia. He attended Columbia University as a John Jay National Scholar, graduating with honors in 1979 (Math/Psych). He did graduate work in mathematics, studying with the world-renowned algebraist Samuel Eilenberg. He was recipient of the W.W. Cumming Prize in Psychology.

Marc is the owner/inventor of patented and patent-pending financial instruments, gaming systems, valuation methods, and mechanisms for protecting privacy in the digital age. He is married and has two sons.

Introduction: Becoming a Savvy Investor

"The times are changed, and we change with them."

—Roman proverb

What a difference a decade makes! Ten years ago, when the first edition of *Forbes® Guide to the Markets* was published, the global economy was booming. "Dot com" was the watchword of the day—everybody wanted to work for one. "Dow 36000" was supposed to be just around the corner.

Today, the global economy is suffering. Bad news is everywhere. Everybody just wants to keep their job. We're closer to Dow 3600 than Dow 36000. Some argue that economic conditions are akin to the Great Depression of the 1930s. Others see the buying opportunity of a lifetime, arguing that the prices of assets have fallen far below their true value. A third group sees some great opportunities amidst the carnage, but expects years to pass before the markets get back to normal.

How does one go about investing in times like these? Will things ever get back to normal? What is "normal," anyway?

This question calls for some serious detective work, as practiced by a serious—if fictional—detective: Sam Spade. In *The Maltese Falcon*, Spade confronts the case of a man who disappeared apparently without any cause: "a man named Flitcraft." It turns out that Flitcraft who, by all accounts had a great life, had simply disappeared: "'He went like that,' Spade said, 'like a fist when you open your hand.'"

Spade first learns of the case five years after the disappearance; it turns out that Flitcraft had been walking to lunch and passed a construction site that had just the skeleton of an office building. "A beam or something fell eight or ten stories down and smacked the sidewalk alongside him . . . a piece of sidewalk was chipped off and flew up and hit his cheek . . . he still had the scar when I saw him. . . ."

Spade continues, "He was more shocked than frightened. He felt like somebody had taken the lid off life and let him look at the works." This, it turns out, accounts for Flitcraft's sudden disappearance. Though he "had been a good citizen and a good husband and father," he knew now that men "lived only while blind chance spared them."

I will come back to Spade's story in a moment, but first we need to take a detour and talk about a close relative to "blind chance," the concept of risk (a subject that deserves and has its own chapter). The financial crisis has brought the concept of risk to the center of investors' collective awareness. In happier times, people focus on the expected return on their investments. Today, as Will Rogers once said, "I'm not so much concerned with the return *on* capital as I am with the return *of* capital."

As a former chief risk officer of two multi-billion dollar hedge funds, I have thought a great deal about risk. From my perspective, it is important to recognize that risk changes over time, along with people's perspective about it. From this standpoint, there was plenty of risk around in the late 90s, but it appeared in a different form—risk of losing ground against one's peers, of not "keeping up with the Joneses." Later, after the Internet bubble burst, the fear of losing what one had came to dominate the fear of not getting more.

Still later, as the housing bubble inflated in this decade, a new fear of missing out (and desire to profit) came to dominate. By early 2009, however, the collective risk profile of investors had transformed yet again, with ready cash valued as highly as "dot com" stock options were a decade earlier.

As we can see, a society's ideas of "normal" or "expected" evolves over time. Ten years ago, at the end of a long secular bull market, most Americans were too young to remember the Great Depression of the 1930s. Many had grown up or were born after the stagflation of the 1970s. It was all too easy for the hard-earned lessons of those times to be written off as ancient history. From the standpoint of 2009, we are led to wonder: "What will the world look like in five or ten years? What existing data and theories are relevant to us as investors?"

These are excellent questions, for which there are no simple answers (which is probably the definition of an excellent question). The truth is that investors should always ask themselves which data and theories are relevant right now, and which are noise that should be ignored. In easier times, these questions tend to be given short shrift. Today, the opposite danger lurks, the danger of too much uncertainty leading to inability to make decisions—which can lead to significant regret over missed opportunities down the road.

As investors, we must strive to keep an emotional equilibrium conducive to intelligent decision making; we mustn't yield to the twin temptations of impulsiveness and procrastination. We must "make haste slowly"!

In this spirit, I invite you to read the new edition of *Forbes® Guide to the Markets*. It has changed with the times, yet strives to reveal what is unchanging in markets—and in human nature.

So what became of Flitcraft? After the accident he disappears, wandering around for a few years, eventually settling down again and re-establishing a normal life like the one he'd had prior to the falling beam. As Spade tells it, "he had settled back naturally into the same groove he had jumped out of . . . that's the part of it I always liked. He adjusted himself to beams falling, and then no more of them fell, and he adjusted himself to them not falling."

—MARC M. GROZ
Stamford, Connecticut
April 25, 2009

Section One
Establishing a Frame of Reference

Chapter 1

FROM "DUMB" BARTER TO INTELLIGENT AGENTS

A Genealogy of Markets

Where did financial markets come from? What distinguishes financial markets from other forms of trade? How do financial markets work? We will briefly address the first two questions in this introduction; answering the third question is the goal of this book.

Markets for the purchase and sale of financial **securities** such as stocks and bonds have existed for hundreds of years. Typically, these markets began with a small group of men (and maybe a few women) who met informally at a coffeehouse or restaurant to act as intermediaries between buyers and sellers of securities (here we're talking pieces of paper). As the volume of their business increased, these loose-knit groups formed associations with rules of conduct. In London, for example, The Stock Exchange was

securities   *Paper or computerized documents expressing financial claims to an issuer's assets; abstractly, the claim itself, independent of the form in which it is represented.*

established in 1773 in a room in Sweeting's Alley. The building became known as The Stock Exchange Coffee House, still showing the link to its former home, a coffeehouse named Jonathan's located in Change Alley.

Nineteen years later, in 1792, a small group of New York stockbrokers, who had been trading under an old buttonwood tree on Wall Street since the days following the Revolutionary War, signed a business agreement. Twenty-five years later, in 1817, the Buttonwood Group created an association—The New York Stock and Exchange Board—and arranged to move indoors.

What Is a Security?

Securities are usually thought of as the pieces of paper that prove ownership (stock certificates), ownership-related rights (option or warrant certificate), or a creditor relationship (bond certificates). Most of these pieces of paper, however, no longer exist, having been replaced by book entries in electronic form. Some dictionaries dodge the question neatly, defining *securities* as "financial instruments" and leaving it at that. In the United States, securities are more narrowly defined as a subset of financial instruments that pass what is called the Howey Test. Like Gaul, the Howey Test is divided into three parts: (1) money must be invested in a business; (2) where there is the expectation of a profit; (3) with no effort required on the part of the investor.

This still leaves us in want of a definition of *financial instrument*. We will define financial instruments as *rightful claims to assets represented in some fashion, whether on paper, in a computer's memory, or in any other verifiable way.* Defined in this way, the financial instrument still exists even if the certificate is lost or the computer crashes.

Under the Old Buttonwood Tree: The First Trading Post

The tree that started it all was a buttonwood tree, *Platanus occidentalis.* According to the New York Stock Exchange, the tree was located near the eastern end of Wall Street, on the north side of the street between Pearl and William Streets. How tall a tree was it? Some buttonwood trees grow to

(Continued)

150 feet. How old a tree was it? It is thought to have been a seedling a century before Columbus's voyage of discovery. Many of its neighbors were felled by British axes when Manhattan was occupied during the Revolutionary War. The buttonwood survived, becoming a popular place for brokers and other traders to gather.

As to the legend itself, did 24 brokers meet beneath this tree on May 17, 1792, to sign the Buttonwood Agreement? The prevailing view is that the agreement was signed indoors, at a local hotel. One thing is certain: Whether the signing under the tree was literally true or a fanciful fable, the agreement has borne plentiful fruit.

What distinguishes financial markets from nonfinancial markets? Financial markets can be seen more clearly if placed in the larger context of markets in general. Markets, in turn, are more easily understood if looked at in the still larger context of forms of trade between individuals and groups.

Both market and nonmarket forms of trade are as old as civilization. Both have existed even in cultures that traded goods without the use of money. Nonmonetary trade has taken many forms, most notably **barter** (i.e., exchange of goods and/or services for other goods and/or services) and various forms of ritualized gift giving. Extensive barter markets existed in Ancient Egypt and in Mesopotamia 5,000 years ago.

An early type of barter trade that required neither money nor even a shared language is mentioned by Herodotus, the Ancient Greek historian known as the Father of History. Writing nearly 2,500 years ago, he tells of Carthaginians engaged in "dumb barter" with tribes from beyond the Pillars of Hercules. Also known as "depot trade," or "silent trade," the widespread custom was practiced at one time or another in such diverse places as northern Russia, western Africa, Sumatra, and India. It worked roughly as follows.

One of the parties to a silent trade went at the appointed time to the traditional spot designated for trading (how these times and places were selected we do not know). The first party set down the goods being offered and then retreated to another location, signaling the other party with a call or other sound. On hearing the signal, the second party went to the spot, placing items considered of equal value alongside the items offered by the first party. Then that individual, too, retreated, allowing the first party to return and look over the wares offered by the second party. At this point the first party either completed the trade by removing the second party's wares or, if not satisfied, left those wares in place until the second party sweetened the offer with additional goods.

Did this type of barter constitute a market? It appears that markets require, at minimum, some goods or services for sale and a means for traders to place bids and make offers on these goods with other traders. Thus "dumb" barter does possess two of the salient features of markets: items for sale and the establishment of a fixed time and place for traders looking to make deals.

But it takes more than fixing a time and a place to constitute a market and to distinguish it from other kinds of trading. It takes only two to trade, but markets need at least three participants. This gives the participants the ability to compare what is being offered (and/or asked for) by one party with what is being offered (and/or asked for) by another. Dumb barter does not provide a means to look for a better deal from a different trader; there are only two parties to the trading. It does not even require a common language. On this reckoning, it falls short of being a true market.

Notice that in the preceding paragraph we studiously avoided the terms *buyer* and *seller*. That is because, in the absence of money, there is no clear distinction between buyers and sellers: Each party is a little bit of both. While this lack of distinction between buyers and sellers might seem to be an artifact of primitive societies, we will see in Chapter Sixteen (on options) that a curious aspect of the Information Age is a form of trading known as *swaps,* in which the distinction between buyers and sellers is once again blurred.

The creation of barter markets was an important development in human history. Even so, its limitations are readily apparent. In a barter market, a potential buyer may not have the item that a potential seller wants. Alice may have almonds that she wants to trade for butter. Bob may have butter but needs chocolate. Charlie, who has chocolate, wants almonds. In order for Alice to get butter, she must first get chocolate (see Table 1–1). In the absence of a medium of exchange, even a simple shopping expedition can require a high degree of knowledge of the marketplace. Furthermore, buyers and sellers find it difficult to calculate prices when restricted to barter.

It is wasteful to have to engage in multiple transactions in order to get a single needed product. Not only can this type of barter be complicated,

Table 1-1 A Comparison of Barter and Money-Based Trading

Barter-Based Trading

	Has	Wants	Owned By	Must Sell To
Alice	Almonds	Butter	Bob	Charlie
Bob	Butter	Chocolate	Charlie	Alice
Charlie	Chocolate	Almonds	Alice	Bob

Alice can exchange her almonds for Charlie's chocolate, then use Charlie's chocolate as a medium of exchange to get Bob's butter.

Bob can exchange his butter for Alice's almonds, then use the almonds as a medium of exchange to get Charlie's chocolate.

Charlie can exchange his chocolate for Bob's butter, then use Bob's butter as a medium of exchange for Alice's almonds.

or

Money-Based Trading

	Has	Wants	Owned By	Can Pay Dollars To
Alice	Almonds, dollars	Butter	Bob	Bob
Bob	Butter, dollars	Chocolate	Charlie	Charlie
Charlie	Chocolate, dollars	Almonds	Alice	Alice
Dave	Dollars	BCA	BCA	BCA

Dave, who distributes the dollars, sits at the center of the money-based system. He makes transactions much easier, as long as his dollars retain the confidence of Alice, Bob, and Charlie. He must not create more money than the market can bear.

but to complete a transaction, a trader may need a great deal of information about price and availability of products he or she doesn't want and about the needs of other traders.

Even with only three people trading three products, barter can be complicated. This complexity increases exponentially with the number of products and services being traded. In a growing economy, with thousands of products and services, barter is a less and less efficient means of trade. At some point along the way, a barter system becomes unworkable. Something has to change. In the language of the theory of complex systems, a critical point has been reached. At that point something new emerges.

That something new is money. Consider Dave the banker. Dave has dollars. Instead of everyone running around in circles trying to complete increasingly labyrinthine transactions, they go to Dave and get dollars in exchange for their goods. Now, with Dave's dollars serving as a universal medium of exchange, Alice can sell her almonds directly to Charlie and buy butter directly from Bob.

Where Do Dollars Come From?

The word *dollar* originally entered the English language as the name of a sixteenth-century Bohemian silver coin, the *taler* or *thaler,* shortened from *Joachimstaler,* named after Joachimsthal, a town in Bohemia. Later, *dollar* was used to refer to the Spanish *peso,* or *piece of eight,* a coin used not only in Spain but in North America, and in widespread use at the time of the American Revolutionary War. From *piece of eight* we get the value of a quarter as *two bits,* long before the word *bit*—a contraction of *binary digit*—became associated with computers.

The emergence of money provides both a medium of exchange and a common denominator that enables traders to compare the various goods (or services) offered. Initially, this was done by selecting one item to be the standard of comparison.

With a universal medium of exchange operating in a market, the ability to discover price emerges. At any given time and place, a unique price is created for items on sale in a market. This price is sometimes called the *equilibrium price*, because it is the price that theoretically equalizes supply and demand. In practice, this equilibrium may not be so obvious or stable. One reason for this is that the exchanges that are supposed to set the equilibrium price are hypothetical, not actual, trades. When real trading commences, it may be affected by influences not taken into account by theory, such as the continual introduction of new products and services that compete with existing wares and the periodic revolutionary changes wrought by the emergence of new forms of trading.

Money simplifies transactions by providing a universal intermediary for goods and services. But it also serves other important purposes. Thousands of years ago, human societies began to move away from prehistoric subsistence economies in which little was produced beyond the bare necessities of life. Cities emerged, and with them came economies that produced a surplus. In these long-ago times, money began to function as a means of representing that surplus.

Money Changes Everything

The word *money* comes from an epithet applied to the Roman goddess Juno. She was referred to as Juno Moneta. In addition to *money*, the words *monetary* and *mint* are also derived from that epithet. In fact, the temple of Juno Moneta *was* the Roman mint.

When the surplus is **invested** (put to use in a productive enterprise), it is known as **capital**. When used as capital, money is not only a convenience for facilitating transactions, but is an essential means of organizing complex projects and enterprises.

capital Surplus goods and/or money used to create more goods and/or money.

The ability to invest money gave rise to a multiplicity of new kinds of wealth. The existence of multiple currencies gave rise to a new kind of transaction. Beyond barter, where goods and/or services are exchanged, and beyond the purchase or sale of goods and services, a purely monetary transaction could now take place, with one kind of money being exchanged for another kind—in essence, exchanging symbol for symbol. In these purely financial transactions, we can see the beginnings of the financial markets.

Trade has developed in two independent, yet related, ways. First, it has grown more and more abstract. Second, it has grown to include larger and larger groups of people. The increasingly abstract nature of trading has fed its tendency to include larger and larger groups, while the involvement of larger and larger groups has reinforced the abstract nature of trading.

The details of how potential participants interact with each other varies from market to market, as does the amount and quality of information exchanged. There is also considerable variation in ownership and control of markets.

We can visualize the history of commerce as an increasingly specialized and complex hierarchy of trading. As we have seen, the simplest kind of trade requires neither money nor market, nor even language. Language makes it possible to negotiate over price and terms, leading to the kind of barter arrangements that exist today. When these are organized into a market, pricing is no longer simply a matter of two-way negotiation, but is derived from the interaction of supply and demand on the part of market participants. We can also have nonmarket trades that involve money. The combination of money and markets leads to still more elaborate forms of trading—and thus to the beginnings of financial markets.

Markets have become so widespread and popular that it is becoming hard to imagine a social order without well-developed markets. Yet it is helpful to recall that until very recently, markets were anathema in many parts of the world. In the former Soviet Union, in Communist China, and in other places, many forms of markets were illegal. The official line was that a "command economy" was best, with centralized planning and sharp limits on what could be bought and sold and who could buy and sell it.

Intelligent Agents: Computer Programs as Financial Intermediaries

The evolution of computer networks has given rise to a qualitatively different kind of program usually known as an **intelligent agent** (also referred to as *smart agents* or *bots,* short for robots). These programs operate autonomously, according to guidelines you specify. If you have used an Internet search engine to locate information or a web site, you have already used an early form of this technology. Intelligent agents go one step further than search engines. They do not merely find a piece of information or a web site for you. They negotiate transactions with counterparties, usually other intelligent agents. Still in an early phase of development, intelligent agents hold the promise of allowing investors to specify guidelines and let the software do the negotiating.

Until recently, the use of barter was a very strong component of the Russian economy. Elaborate barter networks operated in a virtual economy, hiding the true extent of Russian economic activity and preventing the government from collecting taxes. By some estimates, as much as two-thirds of that economy was barter-based. In the aftermath of the financial and economic crises of 2008, we may be observing a resurgence of barter on a global scale, to supplement or replace broken financial systems.

Sophisticated commodities trading with future delivery of goods requires that traders develop the capacity to understand the time value of money. From here it is but a short step to the issuance of bonds and other debt securities, and to their trading. This develops both in the open marketplace and behind closed doors. In either case, technology facilitates the creation and distribution of more and more abstract forms of financial instruments. The constant evaluation of these instruments by buyers and sellers exerts a kind of evolutionary pressure on the whole complex system made up of stocks, markets, and the organizations and individuals who use them. Thus the cycle of innovation continues, from the dumb barter of ancient history to the intelligent agents at the cutting edge of today's financial technology.

Chapter 2

POINT-COUNTERPOINT

Six Investment Approaches

How should you invest your money? There's no shortage of opinions on the subject, no shortage of advice. All too often, however, such opinions and advice are based on a selective presentation of the facts, perhaps colored by the advice-giver's motives and affected by day-to-day news and fads.

One person will tell you that stocks are the solution. Another will insist that mutual funds give you the most for your money. A third will tell you to bet on bonds. Others will espouse exchange traded funds (ETFs), opt for options, or become fascinated by futures.

Investing is not just a theoretical exercise. You have, or will have, money that you want to invest. In fact, *need* is probably a more accurate word. You need (or will soon need) to invest the money that you have earned, saved, and/or inherited so that you can meet your financial goals, responsibilities, and commitments. And you would like to understand as much as possible about this sometimes confusing but vitally important subject.

So, how should you invest your money? As a warm-up for our voyage through the world of financial markets, we'll begin by looking a bit more closely at some of the most common answers to this question. Then we'll take you, one step at a time, through what you need to know in order to arrive at your own answer—the one that is best for you.

Stocks

Many market advisors urge investors to invest in good stocks. There is a great diversity of opinion, however, on what constitutes a good stock. Some analysts favor the stocks of large corporations, such as the 30 stocks that constitute the **Dow Jones Industrial Average (DJIA)** or the 500 stocks that make up the **Standard & Poor's (S&P) 500 Index.** Others argue the merits of small, fast-growing companies (sometimes called *growth stocks*), while still others believe in an approach that looks for value in stocks that are currently out of favor.

Standard & Poor's (S&P) 500 Index   Index of large capitalization stocks.

Mutual Funds

Other analysts believe in the value of **mutual funds.** Mutual funds are investment companies, that is, companies that invest in stocks, bonds, and other financial instruments such as futures and options. Funds offer a number of advantages, including professional money management and portfolio **diversification.** Analysts who favor funds will often argue that the average individual investor is likely to do better by choosing a few good funds than by trying to manage a portfolio on his or her own. They are better off, the argument goes, choosing an outstanding mutual fund with a great track record and a really smart portfolio management team.

diversification
Investing in a broad range of securities to lower risk and/or enhance return.

Mutual funds also have their share of critics, including prominent members of the fund industry. The two most frequent criticisms are that average costs are too high and average performance is too low. One of the ways that the fund industry has responded is to offer an increasing number of **index funds.** These are funds designed to match the return on an **index** such as the Dow Jones Industrial Average or the S&P 500. Typically, the costs associated with index funds are significantly lower, while the performance is designed to closely track the index. After all, indexes are the barometers of

Wall Street. Their minute-by-minute fluctuations are watched by many millions of investors all over the world, while hundreds of millions hear, watch, or read about them to learn how the market did.

Bonds

Bonds have their advocates as well. Some analysts point out that investing a portion of one's wealth in bonds is a good way to diversify a stock portfolio, while others emphasize the security of principal and interest payments offered by bonds of high credit quality. Still others point to the tax advantages of bonds, especially municipal bonds.

On the negative side, critics believe that bonds do not offer a good return relative to stocks and that they have their own risks, including default risk, sensitivity to interest rates, currency exchange rates, and the business cycle.

ETFs

Exchange traded funds (ETFs) are similar to index-based mutual funds, however, they trade on stock exchanges and may be purchased or sold throughout the day at or close to their net asset value. Among their potential advantages are liquidity, tax efficiency, and generally lower costs. These features have made them extremely popular and among the fastest growing segments of the investment business.

On the other hand, some critics argue that ETFs encourage speculation and that the costs associated with frequent trading can be extremely high. Another potential problem is the proliferation of ETFs into so many obscure indexes and trading ideas with the result that liquidity and market cap evaporate.

Options

Options can be used in a variety of ways, ranging from portfolio risk reduction to outright speculation. Most options are short-term investments and must be monitored closely. Advocates of options for individual investors commonly point to the potential for spectacular returns through financial **leverage,** though sometimes they are marketed as a way of "insuring" your portfolio against a market downturn. Critics contend that the cost of trading options is frequently very high for individual investors and that most individuals who use options to speculate lose money.

Futures

Futures have many of the same uses as options, with similar potential for high returns arising from leverage. Unlike options, however, futures bear the added risk of **margin calls**. For this reason, futures investments must be monitored very closely. An alternative to direct investment in futures is a **managed futures account,** which is like a mutual fund for futures. Costs of managed futures can be much higher than those for mutual funds. Furthermore, while some managed futures have had spectacular returns for a year or more, critics contend that most managed futures accounts, particularly the ones available to the general public, are poor investments.

Summary

This chapter reviewed some frequently heard arguments, pro and con, for the six major classes of investment vehicles: stocks, mutual funds, bonds, ETFs, options, and futures. In the succeeding sections of this book, we will examine these vehicles in far greater detail.

Chapter 3

CONFRONTING INFORMATION OVERLOAD

There's no getting around it: The financial markets are complicated and getting more so every day. The sheer range of financial products and services, accompanied by an expanding mass of marketing materials and messages, can lead to frustration about whether it is even possible to make sense of it all. While there are no easy, one-size-fits-all solutions in the world of investing, it is certainly possible to get a good understanding of how the financial markets work and how you can use them to your advantage. Reading this book is an essential start.

What makes financial markets so complicated? In a strong sense, the markets' complexity is a mirror of the complex global economy and of the billions of individuals whose daily actions underlie both. If all investors had the exact same financial goals and timetables, financial markets might never have developed at all. It is because people view their financial goals with different time horizons, with different risk tolerances, from within different national and geographical boundaries, and with different aptitudes, tastes, and ambitions that the necessity of trading in financial instruments arises. Consider the following two examples:

1. The Lerner family is saving for a child's college education, for which they will need money in five years. It might make sense for them to invest in, say, a U.S. government bond with a maturity of five years in order to deal with their expected future liability.

2. Meanwhile, the Transit family needs to buy a car to enable one of its members to commute to a new job. They need to sell a portion of their investments, perhaps withdrawing cash from a stock fund, in order to make a down payment on the car.

From these examples, we learn a basic principle that drives markets: Investors' divergent financial needs create a demand for markets in financial instruments. At one time, it might make sense for one investor to buy stock, while his or her neighbor could be better served by investing in a mutual fund. At a later time, their situations might reverse. Markets allow investors to buy and sell a wide variety of financial products at prices that derive from the collective actions and judgments of market participants. Note that while each family may need the same amount of money, the time frame in which those funds are necessary is very different.

Despite individual differences in risk tolerance, time horizon, and other factors, there are many things that investors share in common. In general, it can be said that all investors seek the maximum return on their investment, subject to a variety of limitations, including investor constraints (what they are allowed to invest in), investor choices (what they want to invest in), and investor safety (what they believe to be a sufficiently safe investment).

Investor Constraints

Every investor, from the individual of limited means to the manager of a large pension fund, has constraints on what he or she can buy. Sometimes these constraints are financial, such as minimum income or net worth requirements that must be met for investing in so-called hedge funds and for trading in futures and options markets. Frequently, such financial constraints are coupled with a requirement that the investor have some prior experience in the financial markets so that he or she is not starting out with an inappropriately risky investment.

Sometimes there are legal constraints, for example when foreign investors are precluded from owning more than a certain percentage of a domestic company. Other constraints may result from the practice of **socially responsible investing,** which takes into account the moral values of the investor or investment policy committee, who may wish to avoid investing in a certain industry or country. On still other occasions, the constraint is determined by practical considerations, such as the need for a certain level of return (a so-called **hurdle rate**) or for a high degree of correlation with a **benchmark.**

benchmark *A standard used for valuation purposes.*

Investor Choices

Despite all the talk about herd mentality, all investors do not think alike. Some investors avoid the financial markets entirely, choosing instead to invest their savings in real estate, family businesses, art, and so forth, while keeping an adequate supply of readily available cash on deposit with a federally insured bank. Others, while feeling comfortable with some combination of bonds (U.S. government, AAA-rated corporate, and tax-exempt), avoid investing in the stock market because they perceive it as too risky. Still others prefer to invest in stock only indirectly, through the purchase of top-performing equity mutual funds, perhaps within a tax-deferred IRA or 401(k) retirement plan. Finally, there are investors who take a passionate interest in finding the next great **growth** or **story stock**, or who painstakingly assemble and monitor a long-term portfolio of stocks chosen for their **intrinsic value**, perhaps according to some **indicator**, **financial ratio**, or **quantitative model.**

growth stock *Stock of a company with growing earnings and/or sales.*

story stock *Stock of a new company without real earnings, but with an exciting idea, opportunity, or technology.*

Behind all of these choices are the varied lessons that different people have taken from recent (and not-so-recent) economic history. Those old enough to remember the Great Depression may tend to view things through a different lens than those of us whose formative years were in the postwar boom era, the **stagflation**, gasoline lines, and gold boom of the 1970s, or the great stock market boom of the 1980s and 1990s. This makes good sense. It also makes markets, as investors chase different objectives with different views of value.

Notwithstanding the differences with which investors come to the markets, there are also common threads that affect us all. In particular, the impact of recent news—good or bad—tends to exert a powerful influence on investors' perceptions about what to buy and sell. Many studies suggest that investors tend to give too much weight to recent events, and to forget the old adage "this too shall pass." In consequence, many investors wind up buying overpriced securities, caught up in the enthusiasm of the moment, or on the other hand, selling undervalued securities with the mistaken belief that their price reflects the securities' true value. We will look at the difficulties and opportunities that stem from these all-too-human tendencies in Section VI, "Summing Up Risk and Return."

Investment Alternatives

You've probably seen this type of list before. No list of this type can be both comprehensive and usable. Aside from this problem, lists frequently convey the illusion that the alternatives are not only exhaustive but mutually exclusive. This, too, is usually false. There is a great deal of overlap among different kinds of investments; sometimes, the biggest difference between two investments is how they are packaged and marketed.

Investment Alternatives

Real estate

Family business

Art and other collectibles

Precious metals

Gems

Bank certificate of deposit

Bond

Stock

Mutual fund

Option

Future

Hedge fund

Wrap fee account

Funds of funds

Annuity

Insurance policy

Cash

Investor Safety

Many investors hold back from committing their capital to an otherwise attractive investment because of its perceived risk. People accustomed to the safety of federally guaranteed bank deposits are frequently ambivalent about investing in financial markets, particularly the stock market. They are attracted by the return potential, but are discouraged by the lack of principal guarantees. Too often, however, decisions about risk are made from a purely emotional standpoint and without a proper understanding of the relationship between risk and return. Reading this book will help you to achieve a fuller understanding of risk/return trade-offs, and you will be less likely to be swayed by appeals to the twin emotions that drive the markets: fear and greed. You will be able to make more informed, intelligent choices about your financial needs and goals.

Section Two
Stocks and Equity Markets

STOCKS AND EQUITY MARKETS

This section is about stocks and the people and organizations who use them. We begin, in Chapter Four, by discussing the various forms of stocks that exist and how issuers (who use stock to finance their business activities) and investment bankers (who help them) work together to create new shares of stock. In Chapter Five, we discuss the various settings in which stock is bought and sold, from the traditional "open outcry" markets, with their floor brokers representing customers and specialists making markets, to the latest digital exchanges that exist only in cyberspace, matching bids and offers of buyers and sellers who may never see each other or learn the other's identity.

Discussion of the settings in which trading takes place leads naturally into Chapter Six, a discussion of the different styles of investing used by stock market participants. Investment styles, of course, are dependent on access to many sources of information, the focus of Chapter Seven.

Finally, having looked at what stock is, who trades it, where and when it is traded, and by which methods of analysis it is deemed a buy, a sell, or a hold, we come to Chapter Eight, which offers a framework for deciding how to put all this information to good use.

special purpose acquisition companies (SPACs), private investments in public equity (PIPEs), and alternative public offerings (APOs) have transformed the issuing landscape.

- DPOs are means by which companies may raise capital by marketing directly to their own employees, customers, and friends, without the need for an underwriter. SPACs are publicly traded shell companies created with the goal of acquiring a private company with the capital raised through an IPO.

- PIPEs are deals that involve publicly traded stock, which may or may not be registered with the SEC.

- APOs combine a PIPE deal with a so-called "reverse merger" to create yet another alternative to a traditional IPO.

The idea behind the Internet investment banking business is simple yet potentially powerful. Instead of seeing IPOs as the permanent preserve of institutional insiders, the Internet is used as an enabling technology to bring issuers into contact with a broad group of potential individual investors. This could be a good thing for individuals. Until now, studies have shown that most individuals investing in IPOs get in too late to share in the early price run-ups. And who stands to lose? Traditional underwriters, who stay away from this technology, and institutions, who will lose their monopoly on IPOs and, perhaps more important, may lose some of their ability to "juice" portfolios with issues that almost always go up—initially.

Prospectus of "IJK Inc."

INFORMATION CONTAINED HEREIN IS SUBJECT TO COMPLETION OR AMENDMENT. A REGISTRATION STATEMENT RELATING TO THESE SECURITIES HAS BEEN FILED WITH THE SECURITIES AND EXCHANGE COMMISSION. THESE SECURITIES MAY NOT BE SOLD NOR MAY OFFERS TO BUY BE ACCEPTED PRIOR TO THE TIME THE REGISTRATION STATEMENT BECOMES EFFECTIVE. THIS PROSPECTUS SHALL NOT CONSTITUTE AN OFFER TO SELL OR THE SOLICITATION OF AN OFFER TO BUY NOR SHALL THERE BE ANY SALE OF THESE SECURITIES IN ANY STATE IN WHICH SUCH OFFER, SOLICITATION, OR SALE WOULD BE UNLAWFUL PRIOR TO REGISTRATION OR QUALIFICATION UNDER THE SECURITIES LAWS OF ANY STATE.

(Continued)

Chapter 4

VARIETIES OF STOCKS

Just What is a Security, Anyway?

What is a security (or financial instrument)? What makes stock different from other securities? As we mentioned in the previous chapter, a security (such as a stock, bond, or option) can be defined in three different ways:

1. A paper document providing proof of a financial stake of some kind.

2. An electronic/computer system equivalent to such a document.

3. An abstract but verifiable financial stake that may be represented through a paper document or a computer system, but does not disappear just because something happens to the piece of paper (or the computer) on which it was recorded.

The third definition has the advantage of recognizing that 100 shares of IBM do not become a different security when the certificate is turned over to a broker who records the shares in book entry form.

The financial stakes represented by securities are stakes in some business, government, or other legal entity.

stock *Securities representing an ownership interest in a corporation's undivided assets.*

bond *Long-term debt securities issued by governments and corporations; also used generically to refer to debt of any maturity.*

proxy *Someone to whom you give the right to vote your shares at a shareholder meeting.*

- If the security is a **stock**, then the investor's role is ownership (together with other investing **shareholders**, if any). Ownership in a corporation that is divided among a group of shareholders is sometimes referred to as an **ownership interest.**

- If the security is a **bond**, then the investor is a **creditor**, and the other entity can be corporate or governmental.

- If the security is an **option**, then the investor has certain well-defined rights and the other entity has corresponding obligations. (Some options are not considered securities, because the underlying asset is not a security. Even so, such options are still considered financial instruments.)

- **Futures** contracts, though they share many of the characteristics of securities, are separately regulated and therefore are generally said not to be securities at all, although they are financial instruments. This may change, especially if the "on-again, off-again" merger between the Securities Exchange Commission (SEC) and Commodity Futures Trading Commission (CFTC) ever becomes reality.

Bonds, options, and futures will all be discussed in much greater detail in later sections of this book.

Stock is denominated in units called **shares**. The share-issuing entity is always a corporation (investors cannot buy partial ownership of a government!). Shares in a mutual fund, whether of the **open-end** or **closed-end** variety, are a specialized form of stock. Mutual funds have become so important to investors that they are given a section of their own in this book.

Normally, as a shareholder, you have certain basic rights, including the following:

1. *A claim, proportional to the number of shares held, to a portion of the corporation's assets.* This does not mean, however, that you can go into corporate headquarters and walk off with a desk! Your claim is on the undivided assets of the corporation, not on any specific piece of property.

2. *The power to vote on company business at shareholder meetings, again in proportion to shares held.* Specifically, you are entitled to vote for **directors**, either in person or by **proxy.** Not all stock, however, comes with voting rights. In any event, relatively few individual investors who are shareholders attend the annual meeting of the corporation. Many do not

even bother to mail in the proxy that accompanies the announceme of a meeting.

3. *The right to* **dividends** *that may be voted by the board of directors.* Howevei not all stocks pay dividends.

4. *Sometimes, a* **preemptive right** *to purchase new shares before they are offered to the general public.* This right, however, may be abridged under certain circumstances (e.g., corporate mergers) or by the articles of incorporation.

So what does it really mean to own shares of stock in a corporation? It seems that if there is an essential component to stock ownership, it is a sharing of the underlying assets jointly with other shareholders.

Issuers and Underwriters: Why Does a Corporation Sell Stock to the Public?

Historically, **public companies**—that is, companies that issue stock to the public—came about in response to the need to finance large commercial enterprises on a scale that was either too grand or too risky for even the wealthiest individuals or families to undertake alone. By reaching out to the public at large, a small group of entrepreneurs can collect the enormous sums of money needed to finance new corporate undertakings, or even entirely new enterprises.

When corporations issue stock (or other securities), they are referred to as **issuers**. Stock can be issued for sale to the public or for **private placement.** When issuers prepare to sell securities to the public, they usually call upon investment bankers to act as **underwriters.** The underwriters' names are literally "written under" the copy at the bottom of the cover page of the **prospectus**, a legal document that, together with a **registration** statement, must be filed with the SEC, the government agency charged with regulating the securities industry. An initial or preliminary prospectus is often referred to as a *red herring* because of the red ink that connotes its preliminary status (see "Prospectus of IJK Inc.").

Beginning in the "dot.com" era, some issuers, particularly of **initial public offerings (IPOs)** have taken advantage of the low marketing costs of the Internet to offer **direct IPOs**, bypassing underwriters entirely. And some have become a new kind of underwriter, offering direct IPOs over the Internet. Over the last decade, **direct public offerings (DPOs)**, as well as

initial public offering (IPO) *First offering of a company's stock to the public.*

PROSPECTUS (Subject to Completion)

Issued April   , 2000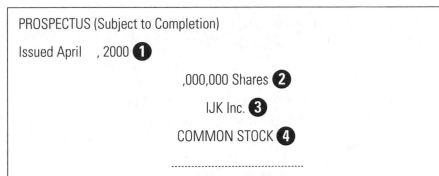

,000,000 Shares ❷

IJK Inc. ❸

COMMON STOCK ❹

ALL OF THE SHARES OF COMMON STOCK OFFERED HEREBY ARE BEING
SOLD BY THE COMPANY. OF THE SHARES OF COMMON STOCK BEING
OFFERED HEREBY,   ,000,000 SHARES ARE BEING OFFERED INITIALLY
IN THE UNITED STATES AND CANADA BY THE U.S. UNDERWRITERS
AND   ,000,000 SHARES ARE BEING OFFERED INITIALLY OUTSIDE THE
UNITED STATES AND CANADA BY THE INTERNATIONAL UNDERWRITERS.
SEE "UNDERWRITERS." PRIOR TO THE OFFERING, THERE HAS BEEN NO
PUBLIC MARKET FOR COMMON STOCK OF THE COMPANY. IT IS CURRENTLY
ANTICIPATED THAT THE INITIAL PUBLIC OFFERING PRICE WILL BE BETWEEN
$ AND $ PER SHARE. SEE "UNDERWRITERS" FOR A DISCUSSION OF
THE FACTORS TO BE CONSIDERED IN DETERMINING THE INITIAL PUBLIC
OFFERING PRICE. ❺

CONCURRENTLY WITH THE OFFERING BEING MADE HEREBY, THE
COMPANY IS OFFERING, BY MEANS OF A SEPARATE PROSPECTUS, $400
MILLION AGGREGATE PRINCIPAL AMOUNT OF ITS   % SENIOR NOTES
DUE 20   (THE "NOTES OFFERING" AND, TOGETHER WITH THE OFFERING,
THE "OFFERINGS"). THE CONSUMMATION OF EACH OF THE OFFERINGS
IS CONDITIONED UPON, AND WILL OCCUR SIMULTANEOUSLY WITH, THE
CONSUMMATION OF THE OTHER. SEE "USE OF PROCEEDS." ❻

UPON COMPLETION OF THE OFFERINGS, AFFILIATES OF THE COMPANY
WILL RETAIN APPROXIMATELY   % OF THE OUTSTANDING VOTING POWER
OF THE COMPANY. SEE "PRINCIPAL STOCKHOLDERS." ❼

(Continued)

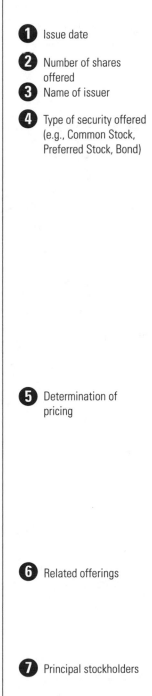

❶ Issue date

❷ Number of shares offered

❸ Name of issuer

❹ Type of security offered (e.g., Common Stock, Preferred Stock, Bond)

❺ Determination of pricing

❻ Related offerings

❼ Principal stockholders

8 Stock exchange listing
and ticker symbol

9 Risk factor

10 SEC disclaimer

11 Price

APPLICATION WILL BE MADE TO LIST THE COMMON STOCK ON THE NEW YORK STOCK EXCHANGE UNDER THE SYMBOL "IJK." **8**

SEE "RISK FACTORS" BEGINNING ON PAGE   FOR A DISCUSSION OF CERTAIN FACTORS THAT SHOULD BE CONSIDERED BY PROSPECTIVE INVESTORS. **9**

THESE SECURITIES HAVE NOT BEEN APPROVED OR DISAPPROVED BY THE SECURITIES AND EXCHANGE COMMISSION OR ANY STATE SECURITIES COMMISSION NOR HAS THE SECURITIES AND EXCHANGE COMMISSION OR ANY STATE SECURITIES COMMISSION PASSED UPON THE ACCURACY OR ADEQUACY OF THIS PROSPECTUS. ANY REPRESENTATION TO THE CONTRARY IS A CRIMINAL OFFENSE. **10**

PRICE $ A SHARE **11**

UNDERWRITING

	PRICE TO PUBLIC	DISCOUNTS AND COMMISSIONS(1)	PROCEEDS TO COMPANY(2)
Per share	$	$	$
Total (3)	$	$	$

----

1. The Company has agreed to indemnify the Underwriters against certain liabilities, including liabilities under the Securities Act of 1933, as amended. See "Underwriters."

(Continued)

2. Before deducting expenses payable by the Company, estimated at $

3. The Company has granted to the U.S. Underwriters an option, exercisable within 30 days of the date hereof, to purchase up to an aggregate of   additional Shares of Common Stock at the Price to Public less Underwriting Discounts and Commissions, for the purpose of covering over-allotments, if any. If the U.S. Underwriters exercise such option in full, the total Price to Public, Underwriting Discounts and Commissions and Proceeds to Company will be $, $ and $, respectively. See "Underwriters."

The Shares of Common Stock are offered, subject to prior sale, when, as and if accepted by the Underwriters named herein and subject to approval of certain legal matters by BIG LAW FIRM, counsel for the Underwriters. It is expected that delivery of the Shares will be made on or about April   , 200X at the office of LEAD UNDERWRITER, New York, NY against payment therefore in immediately available funds.

LEAD UNDERWRITER

UNDERWRITER #2

UNDERWRITER #3

UNDERWRITER #4

April   , 200X

Why Investors Buy Stock

All well and good for the entrepreneur and the corporation. But why should anyone buy stock? It all goes back to the investor's current mix of assets and liabilities, along with his or her financial goals and expectation of future needs. An investor with available cash or credit will buy stock if such a purchase fits his or her financial framework. In broad terms, most investors are motivated by both long-term and short-term needs.

- *Long-term* **capital appreciation.** As a long-term investor, you want the total value of your stocks to increase. The value of your stock position can increase in a number of ways, including a rise in the price per share, a share **split** which gives you additional shares at the same price, or the reinvestment of dividends. Reinvestment can be done automatically through a **dividend reinvestment program (DRIP).**
- *Short-term income.* Aside from your needs as a long-term investor, you may have an immediate need for income from your investments. For short-term income, many investors choose bonds (or bond mutual funds) rather than dividend-paying stocks, because dividend payments are not as reliable as interest payments.

Other, more specific motivating factors may include the following:

- Attraction to a company or one of its products or services
- Confidence in an entrepreneur, portfolio manager, or stock analyst
- Recommendation of friend or financial advisor
- Results of personal research

A *dividend reinvestment program (DRIP),* a service offered by an increasing number of public companies, automatically uses your cash dividend to purchase additional shares of the company's stock without the involvement of a broker. Starting with a trickle of companies in the 1970s—AT&T was among the first—today DRIPs have flooded the marketplace, with about 1,000 public companies sponsoring programs.

(Continued)

Many sponsoring companies allow you to purchase additional shares directly from them. This has led to a major new kind of stock investing, known as *no-load stocks,* which are offered to the public directly by the issuing corporation, bypassing brokers even for the initial purchase of shares. We will discuss this phenomenon in detail in Chapter Eight (buying and selling stock).

What unites these and other motivating factors? For some investors, it is the belief that the potential return from investing in stock is worth the risk of loss of capital. Others may have just taken the plunge without reflecting on the possibility of loss.

We turn now to consider the two potential components of return on an investment in shares of stock: dividends and capital gains.

Summing Up Total Return: Dividends and Capital Gains

Traditionally, one of the defining characteristics of common stock is that it pays dividends to its shareholders. The word *dividend* means "that which is divided." Dividends, then, are a dividing up and distribution to shareholders of a portion of the corporation's earnings. The amount and timing of dividend payments, if any, is voted upon by the **board of directors** of the corporation.

The importance of dividends as a component of return to an investor varies from stock to stock. Stocks that have been around a long time are more likely to pay dividends than is the latest IPO. You might think that this means stocks paying regular dividends have a higher survival rate, but paying dividends is no guarantee of survival.

Perhaps companies that have been around a long time are, on average, more able to pay dividends. If so, this would be a reflection of the life cycle of a corporation. In the early years, when a company is growing fast, its need for capital is likely to be greater than its desire to pay dividends. More mature companies, whose growth prospects are diminished, need less capital and can return more to investors in the form of dividends. While you may feel good getting that dividend check, the board of directors owes it to you to make sure that the company is not missing out on worthwhile investment opportunities that would make your investment more profitable.

There is an argument made by some financial analysts that dividend payments are not in the best interest of shareholders. The reason? Dividend payments are taxed as ordinary income in the year that they are received. For most shareholders, ordinary income is taxed at a higher rate than **capital gains**, giving those investors an incentive to seek out stocks that do not pay dividends at all, generating returns to shareholders exclusively through capital appreciation—that is, increases in the value of the stock itself.

capital gain   *Increase in the market value of an asset.*

Another argument against paying dividends stems from their tax status from the point of view of the corporation. A corporation cannot deduct the amount it pays in dividends from its income. The situation is different when a corporation issues bonds. Interest payments on corporate bonds are considered deductible expenses of the corporation. This may create an incentive to issue bonds instead of stock and to avoid paying dividends altogether.

Though linked to the earnings of the corporation, dividend payments in practice are a combination of tradition, shareholder expectation, and corporate strategy. In earlier days, examination of a stock's dividend record was high on most investors' checklists. Some stocks have unbroken records of decades of quarterly dividend payments.

blue chip   *Stock of a large-capitalization, financially sound corporation.*

Regular dividend payments are historically associated with large, **blue chip** companies and stocks of electric power, gas, and other utility sector companies. But things have changed dramatically in recent years. IBM, the bluest of blue chips, drastically cut its dividend some years ago as part of its aggressive restructuring program. Microsoft, which now has a market value greater than IBM, did not pay a dividend until 2003.

While most dividends are paid in cash, there are also **stock dividends**, so-called **scrip** dividends, and occasionally even dividends in the form of company products or other property. When voting on the amount and form of a dividend, the board of directors also provides two dates: a **record date** and a **pay date.** The record date is the point of reference for determining shareholder eligibility for the dividend. The pay date is typically a couple of weeks after the record date.

Three days before the record date, and about three weeks before the pay date, the stock goes **ex-dividend.** Investors who purchase shares between the **ex-dividend date** (sometimes just called the *ex date*) and the pay date are not entitled to the dividend. Instead, it is paid to the previous shareholder. When a stock goes ex-dividend, its price usually drops by the (after tax) amount of the anticipated payment.

ex-dividend   *No longer eligible for a dividend, because dividend has been announced and payment date scheduled.*

Many investors keep a sharp lookout for changes in dividend payouts. A popular view is that dividend increases are an indicator of a stock that will outperform the market, while stocks that decrease or eliminate the dividend tend to underperform. A recent study challenged this view, arguing that at least some of the time, the exact opposite is true. If so, it is not hard to imagine an explanation. Some companies may pay too high a dividend, leaving little money to reinvest in the business. And companies that cut their dividends may be about to embark on an aggressive turnaround. IBM comes to mind as a recent example of a company that cut its dividend, took its lumps, and then rebounded nicely. Other companies that got a positive response from the market after cutting dividend payments include SPX Corporation, Florida Power & Light, and IPALCO Enterprises.

The contrasting theories of the impact of changes in dividend payouts highlights an important insight about dividends. Beyond any easily quantifiable difference between dividends and capital gains, there seems to be a significant psychological dimension to the dividend controversy. Some people just like dividends. We can speculate about why this is so (getting money without having to make a decision about selling stock is one possibility). No doubt, tradition also plays an important role.

If dividends make little financial sense—and many corporations act as though this is the case—how do these corporations reward you as the investor? The answer is capital gains. One way that capital gains can be offered to shareholders is through **share repurchase** programs, sometimes called **stock buyback** programs. When a company buys back its stock, this reduces the number of shares **outstanding** (shares held by investors), which tends to boost the price of the stock. Sometimes, the stock price rises because the company has announced (or is expected to announce) that it will be buying back shares. The underlying reason for the price change is that the remaining individual shares have become more valuable.

tax deferral vehicle
IRA, 401(k), variable annuity, or other mechanism for deferring taxes.

A company's earnings are either paid out as dividends or retained. Retained earnings increase the company's value to investors, which (all other things being equal) translates into a higher price for the stock. If you sell a stock purchased outside of a **tax deferral vehicle** (such as a pension plan) at a profit, a **realized capital gain** is created whereas before there was only an **unrealized capital gain** or **paper profit.** For most investors, capital gains are taxed at a lower rate than dividends or interest. The latter two are considered forms of **ordinary income**.

If the stock you sold was in an individual retirement account (IRA) or some other tax-deferred investment plan, then this distinction between capital gains and ordinary income no longer applies. We will explore the impact of taxes on investment performance in Chapter Fifteen.

Over time, the price of a successful company's stock can get very high. This can discourage new investors from purchasing the stock, because individual shares look expensive. An extreme example is the stock of Berkshire Hathaway, Warren Buffett's company, whose closing price on September 19, 2008, was $147,000 *per share.*

Most companies would find it difficult to attract investors with such a high per-share price. Eventually, if the price of an individual share gets too high, the board of directors may vote for a stock split, which increases the total number of shares outstanding without changing the total market value of shares.

For example, in a 2-for-1 stock split, a holder of 100 shares of IJK Corporation common stock receives an additional 100 shares (usually, in **book entry** form, although investors can request a **stock certificate**). If the price of IJK was $144 just before the split, it is $72 after it. For a time, investors purchased stocks right after a split, having noticed a tendency for stocks to rise. After enough investors began to take advantage of this pattern, the pattern changed. The price rise occurred before the split, and the price actually tended to sink after the fact. Such is the self-referential nature of markets.

When a stock's price sags, a reverse split may prevent it from being **delisted**—removed from the list of stocks allowed to be traded on an exchange. This might happen because an exchange sets a minimum price requirement, or simply because investors shy away from stocks with low share prices. What happens if you own, say 100 shares of XYZ Corporation common stock, and the company does a 1-for-12 reverse split? You would be entitled to 100 divided by 12, or $8^1/_3$ shares. Common stocks, unlike mutual funds, do not generally issue fractional shares. So you would receive the cash value of the fractional share.

What if the corporation goes belly-up? Recall that part of a shareholder's ownership interest is a claim on the (undivided) underlying assets of the corporation. In the event that the corporation declares **bankruptcy**, however, the corporation will either get **reorganized** or undergo **liquidation.** In the former case, a reverse split may result. If liquidation happens, though, holders of common stock are not in a strong position. They have a residual claim on any assets that are left over after the corporation has paid its creditors. Generally speaking, bondholders fare better in a corporate bankruptcy, as they have a prior claim. So do holders of preferred stock. Stockholders tend to be far down on the list when it comes to getting paid anything for the shares of a bankrupt corporation.

Priority of Claims in the Event of Bankruptcy

If you own common stock in a company that goes bankrupt, there are a lot of people in line ahead of you whose claim on the corporation's assets takes precedence over yours. This is known as a **creditor hierarchy**. First priorities include accrued wages and salaries to employees, employee benefit plans, and taxes. Next come the secured creditors, usually banks and other financial institutions that have loaned the corporation money. Directly behind them are the bondholders, whose claims vary in strength depending on whether the debt they hold is **senior debt or subordinated debt**. If there are any assets left after the creditors and bondholders have all been paid in full, there may still be people in line ahead of you. Holders of **preferred stock** have priority over holders of common shares. As a result, common shareholders seldom recover any money from a corporation in bankruptcy.

preferred stock *Stock that offers some bondlike characteristics such as income and safety of principal.*

Stock splits and reverse splits are two types of **capital events**, which may be defined as changes in the capital structure of a corporation. Other capital events that can result in capital gains include rights offerings, corporate mergers, and spin-offs:

- **Rights offerings** give existing shareholders an opportunity to purchase (or subscribe to) additional shares of stock at a discount from the public offering price when the company prepares to issue new shares. These rights, which are also called **subscription rights**, are transferrable securities. The right to purchase at a discount is valid only for a short time period. After this period, the right has no further value.

- **Mergers** combine two (or more) companies to form a larger company. Frequently, the acquiring company pays shareholders of the acquired company in shares. For example, Company A may purchase all of Company B's shares on the basis of a predetermined ratio of shares, say two shares of Company A stock for every share of Company B stock outstanding. If you own 100 shares of Company B stock, after the acquisition is complete (and Company B no longer exists as a separate entity) you will own 200 shares of Company A stock.

- **Spin-offs** are like mergers in reverse. Company C decides to split off part of its operations into a separate organization. Let's say the new organization is called Company D. How are shareholders in Company C compensated for the splitting off of part of their ownership interest into a new enterprise? Usually, through issuance of stock at some preset ratio. Let's say you own 100 shares of Company C. After the spin-off of Company D, you still own 100 shares of C, but you also own, say, 50 shares of Company D.

In recent years, most stocks have done very well indeed, as stock market returns have far exceeded their historical averages. In these circumstances, a note of caution is warranted. Corporations do not guarantee that they will pay dividends, nor do they guarantee the price of their stock. Some stocks, of course, are safer than others, and a diversified stock portfolio is safer than the average stock contained in it. In fact, a properly diversified portfolio is safer (as judged by standard measures of risk) than the safest individual stock contained in the portfolio. Even so, *there is no guarantee on any of the money you invest in stocks.*

A Letter to Our Shareholders: Annual and Quarterly Reports (and Filings)

In addition to the prospectus, shareholders are entitled to regular reports from corporate management and the board of directors. These include the company's annual report and other periodic (e.g., quarterly, semiannual) and occasional communications. Shareholders and other interested investors can generally get copies of the corporation's press releases from its investor relations or public relations departments. Last but certainly not least, required quarterly and annual filings with the SEC (Forms 10-K and 10-Q) contain a wealth of additional information on the company's operations and financial condition. Form 10-K contains more financial details than the annual report that is mailed to shareholders. If you are a shareholder, you can request a 10-K directly from the company. The 10-K and related filings are also available at many libraries, through commercial databases, or directly from the SEC via the Internet (www.sec.gov).

Making Sense of Types, Classes, and Other Stock Categories: A Map of the World of Stock

Stocks come in a sometimes bewildering variety. There are many issuers of stock, from small companies to global giants. Many of these issuers offer preferred stock in addition to **common stock.**

Common stock is, as its name suggests, far more common than preferred. So who prefers preferred stock, and why? *Preferred stock* has several features that make it more attractive to some investors. First, it pays dividends at a specified rate. Second, payment of those dividends takes precedence over payment of common stock dividends. No common stock dividends can be paid out until the preferred shareholders have been paid what they were promised. Furthermore, if the assets of a company are sold, or liquidated, due to bankruptcy, preferred stock shareholders take precedence over owners of common stock in their claim on the assets. The main reason for the existence of preferred stock is the tax advantage it provides to corporate investors. When a corporation buys stock in another corporation, a large portion of the dividend payments it receives is tax-exempt. Therefore, when corporations have excess cash they want to invest, they typically look for high-dividend-paying stocks. Because preferred stock pays more dividends than common stock, that is what they buy. If this tax advantage did not exist, few corporations would even issue preferred stock.

Both kinds of stock, however, take a backseat to the bondholders, who have a prior claim both with respect to their interest payments (which are paid before any dividends) and in a bankruptcy. So preferred stock is sort of a hybrid security, something like a common stock, but also resembling a bond. The term **capital stock** is sometimes used informally as a synonym for common stock; at other times, it includes common and preferred stock. It has another, more precise, meaning when it appears on a corporation's **balance sheet.** Balance sheets are discussed in Chapter Six.

Issuers of stock decide how many shares will be authorized and how many of those will be **issued** (made available for sale), and they keep track of how many are **outstanding** (sold). **Authorized** shares (or stock) are the maximum number of shares that a corporation is allowed to create. The number of authorized shares is specified in the articles of incorporation of the company and is legally binding. It can be increased only by share-holder vote. Authorized stock is the total of issued and unissued stock. Since issuing stock costs money, corporations may issue only a small portion of authorized shares to keep down expenses. Issued stock is divided into stock that is owned by investors and stock that is owned by the corporation. The former is referred to as (issued and) outstanding, while the latter is called **treasury stock**. Treasury stock is stock that was sold and then repurchased as part of a stock buyback.

The amount of shares available for trading in the public markets is called the **float**. The float is important, because thinly traded stocks tend to be more volatile, while stocks with large trading volume tend to be less volatile. The float of a **closely held** corporation, with most of the equity in the hands of a few people or institutions, is likely to be significantly lower than the float of a company whose stock is widely held by a large number of shareholders. Even so, closely held corporations are still public companies, in contrast to **closed corporations**, which are also referred to as **close** or **privately held corporations.** (See "Publicly Held versus Closed (Close or Privately Held) Corporations.") Sometimes, one class of a company's stock—the nonvoting shares—has a large float, while the voting shares are closely held.

Publicly Held versus Closed (Close or Privately Held) Corporations

The rights of shareholders are set forth in a legal document. For a closed (or close or privately held) corporation, this document may simply be the articles of incorporation, setting forth the purpose of the corporation, number of shares issued, number of shares outstanding, who owns shares, officers and directors of the corporation, and so forth.

For a public company, there are much stricter disclosure requirements, corresponding to the greater need for information when investments are offered to the general public. For example, investors in a public offering must receive a document called a *prospectus,* which is a formal written offer to sell stock, either in a proposed new enterprise or in an existing company.

A note of caution: The term *closely held* refers to a kind of *publicly* held corporation. Confusingly, the term *private corporation* is also sometimes used to refer to a publicly held corporation to emphasize that it is owned by private shareholders (a category that includes individuals, corporations, and other private institutions) and not by the government. For example, the Federal National Mortgage Association (Fannie Mae) refers to itself as a "private corporation" to distinguish itself from the Government National Mortgage Association (Ginnie Mae), a corporation owned by the federal government. In this sense, Fannie Mae is a "private" corporation—but with over 300,000 shareholders and $400 billion in assets, it is not "privately held"! Both of these companies will be described in more detail in Chapter Fifteen.

Some companies offer numerous classes of stocks, varying in price and voting rights. When stock is described as **classified**, this does not refer to secrecy, but rather to different classes of stock authorized by the articles of incorporation. For example, a corporation may authorize the creation of two classes of stock, Class A and Class B. Classified stock is used to pre-serve certain rights for shareholders of one class of stock. Typically, this is done by restricting the voting rights to shareholders of a particular class, thereby keeping control of the corporation in the hands of those shareholders. Classified stock, which was widespread in the 1920s, fell out of favor after the **crash of 1929** and the **Great Depression** of the 1930s, but it has been making a comeback in recent years. **Control stock** is the stock owned by a shareholder or group of shareholders who own a sufficient number of voting shares to control the corporation. While, theoretically, control can require more than half of the voting shares of a corporation, in many cases a much smaller percentage is sufficient, as long as most of the other shares are held by inactive shareholders.

Voting, Nonvoting, and the Rights of Minority Shareholders

Ownership of common stock ordinarily entitles the shareholder to vote on issues affecting the corporation or to designate a proxy to vote on his or her behalf. Sometimes, however, the founders of a company create more than one class of stock, using the voting stock to retain control for themselves, while selling nonvoting stock to raise capital.

Most public companies have only one class of stock—with voting rights. These rights are in proportion to the amount of common stock owned. Even so, the most common method of voting, known as **statutory voting**, gives a **majority shareholder** the ability to elect directors of his or her own choosing, by giving each share one vote for each open position on the board of directors. Votes cannot be accumulated to be cast for a single director, who might be an advocate of other, **minority shareholders**.

An alternative system, known as **cumulative voting**, works as follows. Say there are six open positions on the board of IJK Corporation. A holder of 100 shares would have a total of 100 votes for each of six positions. Under statutory voting, such a shareholder could not vote more than 100 shares for any position, but under cumulative voting, that individual could vote all 600 shares for one candidate, making it more likely that the shareholder would have at least one director representing his or her interests.

Under certain circumstances, a shareholder or bondholder may be given coupons or other means to receive special "sweet deals," whether discounts on additional purchases of the same security or incentives to buy or trade for another security offered by the same company. Shareholders, and frequently bondholders, may have certain rights to exchange one security for another. This makes extra work for investors, who have to figure out how much the stock is really worth. Various other investments, including convertible preferred stock, **convertible** bonds, **stock options**, and **warrants**, can all be converted into common stock. The conditions under which conversion is both possible and advantageous to the owner of the convertible instrument vary from instrument to instrument and from owner to owner. For example, an executive may hold a significant number of options that can be **exercised** only at certain times. New accounting rules guide a corporation's accountants (and industry **analysts**) in calculating the **earnings per share (EPS)** on a **diluted** basis.

earnings per share (EPS) Measure of a stock's profitability, either historically (trailing EPS) or prospectively (forecast EPS).

There are many more varieties of stocks. Some are blue chip, others red chip. *Blue chip stocks* are stocks in the largest public companies with high name recognition. Traditionally, blue chips have appealed to individuals seeking both long-term growth and current income through dividends, and to institutions as one of the two pillars of their investment portfolios (the other being bonds). *Red chips*, in contrast, refer to the shares of smaller, newer companies, which may be both riskier and potentially more rewarding than their blue chip brethren. The term *red chip* has also been used in a more specialized context, to refer to the shares of companies based in (the People's Republic of) China. Some of these companies are quite large; the red chip label stems from the risk of investing in an emerging market without a well-developed regulatory and legal framework (as well as a wordplay, of course, on the old term "Red China").

We will encounter even more varieties of stock in the remaining chapters of this section. A brief mention will suffice for now. Some companies offer additional shares of stock through dividend reinvestment programs, or DRIPs. An increasing number of companies large and small are taking advantage of new technologies to sell their stock directly to the public, bypassing brokers and sometimes even underwriters. These are discussed in Chapter Eight (on buying and selling stock). **American Depository Receipts**

(ADRs) are making it easier for U.S. investors to own foreign stock. ADRs are described in the section on sources of information about stocks (Chapter Seven). Finally, all this growth and change has brought with it a new wave of scamsters, selling **chop stocks** to defraud the unwary public. These dangers are explained in Chapter Eight.

Chapter 5

STOCK MARKETS

From the Buttonwood Tree to the World Wide Web

For the vast majority of investors, stocks are bought and sold in the markets. Your success as an investor, and your comfort with your investments, is at least in part coupled with how well you understand the markets in which your stock trades. To help you achieve a broader perspective, this chapter pulls back from the close-up view of stocks offered in the previous chapter to take in the bigger picture: the markets themselves.

Whereas once you could point to a building and say, "There is the stock market," technology has changed all that forever. The change, though most obvious in the last few years, has been decades in the making. It no longer makes any sense to think of a market, even the **New York Stock Exchange (NYSE)**, that one-time bastion of **open-outcry markets**, as being limited to the floor of its exchange building. Not only is the New York Stock Exchange no longer primarily based on "open outcry," it has in the last decade transformed itself into a publicly traded company (ticker NYX), dispensing with its famous "seats" and merging with **Euronext** to form a global financial marketplace.

Table 5-1   Major Stock Markets of the World as of December 2008

Name of Market	Year Founded	Market Cap*	Principal Regulator
NYSE Group	1792	9,209	SEC
Tokyo SE Group	1949	3,116	MoF
Nasdaq	1971	2,396	SEC
Euronext	2000	2,102	various
London SE	1773	1,868	FSA
Shanghai SE	1990	1,425	CSRC
Hong Kong Exchanges	1891	1,329	CFC
Deutsche Börse	1993	1,111	BAFin/ESA
TSX Group (Canada)	1992	1,033	SEC
BME Spanish Exchange	2002	948	SSEC

Source: World Federation of Exchanges, www.world-exchanges.org
*US $billions, year end 2008.

Historically, there were important differences between **stock exchanges** like the NYSE and **over-the-counter (OTC)** dealer-based markets like the **National Association of Securities Dealers Automated Quotation (Nasdaq)** system. Some of these differences persist, while others have blurred as a market like Nasdaq has itself become an **exchange**. Over-the-counter markets operate without a central location where traders can come into physical contact. Instead, all trading is done by computer terminal and/ or telephone. We will focus on these two key markets, highlighting the roles played by economic development, regulatory changes, and innovations in information technology. To further clarify our discussion, we will briefly describe **electronic communications networks (ECNs)**, electronic markets primarily used by institutional traders, and will conclude by describing how the evolution of markets is accelerating in new and sometimes unpredictable ways. (For an overview of the world's major stock markets, see Table 5-1.)

The Big Board

The New York Stock Exchange (often just called the NYSE, pronounced by spelling it out) is the second oldest (the Philadelphia Exchange is the oldest) and the largest (by many measures) stock exchange in the United States. Its origin may be traced to the **Buttonwood Agreement** of 1792, which established common commissions for securities trading. At the time, only five securities were traded in New York: two bank stocks and three government bonds.

Trading activity picked up following the War of 1812, as insurance stocks were added to the growing list of bank stocks and government bonds being traded. In 1817, the New York Stock and Exchange Board was created, traders moved inside, and trading took place in two sessions of a **call market**, one in the morning, another in the afternoon. In a call market, the names of stocks are called out one at a time, with all trading limited to the stock most recently announced. Continuous trading in multiple stocks was still more than 50 years away. In the intervening years, a confluence of economic, technological, and regulatory changes would set the stage for its development:

- The exchange prohibits trading in the street (1836).
- The telegraph is invented (1844).
- Listing standards are tightened (1853).
- The first transatlantic cable is laid (1866).
- Stock ticker brings current market price to investors (1867).
- Member seats become a "property right" and can be bought and sold (1868).
- Listed shares must be registered (1869).

Where Do Ticker Symbols Come From?

In 1867, a man named Edward A. Calahan received a patent for the *ticker*, a small printing machine for transmitting lists of stock symbols and their prices over telegraph lines. It was also used to transmit commodity prices. Calahan worked as an operator for the American Telegraph Company. His coworkers had developed a set of abbreviations, or *ticker symbols,* for the names of stocks they had to transmit (using Morse code) over telegraph lines. One-letter abbreviations went to the most important stocks of the day. Some of those one-letter abbreviations have survived to the present day. For example, Sears, Roebuck still has its *S,* while AT&T retains its *T.*

Eventually, Calahan's device was improved upon by Thomas Edison, whose ticker became a fixture and an emblem of the stock market in the first half of the twentieth century.

Continuous trading was introduced in 1871. Under the new system, brokers who specialized in a stock remained at a fixed location, leading to the creation of trading posts and specialists. From an *annual* trading volume of roughly 50,000 shares in 1829, volume mushroomed to the first million-plus trading *day* on December 15, 1886.

A Seat on the Exchange

From 1953 until 2006, the NYSE was a membership organization with a total of 1,366 "seats." Seats could only be purchased or sold by individuals. The owner had trading privileges and access to the floor of the exchange. Typically, these individuals represent brokerage firms or firms that act as specialists in the stock of a particular company. Seats, like taxicab medallions, were frequently leased for use by third parties.

Continuous Trading

Trading on the NYSE is done by **double auction**, meaning that offers to buy and sell securities proceed side by side. **Specialists** are responsible for maintaining an orderly market in a particular security. This means that they must try to match buyers and sellers in a way that is fair to both. In addition to matching buyers and sellers, specialists are permitted to buy and sell for their own accounts to help maintain liquidity in the security.

Until very recently, all orders placed through the NYSE in a particular security went through the specialist. In 2007, NYSE introduced a **hybrid market** that gave market participants the option of routing their orders to an electronic system *or* using the traditional trading floor with its open outcry. There are two basic types of orders: *market orders* and *limit orders.*

- **Market orders** are instructions to buy or sell stock at the best available price. They are the most common type of orders.

(Continued)

- **Limit orders** tell your broker to buy or sell stock at the limit price or better. The **limit price** is a price you set when placing the order. For a given purchase, it is the most you will pay; for a given sale, it is the minimum you will accept. You can also place a limit order to buy along with one to sell. For example, if IJK Corporation is currently trading at $42 per share, you can place a limit order to buy 100 shares of IJK at $40 or better (less) and to sell 100 shares IJK at $45 or better (more).

There are a variety of terms for special types of limit orders: *day orders, good-till-canceled (GTC),* and *stop orders.*

- **Day orders** are limit orders that are valid only the day they are made.
- **Good-till-canceled (GTC)** are limit orders that continue in force until they are filled or you cancel them.
- **Stop orders** instruct the broker to buy or sell at the market once a certain price target—the stop price—has been achieved. Stop orders are less restrictive than pure limit orders; the market price may be worse than the stop price when the broker executes the order. Stop orders require only that someone bought or sold at the stop price. Pure limit orders require that you get the stipulated price.

In addition to specialists, other members include **floor brokers** who work for member firms and execute trades on behalf of clients. Since 1996, floor brokers have been provided with wireless communication devices that allow them to receive trading instructions. Once the floor broker has instructions, that individual must go to the appropriate trading post on the floor of the exchange where he or she is surrounded by other floor brokers and specialists in the stock (or other security) being bought and sold. The broker executes the transaction at the best available price. Information about the trade is processed and delivered to the client's broker, who communicates it to the client. This can all happen in a matter of seconds, while the customer is on the phone.

Table 5–2 Original 12 Stocks in the DJIA

American Cotton Oil	Laclede Gas
American Sugar	National Lead
American Tobacco	North American
Chicago Gas	Tennessee Coal & Iron
Distilling & Cattle Feeding	U.S. Leather Preferred
General Electric	U.S. Rubber

Ten years later, on May 26, 1896, the Dow Jones Industrial Average was published for the first time. *The Wall Street Journal* began daily publication later in the same year. The starting value of the index was 40.94. The original 12 stocks and the current composition of the list are displayed in Tables 5–2 and 5–3, respectively.

The Dow Jones Industrial Average: Mother of All Stock Indexes

The Dow Jones Industrial Average (DJIA) is the best-known stock market index. An *index* is a list of stocks, bonds, or other securities whose prices are combined in a type of averaging process to come up with a number that represents their collective value. For example, the DJIA is a list of 30 stocks. Not just any 30 stocks, mind you, but 30 of the bluest of the blue chips. See Table 5–3 for a listing of the components of the DJIA as of April 2009, along with each stock's ticker symbol and the year it entered the index. Current components of the Dow may be retrieved at www.djaverages.com.

The simplest type of index gives equal weight to all its components. But not all stocks count equally in the DJIA. It is a **price-weighted** index. This means that stocks with higher prices are counted more heavily in figuring the value of the index. Other indexes, such as the Standard & Poor's 500 Index, are weighted in proportion to the free float market capitalization of the stocks in the index.

Table 5–3   Stocks in the Dow Jones Industrial Average (April, 2009)

Stock	Ticker Symbol	Year First Entered DJIA
3M	MMM	1976 (Minnesota Mining and Manufacturing)
Alcoa[1]	AA	1959 (Aluminum Company of America)
American Express	AXP	1982
AT&T	T	1999 (SBC Communications)
Bank of America	BAC	2008
Boeing	BA	1987
Caterpillar	CAT	1991
Chevron	CHV	1930[†][*]
Citigroup	C	1997 (Travelers Group)
Coca-Cola	KO	1932[†]
Du Pont[2]	DD	1935
ExxonMobil	XOM	1928[*] (Standard Oil)
General Electric	GE	1896[†]
General Motors	GM	1915[*]
Hewlett-Packard	HWP	1997
Home Depot	HD	1999
Intel	INTC	1999
IBM	IBM	1932[†]
Johnson & Johnson	JNJ	1997
JP Morgan Chase	JPM	1991
Kraft Foods	KFT	2008
McDonald's	MCD	1985
Merck	MRK	1979
Microsoft	MSFT	1999
Pfizer	PFE	2004
Procter & Gamble	PG	1932
United Technologies	UTX	1933[*]
Verizon	VZ	2004
Wal-Mart	WMT	1997
Walt Disney	DIS	1991

Source: Dow Jones & Co.

[1]Aluminum Company of America is the official name. If you have trouble locating a ticker, it might be because the official name of the company is different from its more familiar name.
[2]Short for E. I. du Pont de Nemours. Do you look under E. I.? du Pont? de Nemours? Just remember DD.
[*]Name change and/or merger.
[†]Stock not continuously part of the index. For example, GE, the only original DJIA stock currently in the DJIA, was absent from the list from September 1898 to April of 1899 and from April of 1901 to November of 1907.

The DJIA reached a new historic high on September 3, 1929, after a six-year **bull market.** Eight weeks later, on **Black Tuesday,** October 29, 1929, it crashed. Over the next three years, the average would decline 89% from its high. Of course, the great crashes affected not just the NYSE, but markets all over the world.

bull market   *Market characterized by a pronounced upswing in price level.*

bear market   *A*
pronounced downturn in a
market.

Of Bulls and Bears

Colloquially speaking, a **bull market** is a prolonged period of increasing prices in stocks or other securities or commodities. A **bear market** is a prolonged decline in prices. Typically, trading volume increases dramatically during a bull market. Famous bull markets include the U.S. stock market in the 1920s, Japanese stocks in the 1980s, and the Internet Bubble of the 1990s. All of these bull markets were followed by bear markets. Not all bull markets are followed by such severe bear markets. For example, the bull market in U.S. stocks that ended with the **crash of 1987** was not followed by a prolonged price decline, but rather by a gradual recovery to precrash prices that developed into an even stronger bull market. This difference may be attributable to the existence of long-term secular market trends. In this view, such trends (generally lasting 15 to 20 years) contain alternating bull and bear markets within them. A *secular bull market* is a period in which bull markets are more powerful than the bear markets with which they alternate; in contrast, a *secular bear market* is a period in which the bear markets are more damaging and the bull markets are tepid. The period 1982–2000 has been described as a secular bull market for the S&P 500, while the period 1980–1999 can be viewed as a secular bear market for gold. Note that secular bull and bear markets can co-exist in different securities and commodities and may differ in duration and degree of overlap. A more precise definition of bull and bear markets is required in order to make definitive categorizations.

Changing the definition of bull or bear market may result in significantly different beginning and ending dates, as well as changing the number of cycles. For example, some people consider a 20 percent decline from a high to constitute a bear market. By this definition, the most recent complete bull market in the DJIA ended on October 9, 2007 with the Dow over 14,000. A bear market began that day, reached a (closing) low point of 7,552 on November 20, 2008. A rally of slightly less than 20 percent had the DJIA close over 9,030 on January 2, 2009. For some, this marked the end of the bear and the beginning of a new bull market—because the DJIA made an intraday low of 7,449 in November, 2008. Though the difference to the

(Continued)

closing low of 7,552 is small, it is enough to make the rally exceed the 20% threshold this definition requires!

So we can see how tricky it can be to know when you've reached a turning point. In the present instance, one could argue that a more sensible definition would require a 25 percent gain to constitute a bull market. After all, it takes a gain of 25 percent to offset a loss of 20 percent This "sensitive dependence upon initial conditions" is definitely worth "bearing" in mind!

A Tale of Three Crashes

Three times in the last 100 years, the stock markets have collapsed dramatically, sending millions of investors into a panic and erasing billions of dollars in equity. The first of these great crashes occurred in 1929, after a six-year bull market in stocks had sent the DJIA soaring from 85.76 on October 27, 1923, to an all-time high of 381.17 on September 3, 1929. Fifty-five days later, over a two-day period beginning on Monday, October 28, and continuing on Black Tuesday, October 29, 1929, the stock market crashed. Tuesday's closing price was 230.07. Measured from the previous Friday's closing price of 298.97, the index had declined by more than 20percent Measured from the peak attained only 55 days earlier, the index had lost nearly 40 percent.

Many investors were totally wiped out. Some committed suicide. One of the reasons for the devastation (if not for the crash itself) was the widespread use of **margin,** a form of **leverage.** Using margin allows an investor to borrow part of the money needed to buy stock from a broker. In the 1920s, investors were able to buy stocks by paying only a small fraction of the cost up front. They would borrow most of the money from their brokers. For example, in those days you could buy $100,000 worth of stock with 10 percent margin ($10,000), borrowing the remaining 90 percent ($90,000) from your broker.

The catch? Each day the value of your holding is **marked to market.** Let's see what this means by using an example. If the price of the stock falls by 5 percent, the value of the stock decreases by $5,000. But you still owe $90,000 (plus one day's interest). The value of your position, sometimes called your equity, has decreased by 50 percent, from $10,000 to $5,000. The process of
(Continued)

margin   *Cash used to purchase investments with supplemental credit supplied by broker; subject to terms of a margin account agreement.*

marked to market
Calculate the market value of a position; in a margin account, used to ensure that minimum margin is maintained.

figuring out how much equity you have in your account is called *marking it to market*.

A large percentage decline in your equity triggers a **margin call** from your broker. This means that the broker is demanding more money (or eligible securities) to bring your position back up to its minimum margin requirement. This is sometimes referred to as **remargining**. If you do not come up with the money in time, your position may be **closed out**, meaning that the broker can sell your stock in order to recoup (some of) the money you owe. In the crash of 1929, many investors were not only wiped out, but they still owed significant sums to their brokers.

The magnification of losses through borrowing is the great danger of leverage. The use of borrowed money in investing is one example of leverage. Another kind of leverage that does not involve borrowing is the purchase of options (see Chapter Sixteen). Some investors engage in margin-based leverage when they are **bullish** on a stock. A small uptick in the stock brings a magnified profit because of the larger amount of stock in the investor's account. A major reason for the high degree of risk in futures markets is the common use of much higher amounts of leverage than is permissible for stocks.

Leverage is a double-edged sword. It can bring great returns, or it can cost you your shirt. Unless and until you thoroughly understand securities and the markets in which they trade, leverage may be hazardous to your financial health.

One of the many reforms instituted in the years following the crash was the regulation of margin requirements by the **Federal Reserve Board.** Under Federal Reserve **Regulation T,** initial margin has ranged between 50–100 percent for eligible stocks, meaning your broker can lend you up to half of the money needed to buy a stock.

In the months following the crash, stocks traded in a fairly narrow range, with the DJIA recouping some of its losses. It looked like the worst might be over and that prosperity was "just around the corner." In fact, what was just around the corner was the Great Depression. With 20/20 hindsight, the period from the end of 1929 to the spring of 1930 became known as the *sucker's rally*.

(Continued)

Federal Reserve Board   *Governing board of the Federal Reserve System, which serves as the central bank of the United States.*

The second great crash occurred almost 60 years later. It came after a bull market of a little over three years. This bull market began on July 24, 1984, with the DJIA closing at 1,086.57. The market reached its peak of 2,722.42 on August 25, 1987. By a strange coincidence, the crash commenced exactly 55 days after another late-summer all-time high. (See Table 5–4.)

There, were, however, three major differences:

- The market collapse happened faster in 1987 than in 1929.
- Vigorous action by newly appointed Federal Reserve Board Chairman Alan Greenspan provided desperately needed liquidity on the day following the crash. Some analysts believe that it was the Fed's intervention that prevented October 20 from becoming an international financial catastrophe.
- Finally, though it took almost two years for the market to reach precrash levels, no economic collapse followed in the wake of the 1987 crash.

Some economists believe that the roughly 60-year period between the two great crashes is no accident. They point to an underlying cycle of prices and economic activity, the so-called **Kondratieff Wave.** Indeed, looking back 60 years from the 1929 crash brings us face to face with another famous financial panic, the original Black Friday: September 4, 1869, when a business panic was precipitated by a group of financiers trying to corner the gold market.

Table 5–4   The First Two Crashes: Comparative Stats

	October 29, 1929 (Black Tuesday)	October 19, 1987 (Black Monday)
Closing price (DJIA)	230.07	1,738.74
Previous day close	260.64	2,246.74
Percent decline from previous day	11.7%	22.6%
Previous record closing high	381.17	2,722.42
Date of high	September 3, 1929	August 25, 1987
Percent decline from high	39.6%	36.1%
Number of days (from high to crash)	56	55
Interval to regain previous day close	2 days (October 31, 1929)	1 year 5 months (January 24, 1989)
Interval to regain previous high close	25 years (November 24, 1954)	2 years (August 28, 1989)

(Continued)

The third crash began roughly seven years after the bursting of the Internet Bubble. During those seven years, a Housing Bubble unfolded, fueled by extremely easy credit policies in the United States and abroad. By the summer of 2007, these credit policies gave rise to extremely unstable market conditions and an initial round of failures of hedge funds and subprime-related assets. Though the DJIA made a new peak of 14,163.53 on October 9, 2007, it had only barely broken even since 2000 after adjusting for inflation. Seventeen months later, on March 9, 2009, the DJIA was more than cut in half to a low of 6,469.95

The Incredible Growth of Trading and Capital

The total number of shares traded in a given period of time is called the *trading volume*. Trading volume on the NYSE has roughly doubled on average every 11 years, going back for more than a century. This pace of change shows no sign of letting up.

Another way of looking at trading activity focuses on the behavior of a single share. How often does the average share change hands? This number, expressed as an annual percentage, is called the **turnover**: 100% turnover means that, on average, each stock is held for about one year. You might think that the tremendous increase in trading volume has brought with it an increase in the turnover of individual shares. But you'd be in for a surprise. It is worth noting that the expansion of trading on the exchange has not been from an increase in the number of times individual shares of stock get traded. Turnover can be calculated for individual stocks, funds, even for the market as a whole. Turnover in NYSE shares set an all-time record of 319% in 1901, when trading volume was less than one-tenth of 1% of what it is today. (See Table 5–5.)

At the end of 2008, the total market capitalization of the NYSE exceeded $9 trillion. By this metric, it is by far the largest exchange in the world (see Table 5–1). As of December 31, 2008, the combined NYSE Euronext facilitates trading in the stock of the more than 8,000 companies that meet its stringent **listing requirements**. The historic landmark building at 11 Wall Street and 18 Broad Street has housed the exchange since 1903.

turnover The rate at which a stock, portfolio, or market is traded; expressed as an annual percentage.

Market Turnover Through the Years

Annual turnover on the NYSE was over 100 percent many times in the early decades of the twentieth century, before going into a long period of low turnover that began with the **Great Depression** and continued for nearly 50 years. A new uptrend in turnover began in the early 1980s, reaching 73% in 1987, the year of the second great crash, and climbing back into triple digits in the current decade, with a recent monthly peak of 173% (annualized) in October of 2008.

Table 5–5   Volume versus Turnover on NYSE

Year	Annual Trading Volume (millions of shares)	Average No. of Listed (millions of shares)	Turnover (Percent)
1901	222	70	319
1911	126	140	90
1921	173	293	59
1931	577	1,308	44
1941	171	1,459	12
1951	444	2,485	18
1961	1,021	6,773	15
1971	3,891	16,783	23
1981	11,854	36,004	33
1991	45,266	95,177	48
2001	307,509	327,723	94
2008	802,027	432,761	185

Sources: NYSE, World Federation of Exchanges

On October 30, 1929, the second day of the infamous crash of 1929 (see "A Tale of Three Crashes"), the NYSE set a new record for trading volume when 16.4 million shares changed hands. In October of 1997, the NYSE had its first day of more than *1 billion* shares traded. This more than 60-fold increase in trading activity would be impossible to imagine, much less accomplish, without the tremendous technological advances of the intervening decades. On the day of the crash itself, the ticker ran more than two hours late. On October 10, 2008, the NYSE accommodated record trading volume of more than 2.95 billion shares.

NYSE Listing Requirements (minimum standards for domestic equity-listed companies)

1. Number of holders of 100 shares or more (or of a unit of trading if less than 100 shares)
   400*

or

     Total stockholders together with average monthly trading volume (for most recent six months)
   2,200*
   100,000 shares

or

     Total stockholders together with average monthly trading volume (for most recent 12 months)
   500*
   1,000,000 shares

2. Number of publicly held shares[†]

   1,100,000 shares[†]

3. Minimum Market Value of Public Shares
   $100 million, or $60 million for IPOs, spin-offs, carve-outs, and affiliated companies

---

*The number of beneficial holders of stock held in "street name" will be considered in addition to holders of record. The Exchange will make any necessary check of such holdings.
[†]Shares held by directors, officers, or their immediate families and other concentrated holdings of 10 percent or more are excluded in calculating the number of publicly held shares.
[‡]If the unit of trading is less than 100 shares, the requirement relating to number of publicly held shares shall be reduced proportionately.

Source: NYSE. For additional details and changes, see www.nyse.com.

From Ticker Symbols to CUSIPs: How to Get a Quote

Anyone who has ever tried to find the closing price of a stock in their favorite newspaper or online service knows that it can be time-consuming and frustrating. It is seldom enough to know the name of the company whose stock (or other security) has captured your interest. Newspapers and online services don't always provide the company's name, or even a recognizable abbreviation, when listing the stock. If you don't recognize the abbreviation or the ticker symbol for the stock, what can you do? Today, you have a great option that wasn't available when the first edition of this book was published: you can "consult the oracle at Google," i.e., go to finance. google.com and just start typing what you know. This can save a lot of time otherwise spent in looking it up, asking others if they remember the ticker, and so on. Sometimes, you may wish to identify a security through its Committee on Uniform Security Identification Procedure (CUSIP) code. CUSIPs are alphanumeric codes that uniquely identify securities. Colloquially, CUSIPs refers to the identification codes themselves. All U.S. securities have unique CUSIPs. For example, the CUSIP for IBM common stock is 45920010. The first six numbers of the CUSIP are its issuer number or *cnum;* this number uniquely identifies an issuer. The seventh and eighth digits uniquely identify the security. There is a ninth digit. It is called the *check digit* and it is used to mathematically ensure the accuracy of the whole CUSIP number for data transmission. IBM's cnum is 459200. Cnums are useful if you want to get a listing of all of an issuer's securities. This is especially important for corporate bonds and stock options, because a single issuer can have dozens of these.

National Association of Securities Dealers Automated Quotation System (Nasdaq)

Nasdaq, the leading electronic stock exchange in the United States, originally was set up by the National Association of Securities Dealers (NASD) in 1971. Its roots can be traced to the 1950s, when institutional investors first began buying large quantities of common stock. Rather than pay the high brokerage commission costs of the time, these investors traded large blocks of stock off of the exchange floor, using brokers who were not members of the exchange. Aside from saving on commissions, these large investors were trying to avoid moving the market with a large buy or sell order, thus hoping to get a better price.

With the deregulation of broker commissions in May 1975, some of these brokerage firms became members of the exchanges so that they could trade with existing members. In parallel with this development, member firms began trading blocks of stock off of the exchange floor, subject to the rules of the NYSE.

The NASD was a not-for-profit organization, founded in 1939. It was originally sponsored jointly by the Securities and Exchange Commission (SEC) and the Investment Bankers Conference, in compliance with the Maloney Act of 1938. In 1998, Nasdaq merged with the AMEX, the New York-based stock exchange that had for decades lived in the shadow of the NYSE. Nasdaq became independent from NASD in 2000; in July 2007, the NASD's regulatory functions were combined with those of the NYSE under a new **self-regulatory organization (SRO)**, the **Financial Industry Regulatory Authority (FINRA)**.

Nasdaq lists more companies than any other major exchange; its market cap roughly equals that of London and Tokyo, putting them in a virtual three-way tie for second largest equity market (not counting Euronext, which is a **subsidiary** of NYSE Euronext). The role of the market makers in Nasdaq trading will be discussed further in Chapter Nine.

Instinet was an early innovator in electronic trading. Founded in 1969, it pioneered electronic block trading for institutional investors; offered the first quote montage for a U.S.-listed market; introduced direct market access (DMA) to U.S. exchanges; and pioneered after hours trading.

After its 1987 acquisition by Reuters PLC, a British company, in a **hostile takeover**, Instinet CEO Bill Lupien left to form a new alternative trading system (ATS) which ultimately became Optimark Technologies. Though Optimark failed in its ambitious attempt to transform the nature of trading and to make markets more efficient, it inspired a large number of imitators (including Liquidnet and Pipeline) and a burgeoning field of algorithmic trading that continues to grow today.

Users of ATSs include traders and brokers who work for **sell-side** firms, which is Wall Street jargon for brokerage firms. Sell-side firms use alternative trading systems for customer accounts and for their own internal trading. Other users are the traders who work for the **buy side**—mutual fund managers, pension fund managers, and other professional money managers working at banks, insurance companies, and other kinds of investment firms.

What we have been talking about up until now is sometimes referred to as the **secondary market**, to distinguish it from the market for securities that have not been previously sold. These securities, which include the IPOs of corporate stock, as well as additional shares that a company may issue from time to time, are issued in the **primary market.** Proceeds from the sale of stock in a primary market are divided between the issuer and the underwriters, who receive a commission for assuming some of the risk associated with the new issue and facilitating its sale, either directly or through dealers.

sell side Underwriters and brokers/dealers who sell securities to retail and institutional investors.

secondary market Market in which already issued securities trade.

Technology, Dark Pools, and the Evolution of a Unified Market

The great and continuing consolidation of exchanges is being driven by technology and deregulation. Simultaneously, the emergence of "dark pools"—electronic trading systems used by sophisticated traders in search of liquidity—have increased the fragmentation and complexity of orders and trading. The combined impact of these forces is hard to measure, much less extrapolate. Nonetheless, the evolution of a truly international market system seems increasingly likely.

Chapter 6
THREE VIEWS OF THE NUMBERS

Fundamental Analysis, Technical Analysis, and Quantitative Analysis

Whatever label they go by, all market strategies and systems have at least this much in common: They are attempts to invest on a disciplined basis. A disciplined approach is the best defense against being governed by the emotion of the moment, which could be called the strategy of not having a strategy. That being said, however, no market strategy, system, or model works all the time. All have blind spots, in both theoretical and practical terms. Thus, while discipline is important to prevent being governed by emotion, it may be equally important to retain the flexibility of looking at things in more than one way.

In this chapter, we provide an overview of three major ways of analyzing investments: fundamental analysis, technical analysis, and quantitative analysis. Two things should be noted: First, as suggested by the title of this chapter, all three approaches involve numbers. Second, in practice, many investors use a mixed approach. For example, you may decide after studying this chapter that fundamental analysis is a good guide to the value of an investment, but that technical analysis must be used to figure out how other investors are viewing the market.

Fundamental Analysis

As an investment tool, **fundamental analysis*** is a method for determining the intrinsic value of companies. *Intrinsic value* is a theoretical number that reflects what fundamental analysis determines the stock or other security to be really worth. If the market price is greater than the intrinsic value calculated by a fundamental analyst, then the analyst may describe the security as **fully valued** (probably a euphemism for overpriced). Or the analyst may describe it as **rich.** In contrast, if the market price is less than the intrinsic value, the analyst will describe it as undervalued or **cheap** (but not poor!). Cheap stocks gladden the heart of the fundamental analyst.

price target   *The price that a Wall Street analyst forecasts for a stock.*

The primary tools of the fundamental analyst are balance sheets, **profit and loss (P&L) statements**, and other information supplied in 10-Ks, quarterly filings, and annual reports of companies. This information is used to predict future stock prices and earnings of the companies and to determine whether and to what extent a company should be included in a portfolio.

Wall Street's **financial analysts** frequently combine fundamental analysis with visits to the companies they follow when developing their **recommended list**, the list of stocks that a brokerage firm's analysts like. These analysts frequently set **price targets** for the companies they follow. They also generate **earnings estimates** that are closely monitored by investors, especially by institutional investors who own shares in these companies. They may rate a company as **strong buy, buy, accumulate,** or **hold.** "Hold" may be a polite way of saying "sell" (see feature). Analysts may also rank stocks as "market outperform," "market perform," or "market underperform."

---

*The phrase *fundamental analysis* is also applied to a way of analyzing the economy. By studying inventories, inflation, and interest rates, fundamental analysts attempt to forecast future economic conditions.

Do Analysts Tell a Balanced Tale?

Over the years, many studies have called into question the independence and reliability of "**sell-side**" research. For example, one study examined research reports on nearly 4,000 companies for the period 1987 to 1994. These reports were written by over 500 research analysts employed by more than 100 different brokerage firms. The conclusion: Analysts were far more likely to add coverage of "good news stocks" and to drop coverage of "bad news stocks." Not so long ago, the Wall Street analyst's credo appeared to be that "if you can't find anything good to say, drop the stock and find a better one."

This problem persisted for so long that for many it was just a "given." However, in response to some of the more egregious examples of this bias, the NASD in 2004 adopted Rule 1050 that requires sell-side analysts to pass two specialized exams (above and beyond **Series 7**).

A corporate balance sheet (also referred to as a *statement of financial position,* or a *statement of condition*) is a financial report providing a snapshot of a corporation's **assets, liabilities,** and **owners' equity** rendered on a particular day, typically at the end of a financial reporting period (e.g., month-end or year-end). By definition, assets must equal liabilities plus owners' equity—this is the fundamental equation implied by the balance sheet.

$$\text{Assets} = \text{liabilities} + \text{owners' equity}$$

The balance sheet provides information about a company's condition only on a particular date; by itself, it cannot tell you anything about the company's operations over time. Comparison of balance sheets for different periods can show how assets, liabilities, and owners' equity have evolved over time. But you would need to infer this information by calculating the changes in the balance sheet on a line-by-line basis, being careful to know any adjustments that might be noted in the **footnotes to the financial statement.**

A more direct approach to seeing a company's operations over time is through its profit and loss statement (P&L), also called the *income statement, statement of profit and loss, operating statement,* or *income and expense statement*. The P&L provides information about **revenue**, costs, expenses, and earnings for a particular period.

The balance sheet, together with the P&L statement, constitutes a company's financial statement. These statements must be prepared and presented in conformity with **Generally Accepted Accounting Principles (GAAP)** accounting standards defined by the **Financial Accounting Standards Board (FASB)**, an independent self-regulatory body established in 1973 as a successor to the Accounting Principles Board.

Example of a Corporate Balance Sheet for the IJK Corporation

You set up a company, the IJK Corporation, with initial capital of $5 million. Its initial balance sheet, simplified, would look like this:

Assets		Liabilities and Shareholders' Equity	
Cash:	$5,000,000	Shareholders' equity:	$5,000,000

Having set up the company, you buy a million-dollar machine for your business. This purchase changes your assets, but leaves the liability/shareholder equity side the same. Now the balance sheet looks like this:

Assets		Liabilities and Shareholders' Equity	
Cash:	$4,000,000	Shareholders' equity: $5,000,000	
Machinery:	1,000,000		
	$5,000,000	$5,000,000	

Now you go to the bank and borrow $5 million. This creates a liability and an equal addition to the asset side to keep the two sides in balance. Let's assume that the asset is in the form of cash for now:

Assets		Liabilities and Shareholders' Equity	
Cash:	$9,000,000	Bank debt:	$ 5,000,000
Machinery:	1,000,000	Shareholders' equity:	5,000,000
	$10,000,000		$10,000,000

Book Value versus Market Value of Companies and Their Assets

Corporate assets are expressed on the balance sheet in terms of **book value.** The book value of an asset is defined by accounting conventions. These rules allow a company to recover its costs over time through a process called **depreciation.** For example, a piece of machinery is purchased for $100,000. Initially, its book value is simply its cost. Each year, the value of that asset is reduced according to a depreciation formula that allows the company to gradually lower the value at which the asset is "held," while receiving a tax benefit for the amount depreciated.

In contrast, the **market value** of an asset is the price that it could be sold for today. There is no general rule or formula to relate these two numbers. Using the $100,000 machine as an example, one year after purchase it might have a resale value of $60,000, while its book value might be $80,000. On the other hand, fully depreciated equipment has a book value of $0, but may still have a positive market value.

The concept of book value is also applied by fundamental analysts to determine the book value per share of a company's securities. It can be thought of as one way of measuring intrinsic value. Why is this important? The book (or other intrinsic) value can be compared to the market value of the security to help identify stocks or bonds that may be worth more or less than their current market price.

For example, to calculate the book value per share of IJK Corporation common stock, simply divide **stockholders' equity,** which can be found on the company's balance sheet, by the number of shares outstanding. Say that stockholders' equity is $135 million. Divide this number by the number of IJK common shares outstanding, say 2.7 million shares, to come up with the book value per share for IJK common: $50.

stockholders' equity
From an accounting standpoint, the portion of a company's assets belonging to shareholders.

$$\frac{\$135,000,000}{2,700,000} \text{ shares } = \$50 \text{ per share}$$

The ratio of the market value of a company's securities to its book value is a traditional measure of whether those securities are underpriced or overpriced. In recent years, however, the usefulness of this ratio has decreased as the proliferation of **off-balance-sheet investments** have tended to make book value a less useful number.

In actual practice, financial analysts who work for sell-side brokers or buy-side money management firms supplement their fundamental analysis of the companies they cover with careful study of the competitive position of companies in a particular **sector** or portion thereof, consideration of prospects for the comparison group as a whole, and **interviews with management** of the corporation. On this basis they develop or revise buy/sell/hold recommendations and formulate price targets and earnings forecasts.

Technical Analysis

If, as the saying goes, a picture is worth a thousand words, a technical analyst's chart collection may be worth millions. **Technical analysis** is an intuitive, graphic approach to understanding what the market, or a particular stock, is doing. It includes many charting techniques (in the precomputer era, technical analysts were sometimes referred to as *chartists*). Through their charts and interpretations of those charts, technical analysts attempt to read the mind of the market, sometimes with great success. Skeptics suggest that technical analysis is a rubber-band theory—they say it can be stretched to fit any new data that comes its way.

Pure technical analysts do not worry about the financial condition of a company or commodity they are interested in. Nor do they worry much about the skeptics. From their standpoint, all important information is already in the chart.

Traditional technicians charted prices and volumes. Today, many continue to chart those things, but the list has expanded to include return data, **volatility**, and other risk measures, and moving averages and other **smoothed** or **transformed** versions of the underlying data sets.

volatility A measure of how much the price of a security moves around its mean, or average, value; more generally, the tendency of security prices to fluctuate.

As an example of smoothing, instead of plotting the daily price of IBM, a technician might examine a 200-day moving average of the price (by each day looking back on and taking a simple average of the previous 200 closing prices). For the average to be meaningful, adjustments for dividends and capital events such as **stock splits** may be necessary.

Smoothing can be regarded as one kind of data transformation. Another frequently encountered transformation, called **exponential weighting**, assigns weights to prices depending on their position in time—the further back they are, the less weight they are given. The idea is to make an average that weighs recent numbers more heavily than older ones. There are countless variations on these themes.

What Is Volatility?

In general terms, volatility is the tendency for the price of a security or commodity to jump around. When J.P. Morgan answered the question, "What will the market do next?" by saying, "It will fluctuate," he was talking about volatility.

The term *volatility* is also used to refer to a measure of how much the price of a security moves around its mean, or average, value. When used in this way, it has important applications to calculating the historical performance of a stock or other security on a risk-adjusted basis. It is also used in estimating future performance and in the pricing of options. These topics are discussed in later chapters.

Much of the language of technical analysis is anthropomorphic. Technicians speak about what the market wants to do as though the market has a mind of its own. This is hardly accidental. Almost anyone who spends a lot of time in the market comes to act as though the market has a mind, whatever the philosophical ramifications or scientific plausibility of such a position.

Some of the many charting strategies that have been used by technicians include the following.

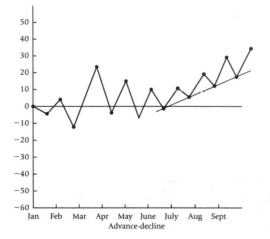

Advance-decline

- **Advance-decline (A-D) lines.** A way to chart the ratio of advancing to declining stocks (or other securities) over a given period (e.g., six months). Each point on the chart shows the ratio of the advancing stocks (stocks whose value increased) to the number of declining stocks on a particular day (or other sub-period). In general, the higher this ratio, the more bullish the interpretation. *Changes* in this ratio are also believed by some to be significant.

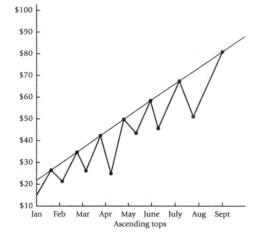

Ascending tops

- **Ascending tops.** A charting technique that draws a straight line connecting a series of market tops that get progressively higher as time goes on. This is considered a bullish signal, in contrast to *descending tops* (see page 73).

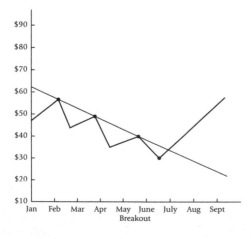

Breakout

- **Breakout.** A rise above a resistance level (e.g., a previous high) or a fall below a support level (e.g., a previous low). See pages 77 and 79 for more on resistance and support, both key technical concepts. See also *reversal* on page 78.

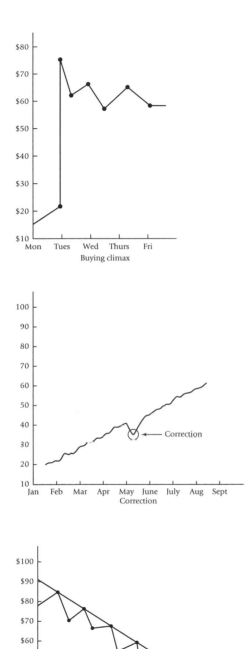

- **Buying climax.** A sharp run-up in prices that occurs when everyone wants in; taken by some technicians to presage the end of a bull market.

- **Correction.** An expected downward move in stock prices that are generally moving upward. Seen as a temporary blip. Compare to *dip* on page 74.

- **Descending tops.** Akin to ascending tops, except moving lower. Considered bearish.

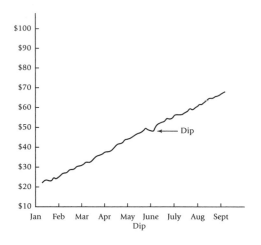

Dip

- **Dip.** A slight drop during an uptrend. Technicians often say that it's a good time to buy a stock.

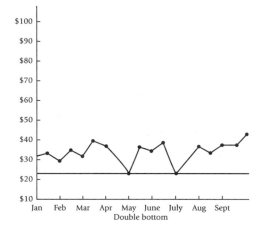

Double bottom

- **Double bottom.** If a stock hits the same number on the downside twice, then recovers without going lower, this is viewed by technicians as indicating *support* at that price. If, however, it does go lower, it is taken as a sign that it is headed lower still.

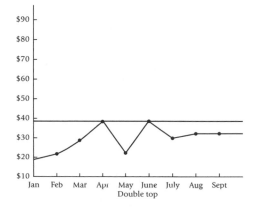

Double top

- **Double top.** Analogously, if a stock hits the same number going up, but does not go any higher, it is thought to indicate *resistance*. If the market breaks through to a higher level, it is taken as a sign of further advance (compare to *breakout*).

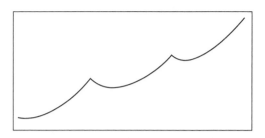

- **Elliott Wave.** A theory of market movements that makes use of **Fibonacci numbers.** The waves referred to are the cycles of up-and-down movements in market prices predicted by Elliott Wave theorists. Spectacular successes have been claimed for this approach. There have also been some spectacular erroneous predictions made by formerly widely followed market gurus.

Fibonacci Numbers

Fibonacci numbers are a series of numbers named after the thirteenth-century mathematician Fibonacci, a.k.a. Leonardo of Pisa—the "other" Leonardo—who first described them in his famous book, *Liber Abaci*. This work is credited with introducing Hindu-Arabic numerals to Europe, thus facilitating the great mathematical advances of later centuries and the technological marvels of the modern age.

Fibonacci numbers start with 0 and 1 as seed numbers. All following numbers in the series are generated by adding the previous two. Thus the series begins 0, 1, 1, 2, 3, 5, 8, 13, 21, . . . The list goes on forever. It turns out that Fibonacci numbers occur in all kinds of unlikely places, such as the number of petals in a flower. Furthermore, the ratio of a Fibonacci number to its predecessor gets closer and closer to a fixed value (approximately 1.6)—itself an important number in nature.

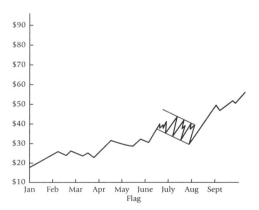

- **Flag.** A somewhat more arcane technical chart, purporting to show a period of consolidation (narrow movement in price) between either up- or downtrends. It is interpreted as indicating a continuation of the previous trend, whether up or down.

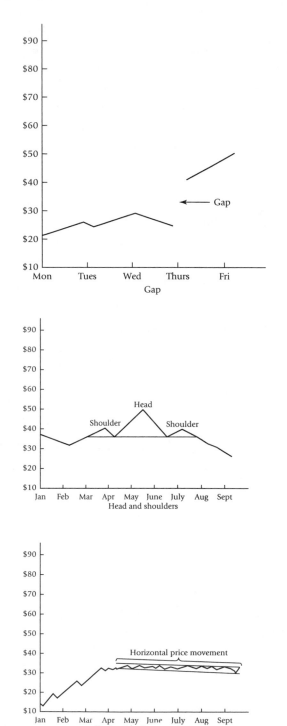

- **Gap.** A sharp discontinuity in price (up or down), frequently occurring between the close of one day's trading and the opening of the next, in response to unexpected news.

- **Head and shoulders.** A chart interpreted to indicate the reversal of a trend. If the head is above the shoulders, it is taken as bearish. If the head and shoulders are upside down, the trend is viewed as bullish.

- **Horizontal price movement.** A phrase used to describe a stock or a market that isn't doing much of anything, up *or* down. Also called a *sideways price move* or (for markets) a *flat market*.

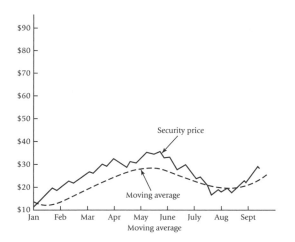

Moving average

- **Moving average.** A smoothing technique borrowed from statisticians to remove the **noise** (random fluctuations) from a set of financial data. It involves calculating an average value for a subset of data from some longer time period. For example, you could calculate a 12-month moving average of IBM month-end closing prices for a 20-year interval, say, 1989 to 2008. Notice that there are 240 months in the 20-year period, but only 229 12-month periods (with the first period ending December 1989 and the last period ending December 2008).

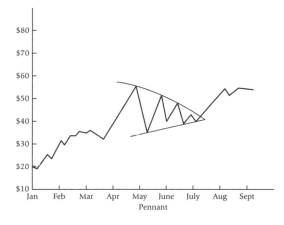

Pennant

- **Pennant.** A chart that is supposed to presage a sharp up or down move after it has completed itself.

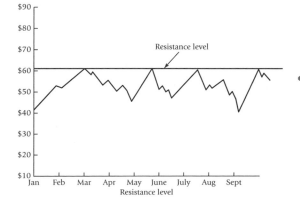

Resistance level

- **Resistance level.** A key concept of technical analysis, this is a price or other value above which the market seems unable or unwilling to go.

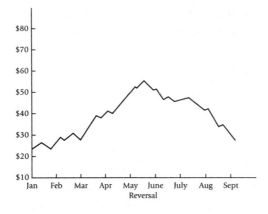

Reversal

- **Reversal.** Simply what it says, a (sustained) change in the direction of the market. Contrast to *correction, dip*.

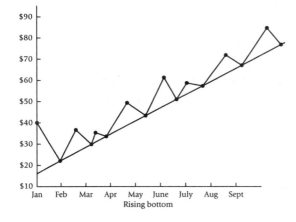

Rising bottom

- **Rising bottom.** Chart that shows a straight line connecting a series of market bottoms that get higher over time; believed to indicate higher support levels; bullish when combined with ascending tops.

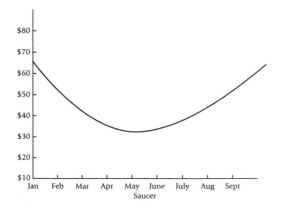

Saucer

- **Saucer.** A pattern like the Cheshire cat's smile, indicating a bottom is behind you and there's something to smile about (unless it's an inverted saucer, in which case spilled milk comes to mind).

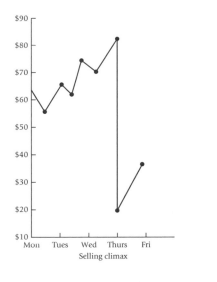

Selling climax

- **Selling climax.** A sharp drop in prices as everybody tries to sell at once. In a word, *panic* (or if you prefer, *crash*). Taken by some technicians to indicate the end of a bear market.

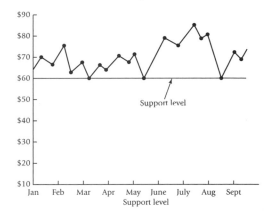

Support level

- **Support level.** The complement to resistance, a price or other value below which the market seems unable or unwilling to go.

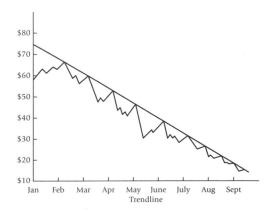

Trendline

- **Trendline.** A straight line drawn over (or under) past prices used by technicians to predict future prices. Interpret with caution. If the "trend is your friend," then perhaps the reversal is your enemy.

Technical analysis is a vast subject, with hundreds of books describing many thousands of variations on the preceding charting methods and many others. Believers in technical analysis can point to startlingly accurate predictions, including some that are well documented. Skeptics reply that technical analysis has even more impressive failures, including repeatedly wrong predictions by prominent technicians about imminent market crashes.

At the extremes of belief and skepticism, there is probably no conceivable evidence that could convert a believer into a skeptic or vice versa. In the middle ground, many investors, including many professionals, use some technical analysis methods some of the time. Some argue that the best reason to use technical analysis tools is because other people use them, so they provide a window into market sentiment. While there is certainly some truth in that argument, the window is not a very clear one, and the picture that is perceived is sometimes more like a mirror's reflection than anything else.

If you would like to experiment with technical analysis, here are two highly regarded computer programs that greatly simplify data gathering and do a great job of generating charts:

Telechart 2007 has been voted "best trading software under $500" in 2008 by *Stocks & Commodities* magazine. It can be tried out free for 30 days (800–776–4940, www.worden.com). If you decide to buy, costs begin at $29.99/month.

Metastock is more expensive (list price for their entry-level "end of day" product is $499 or $59/month). Barron's describes it as the "Rolls Royce" of technical analysis programs (Equis International, 800–882–3040, www.equis.com).

Quantitative Analysis

Quantitative analysis, as applied to investments, can be broadly defined as a method that restricts its outlook to measurable factors in determining the value and/or future price of a stock or other security. In this sense, the term **quantitative analysis** embraces nearly all of the discipline of the fundamental analyst and much of what the technical analyst does as well. The only things that are off limits are subjective judgments that are qualitative in nature, which cannot be objectively measured.

Given the broad scope of this definition, it should come as no surprise to find that Wall Street is filled with people who describe themselves as quantitative analysts. This was not always the case. In earlier times, qualitative factors such as an investor's subjective impression of a corporation's management team were given more emphasis. Relatively few quantitative analysts worked on Wall Street at the time. Computers were expensive and hard to use, making it harder and more time-consuming to create **financial market models.** The models that could be created were often not very prepossessing. Quantitative analysts were sometimes disparaged as mere **number crunchers.**

Beginning in the early 1980s, dramatically cheaper computer technology, such as PCs running Lotus 1–2–3, facilitated a move to a more quantitative approach to investing. All of a sudden the number crunchers, many of them with PhDs in physics or math, were being called **rocket scientists** and given financial problems that required complex mathematical calculations to solve. A new discipline called *financial engineering* was being created. Practitioners, including David Shaw, a former academic recruited by Morgan Stanley in the 1980s, established new brokerage firms and investment boutiques based on their mathematical models. This more elite group of quantitative analysts (sometimes shortened to **quants**) lent cachet to the field as a whole.

quant A mathematician who works in financial markets.

What Is a Model?

A model is a set of mathematical formulas or computer programs intended to represent how something works. Financial market models vary in sophistication, complexity (not the same thing!), and in clarity.

A model can incorporate sophisticated ideas, yet be relatively simple. As Einstein said in talking about models of physical reality, "Everything should be as simple as possible, but not simpler." $E = mc^2$ is an exquisite example of this idea.

Some financial market models are enormously complex, incorporating hundreds of different variables into their designs. Some of these models are open to the criticism that they overinterpret a relatively small amount of financial market data to draw unreliable conclusions.

(Continued)

Finally, some financial market models are sadly lacking in clarity. They demand subtle interpretation, vitiating the time and effort that went into creating them. If they don't make predictions that can be tested, then they really aren't modeling what they claim to be modeling. They aren't even good enough to be wrong.

More recent technological developments, notably the widespread adoption of the Internet as a major means of commerce, have increased the availability of enormous quantities of financial data. Much of it is of good quality, and much of it is inexpensive or even free. Along with this data comes an amazing variety of software tools for charting, analysis, and record keeping. We will provide an overview of this large and important subject in the next chapter. For now, we merely note its connection to the rise of quantitative investing.

An example of the quantitative approach to investing is **discounted cash flow (DCF) analysis**, which is used to relate future cash flows such as interest and dividend payments to current prices and values. A major use of DCF is in **dividend discount models (DDMs)**. Dividend discount models are used by security analysts to figure out an implied return on the money invested in a stock. Most of the major brokerage houses have developed their own proprietary stock valuation models, often based on some form of DDM. Other analysts prefer to look at total earnings projections, rather than just dividends. They use a kind of DCF called an *internal rate of return calculation* to develop an alternative way of judging the intrinsic value of a security.

A very different type of model is based on the impact of the **presidential election cycle (PEC)** on stock market prices. Since 1941, the total return on stocks comprising the S&P 500 have been positive in all of the third years (including 1987 and 2007) and in all but two of the fourth years of presidential terms (the two exceptions being 2000 and 2008). In contrast, total returns in the first and second years of the PEC have been negative fourteen times over the same period and have shown far greater volatility. There have been some great years in the first half of the PEC (e.g., 1954, 1997), but also some really bad ones.

Presidential election cycle models are based on observations linking the behavior of the stock market to the various phases of the four years of a president's term of office. One simple model has investors staying out of the market for the first 18 months of a president's term of office and remaining fully invested during the final 30 months. Variations on the basic strategy look at other factors, such as incumbency and the political party of the president, or even which party controls Congress.

Many well-known investment indicators are incorporated into models:

PEG ratio (a.k.a. *fool ratio*)

Price to sales

Price to cash flow

Positive earnings surprises

Stock buybacks

A large number of simple quantitative investment strategies are presented and analyzed in *The Stock Trader's Almanac 2009* by Yale Hirsch and Jeffrey A. Hirsch.

enhanced indexing
Strategy for outperforming index funds using mathematical models.

Indexing

Indexing is frequently described as a passive investment strategy, in contrast to the active trading strategies pursued by many individual investors and professional money managers. It is passive in the sense that other than adjusting the portfolio of stocks to reflect changes in the index, no trading needs to be done, nor is any investment analysis required. But it is not as static as the portfolio of a unit investment trust, which does not change at all.

The practice of managing money to **replicate** an index began with institutional money managers who decided that such a strategy was reasonable for at least a portion of the assets under their control.

Index investing received a boost from academic theories, notably the Capital Asset Pricing Model (CAPM) developed by William Sharpe. Sharpe, whose work earned him a Nobel Prize, suggests that it is impossible to really beat the market after making adjustments for **risk**. The move toward indexing received additional impetus from studies showing that, for most periods studied, the majority of professional money managers fail to do even as well as benchmark indexes such as Standard & Poor's 500 Index. An increasing number of individual investors are taking advantage of the low fees associated with index investing, jettisoning their actively managed mutual funds and buying index funds like Vanguard's Index 500 portfolio, which has become one of the largest mutual funds in the United States. Others have discovered that they do not even need to buy a mutual fund; they are buying SPDRs (S&P 500 depository receipts, referred to as "spiders"), a stocklike security that trades on the American Stock Exchange and is designed to track the value of the S&P 500.

How Easy Is It to Replicate an Index?

Index investing sounds simple. And in principle, it is. In practice, however, it requires both skill and resources on the part of the professional money manager to make sure that his or her portfolio follows the index as closely as possible.

Part of the difficulty is that an index is merely an abstract set of securities whose values are combined in an ideal world without transaction costs or problem trades. An index portfolio, on the other hand, is made up of real securities (including, possibly, options and futures). Real securities cost money to trade, incurring costs not reflected in the theoretical value of the index. Sometimes, too, mistakes are made, adding to the divergence between actual and theoretical values. If you are investing in an index fund, make sure that it accurately tracks the index it is supposed to mirror.

Divergence in value between a portfolio and the index it is supposed to replicate is sometimes referred to as *tracking error*. Index portfolios should have minimal tracking error—even to the upside. If an index portfolio deviates far from its benchmark, it is failing to meet its investment objective.

Indexing is an increasingly popular response to the complexity and cost of investment management. Recall that an index is a number derived from a set of underlying numbers according to some definite rule. In the investment world, some indexes, like the Dow Jones Industrial Average, are price-weighted. Others, like Standard & Poor's 500 Index, are (free-float) market-value-weighted. Over time, many indexes change, dropping companies that are no longer important (or have merged or gone out of business) and adding newly created companies in their place. Also, the weights accorded to the underlying companies can change on a minute-to-minute basis.

What Is Arbitrage?

Sometimes you may hear the term **arbitrage** used in discussions of the financial markets. Arbitrage refers to a family of related investment strategies with a long and interesting history. In its classic form, arbitrage is the simultaneous buying and selling of the same thing in two different markets in order to profit from a momentary price discrepancy. In order to engage in arbitrage successfully, you must have better information than the average person; you must be able to act quickly in two different markets, possibly on opposite ends of the globe; and you must be able to do it cheaply enough so that the cost of your transaction doesn't devour your profits.

A more complex type of arbitrage involves simultaneous or near-simultaneous purchase and sale of two distinct, but highly correlated, sets of securities. For example, there is index arbitrage, in which the cash and futures markets are monitored for "mispricings" (i.e., occasions when the cash price of a stock index is either higher or lower than it should be relative to the futures price of the same index).

Many investors have concluded that they can't beat the index, nor can they identify a professional whom they believe is likely to beat the index. That being the case, their best and cheapest approach to investing is to "buy the index." This topic is discussed further in Section III.

Chapter 7

WHERE TO FIND INFORMATION ON STOCKS AND FINANCIAL MARKETS

A fter reading this chapter you will know how to get the information, data, and other tools you need to support your investment program and perform the analyses of your choice, whether fundamental, technical, quantitative, or some combination thereof.

As we have seen in Chapter Six on approaches to investment analysis, the process is highly dependent on good information. Where can you get the information you need for investing? This question can be separated into three parts, as follows:

- Who are the sources of the information?
- Who distributes the information?
- What are the delivery mechanisms for the information?

Before you get too comfortable with these distinctions, we must point out that sources and distributors frequently overlap. For example, stock exchanges transmit information about trades to many data vendors. They also distribute some of the same information directly in competition with those vendors. Sometimes, vendors add value by checking the data for errors and providing user-friendly formats for their customers. In the process, they may uncover inconsistencies in the data that the exchange does not know about, giving the distributor cleaner data than the source.

Just as the lines dividing data sources and distributors blur, so do the lines separating various means of accessing data. Sometimes, you can get the same information via a toll-free number or over the Internet. Many cell phones can send and receive electronic messages over the Internet. Increasingly, information is available on multiple delivery mechanisms, sometimes piggybacking on each other. Media such as the Internet and World Wide Web, email, cell phones, fax machines, DVDs, and print are increasingly becoming interoperable (and sometimes interchangeable) at the end user's discretion.

Good Data Is Hard to Find

Not too long ago, a major newspaper published a correction in its financial section, stating that in some editions of the previous Saturday's paper, the closing price of the Dow Jones Industrial Average, the yield on 30-year U.S. Treasury bonds, and the dollar/yen exchange rate were all stated incorrectly. The interesting thing was the size of the errors. The Dow was quoted incorrectly by some 2,000 points! The bond yield and the dollar/yen exchange rate were also far from their correct values.

These kinds of errors happen. Data entry errors, use of the wrong computer file (which might have last year's data), and corruption of data by hardware

(Continued)

failure, software failure, or by malicious persons with access to the records are all possible sources of problems. To guard against such problems, it's a good idea to use and compare multiple sources of data whenever possible. *Always investigate discrepancies in your data.* A helpful practice is to establish ranges of acceptable values for prices and to automatically investigate any price (or other data value) that falls outside of this range. For example, if yesterday IJK Corporation was trading at $100 per share, and today's close is $11 per share, find out what's going on! Did the stock really lose 89 percent of its value? Or did someone leave out a zero somewhere? (The price may really be $101, or perhaps $110 per share.) It could also be that the stock just did a 10-for-1 split and is up 10 percent. It's not unusual for a busy investor to miss an announcement of a stock split, discovering it in a moment of panic when it appears the stock has plummeted. If you get your data in a newspaper, there should be a code telling you that the stock has recently split. But if your data is delivered electronically, it may not be so obvious what has happened.

A cardinal principle of investment analysis is borrowed from the computer programming department: garbage in, garbage out (GIGO). This means that a good investment decision is highly dependent on good data. We have seen how bad data can be very misleading. Sometimes, even accurate data can mislead if it is presented out of context or graphed in a way that fools the eye. For instance, when comparing graphs of stock prices, it is good practice to make sure that the prices are shown according to a consistent scale and over a meaningful time period. Standard mistakes (and/or deliberate misrepresentations) include comparing prices for different time periods with different bases and scaling factors (see Figures 7–1a, b, and c), or even in different currencies.

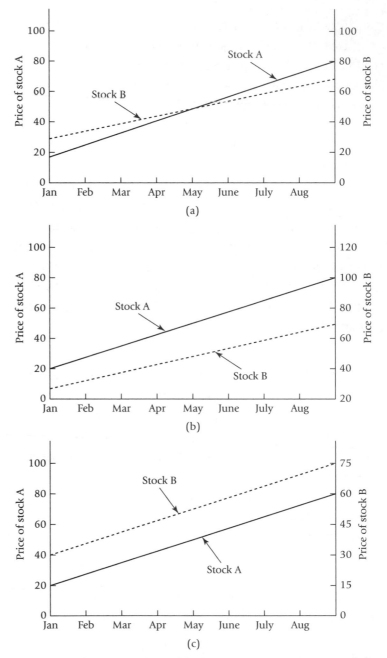

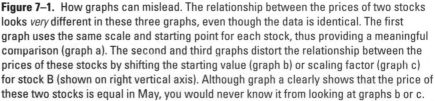

Figure 7–1. How graphs can mislead. The relationship between the prices of two stocks looks *very* different in these three graphs, even though the data is identical. The first graph uses the same scale and starting point for each stock, thus providing a meaningful comparison (graph a). The second and third graphs distort the relationship between the prices of these stocks by shifting the starting value (graph b) or scaling factor (graph c) for stock B (shown on right vertical axis). Although graph a clearly shows that the price of these two stocks is equal in May, you would never know it from looking at graphs b or c.

A Selection of Information Sources on the Financial Markets

There are many thousands of web sites devoted to the financial markets. In addition, a dizzying array of raw data, news, analysis, charts, graphs, radio shows, videos, computer software, and multimedia can leave an investor not knowing where to begin.

Since there is so much overlap in the content of sources of market data, we have organized the information by the category of the source (e.g., governmental agency, nonprofit association, exchange, brokerage firm). Within each category, we have highlighted examples of sources we believe to be useful, indicated *some* of the information and other services available through this source, and listed the formats in which it is currently available. Needless to say, all of this information is changing very rapidly, as new sources spring into existence and offerings change. Nonetheless, we believe that you will find that these resources offer excellent points of departure.

Financial Information Supermarkets

Just as there are some supermarkets for food and other supermarkets for financial services, there are information supermarkets. And some of these specialize in financial information. Here are two worth looking at.

INVESTools (www.investools.com) offers a web site for financial research, providing access to a wide variety of financial newsletters and related products. A free newsletter digest provides weekly summaries from a wide range of newsletters and other advisory services. You can get a free sample issue of many newsletters here. You can also purchase the current issue or get an electronic subscription.

In addition to newsletters, INVESTools gives you access to a database of thousands of companies. You can screen for stocks that meet any of nine preset standards, or create your own screening criteria by choosing from dozens of variables such as revenue growth, earnings per share growth, market cap, and insider ownership percentages.

Yahoo! (www.yahoo.com) is another broad-based resource. It offers "my yahoo," a free, customizable news and portfolio tracking service.

Investor Associations

Some excellent sources of educational and other resource material for investors include the following.

American Association of Individual Investors
625 North Michigan Avenue
Chicago, IL 60611–3110

AAII (www.aaii.org) is an independent, nonprofit corporation, founded 30 years ago with the mission of educating its members and the public on all aspects of individual investing. Membership ($29 per year) includes a subscription to the AAII journal, published 10 times per year. A lifetime membership is available for $290.

BetterInvesting

www.betterinvesting.org

This nonprofit organization (also known as the National Association of Investors Corporation) has operated since 1951 and specializes in helping investors, both as individuals and as members of investment clubs. If you have been thinking about joining or starting your own investment club, this is the organization to contact.

Corporate Issuers

Many corporate web sites give you a good look at a company whose stock or other security you are interested in. These web sites are generally linked to many of the investment-related sites described in this chapter. They can also be found by consulting the "Oracle" at www.google.com.

Financial Markets

The following sources provide education plus data, some of it free.

The New York Stock Exchange, Inc. (NYSE)
11 Wall Street
New York, NY 10005
212–656–3000

A great deal of information is available free of charge at www.nyse.com. The NYSE's web site offers closing stock prices and other market data (previous day's open, high, and low prices and volume; shares outstanding; beginning listing date; industry; type of security; historical graph; links to company web sites) for NYSE-listed companies, information about listed companies, investor protection, educational materials, and a perspective on international stocks. It also has a glossary of market-related terms and a data library containing statistical information, including share volume, block transactions, program trading. The NYSE publishes the Trade and Quote (TAQ) Database, providing intraday trading information on NYSE, AMEX, and Nasdaq National Market System and Small-Cap stocks. TAQ is published monthly and is available by subscription.

The Nasdaq Stock Market, Inc.

The web site at www.nasdaq.com features graphs of the Nasdaq Composite Index and the Dow Jones Industrial Average right on its home page. It also allows you to enter up to 10 quotes at a time and to construct and maintain a portfolio. In contrast to the NYSE web site, which provides information only on NYSE-listed stocks, the Nasdaq site provides information on Nasdaq, NYSE, and AMEX stocks—as well as ETFs and mutual fund quotes and other information. The "infoquotes" facility also provides fundamental information, charting, company news, stock reports, SEC filings, analyst info, and links to corporate web sites. Quotes on Nasdaq stocks are delayed 15 minutes; other stock quotes have a 20-minute lag. Another nice feature of the Nasdaq site is that it provides links to more than a dozen domestic and over 100 foreign web sites of other markets and exchanges.

Market Data Vendors

Reuters
www.reuters.com

Reuters is the largest news and financial information company in the world. An overview of its products and services is available at www.reuters.com. Many of these are geared to financial market professionals, but there is much here also for individual investors including quotes, fundamental data, company news, portfolio tracking, and historical price information.

Bloomberg
www.bloomberg.com

In addition to its radio, television, and magazine publishers, Bloomberg is a major source of financial news to the financial services industry.

Mutual Fund Rating Services

Morningstar (www.morningstar.com) is a leading provider of information on the mutual fund industry. Its web site offers free information on comparative performance, expense ratios, fund volatility, and Morningstar's rating. (See Section III on mutual funds for additional information and resources.)

Software/Computer Vendors

Intuit

www.quicken.com

A highly regarded web site oriented toward personal finance—as befits the publisher of the leading personal financial accounting package. The site includes information on investments, taxes, small business, insurance, home mortgages, banking, retirement, and saving.

Banks, Brokers, and Mutual Funds

As financial service firms try to reinvent themselves in the aftermath of the credit crunch of 2008, they are likely to compete for mind, market, and wallet share with increasingly sophisticated and (we hope) user-friendly financial market information.

J.P. Morgan & Co.

www.jpmorgan.com

J.P. Morgan provides a great deal of information on market, currency, and credit risk. It also has a link to a separate site devoted to American Depositary Receipts (ADRs) (www.adr.com).

Schwab

www.schwab.com

Schwab operates the largest and best-known mutual fund "supermarket," Schwab OneSource.

Vanguard

www.vanguard.com

Vanguard is the leading provider of index mutual funds.

Government Agencies

Securities and Exchange Commission
www.sec.gov

The SEC is the official repository for filings on public companies. This information is available to the public for free, direct from the SEC's so-called **EDGAR** project. EDGAR stands for Electronic Data Gathering, Analysis, and Retrieval system. Originally built by the SEC in the 1980s, it collects corporate filings that are submitted electronically by public companies and makes the data available to the general public within 24 hours. But some investors may prefer to pay for the information to be presented in a more easily digestible way or without having to wait 24 hours.

What Is Available through EDGAR?

Some of the company filings that are or will be available from the SEC web site (www.sec.gov/edgarhp.htm) are as follows:

- Form S-1: Initial Public Offering Registration Statement.
- Form 8-K: Report of recent events that may have a "material effect" on the filing company's business.
- Form 10-K: Annual report (detailed version).
- Form 11-K: Annual report for employee stock purchase and other, similar plans.
- Schedule-13D: Form that must be filed within 10 days by anyone acquiring 5 percent or more of any class of stock in a public company. This form must also be submitted to any exchange on which the shares trade and to the company itself. This form provides information on how the shares were acquired, the name of the acquirer, and the acquirer's future plans with regard to the company. The purpose of this form, which is required under the Securities and Exchange Act of 1934, is to protect the shareholding public from takeover attempts that may affect the value of their stock.
- Form 497: Prospectus for a mutual fund.
- Form N-30D: Mutual fund annual and semiannual reports.

Trade Groups

Securities Industry and Financial Markets Association

www.sifma.org

A valuable resource for information on stocks, bonds, and other securities, this site also contains an enormous number of links to other useful sites.

Investment Company Institute

www.ici.org

This web site, which contains a wealth of mutual fund info, is discussed in Section III (mutual funds).

Magazine and Newspaper Publishers

The Economist

www.economist.com

This site provides an excellent overview of the global markets from a European perspective. Contents of the magazine are published online.

Financial Times

www.ft.com

The web site includes sections on headlines, world, companies, markets, global market indexes, offshore funds, stocks, quotes on over 200 currencies, and financial and fundamental information on 40,000 global companies.

Forbes

www.forbes.com

Forbes provides in-depth analysis and reportage on companies and markets. A wide variety of useful information is also offered without charge at the web site. Mutual fund information available at this site is described in the next section.

Wall Street Journal, Barrons, Smart Money, and other Dow Jones products and services

interactive.wsj.com

Dow Jones offers a vast array of financial information, ranging from the *Wall Street Journal* (the premier American business newspaper) to weekly, monthly and online sources of data. An overview of what is available can be found at www.wsj.com, the web site for the *Wall Street Journal Interactive Edition*. Subscriptions to this service cost $103 per year, or $140 including a subscription to the print edition.

Central Banks

Federal Reserve System
www.federalreserve.gov

An important resource for data on the economy and for purchasing U.S. government bonds directly without paying any brokerage commissions, the Federal Reserve is discussed in Section IV.

Newsletters and Other Sources

Hulbert Financial Digest
Hulbert Interactive
www.hulbertdigest.com

Edited by Mark Hulbert for more than 20 years, HFD is the "go to" source for information on more than 180 financial newsletters. Prices begin at $99 for 1 year. Free trial available.

Forbes Special Situation Survey
www.forbesinc.com/newsletters/sss/index.jsp

FSSS has received high ratings for performance by Hulbert Financial Digest as "one of the oldest continuously published newsletters on the market." Published monthly, FSSS provides a research report on a single stock that, in their analysts' view, "holds the promise for significant capital appreciation over the next 18 to 24 months." Free sample issue and special reports available.

Value Line Publishing, Inc.
220 East 42nd Street
New York, NY 10017
www.valueline.com
212–907–1500

Begun in 1931, Value Line is best known for its Investment Survey, one of the most widely read investment services in the world. The survey provides information on individual stocks and has a long track record for identifying stocks that outperform market averages over time. Value Line Publishing is a wholly owned subsidiary of Value Line, Inc., investment advisors.

Financial Engines, Inc.
www.financialengines.com

This web-based service is based on the financial market theories developed by Nobel Prize winner William F. Sharpe. It is intended to provide individual investors with some of the portfolio management tools used by institutional investors. Prices begin at $149.95 per year.

Chapter 8

HOW TO BUY AND SELL STOCK

In the previous chapter, we have seen a small sampling of the staggering variety of information content and sources available to individual investors today. When it comes time to put this information to use, to actually buy and sell stocks and other securities, we are again faced with many choices.

This wasn't always the case. Until 1975, the brokerage business operated under a system of fixed commissions. There were no discount brokers for the simple reason that no discounting was permitted. (In those days, going "online" meant waiting to pay for your groceries at the checkout counter.) Other financial services companies were prohibited by law from entering the brokerage business. Commercial banks, for instance, were barred from engaging in investment banking (primary market, underwriting) or brokerage (secondary market, broker/dealers). Neither insurance companies nor mutual fund or other money management organizations had a significant presence in brokerage.

With the advent of deregulation on May 1, 1975, everything began to change. Discount brokers sprang into existence. Merrill Lynch introduced the Cash Management Account, offering banklike check-writing privileges in a **marginable** securities account, albeit without FDIC insurance. The mutual fund business began its boom years. The stage was set for a historic bull market.

Today, more than 30 years into the era of deregulation and financial innovation, choice is ubiquitous. To help you make sense of your options, and to figure out which of the many ways of buying and selling securities is right for you, we have grouped your choices into four broad categories: full-service brokers, discount/online brokers, other financial intermediaries, and direct purchase. A brief description of each category is followed by some representative examples. Along the way, we will describe the essential mechanics of buying and selling stock.

What Is SIPC Insurance?

The Securities Investor Protection Corporation (*SIPC,* pronounced "sipick") is a nonprofit organization set up by Congress in 1970. *SIPC insurance* covers the securities and cash in the customer accounts of SEC-registered broker/dealers in the event that the firm fails. It offers no protection against a decline in the value of the securities themselves.

SIPC insures up to $500,000 in securities, including up to $100,000 in cash equivalents (e.g., Treasury bills or money market funds) *per customer.* For insurance purposes, a joint account is considered distinct from an individual account. A family can extend its amount of SIPC protection by allocating securities among several distinct *customer accounts* at the same brokerage firm. You may decide that this is unnecessary. Major brokerage firms offer supplemental private insurance for customers with portfolios that exceed SIPC's coverage limits.

Full-Service Brokers

Full-service brokers are still important players in this business. Though their financial clout has been decimated by the credit crunch, they still possess powerful distribution networks and prodigious data-gathering and research capabilities. On the retail side, Merrill Lynch (www.ml.com), now a unit of Bank of America, remains by most measures the largest and most influential brand; it also retains a strong **institutional** presence. Smith Barney (www.smithbarney.com), another venerable brand, is slated to become part of Morgan Stanley Smith Barney, a joint venture between Citigroup and

Morgan Stanley. The combination is a strong presence in both the institutional and retail arenas.

If you select a full-service broker, you are likely to pay more in commissions than a discount broker charges. There are, however, several points worth noting.

- Commissions are negotiable. Your broker may suggest otherwise, but if you are persistent and if he or she believes that you are a good customer for the long term, you should be able to get lower commissions than the standard rates. Think of the standard commission as their **asking price,** and shop around before you **bid.**

- Commissions are not the only way your broker makes money—far from it. This is true whether you use a full-service broker or a discount broker. There are six additional ways that brokers make money in the course of doing business with you:

  1. You may be surprised to learn that your broker probably makes a lot more money from capturing the **spread**—the difference between bid and asked prices—than from commissions alone.

     spread The difference between bid and asked price.

  2. Your broker is also a **dealer,** meaning that he may have the shares you want in inventory, and may have purchased them at a much lower price, in which case your broker would still make money, even if he sold those shares to you at the bid and charged no commission. A dealer in over the counter (OTC) stocks may also add a charge to the purchase price; this charge is sometimes called his **markup.**

  3. If you buy stock on margin, your broker is effectively making you a secured loan, using the stock he sold you as the **collateral.** He charges you an interest rate above the rate he pays to borrow money from a bank. The difference between these interest rates is another spread—an interest rate spread. This represents additional profit to your broker, as long as the stock is margined.

  4. Furthermore, if you look closely at your broker's **account agreement**, it probably allows your broker under certain circumstances to engage in what is called a **stock loan**—using your securities. The counterparty, who is borrowing your stock, pays your broker for the privilege. Large institutional customers may receive some of the proceeds when their stock is loaned out. Individuals don't see any of this money.

market maker *Broker responsible for maintaining a liquid, orderly market in a stock.*

5. Your broker may be receiving **payment for order flow.** According to the SEC, this could be a penny per share—or more. This can also be done within the brokerage firm, a process called (what else?) **internalization.** More information about these types of payments can be found at www.sec.gov.

    How can payment for order flow wind up costing you money? It may be a disincentive to your broker to get you the best price. It is to be hoped that your broker would put your interest in getting the best price ahead of his interest in receiving order flow money, but it would be better to know that your broker's interests are aligned with yours.

6. In order to encourage such an alignment, some full-service brokerage firms have moved away from commission-based payments, instead introducing compensation schemes that reward brokers for asset retention. By charging you and paying the broker on the basis of how large your account becomes, the brokerage firm is taking away the economic incentive for the illegal practice of **churning** a client's account, thus encouraging a true partnership between client and broker. Nonetheless, these fees can also add up. And some of them are less obvious than others, particularly if you are purchasing money management services.

Many firms have **wrap accounts** that dispense with brokerage commissions entirely, replacing them with an annual money management fee similar to what would be charged by a mutual fund. This is yet another example of the broad convergence of financial businesses.

Discount Brokers

Discount brokers offer much lower commissions to customers willing to forgo services such as research reports and other traditional perks offered by full-service brokers. Commissions, however, represent only a small part of the money that brokers make from your business, as we have seen. Full-service brokers frequently defend their higher commissions by claiming that they achieve better **execution** for their customers, leading to a lower cost overall. Let's look at an example to see how this might be true.

Say you issue a buy order for 5,000 shares of IJK Corporation at the current market price (a market order) and IJK last traded at $144 per share, bid $143³/₄, ask $144¹/₄. FSB, your full-service broker, fills your order at $144, *the midpoint of the bid and asked price.* They charge you $500 commission.

On the same trade ZCB, your zero-commission (superdiscount!) broker would have filled your order "for free," *but at the asking price.* You could have "saved" $500 on commissions, but you would have paid an additional $1,250 for the shares.

There might be a strong argument in favor of full-service brokers if there were credible evidence that the quality of execution at these brokers was much higher than at the discount houses. We know of no such evidence presented by independent third parties, but would be very pleased if brokers began to disclose more information about the true costs of trading to their customers. Such pressure for greater disclosure comes, at present, mainly from brokers' institutional clients. They are (for the most part) savvy enough to ask for the information and big enough to get it. We suspect that full-service customers do not get consistently better execution, but in reality are paying for the higher cost structure of full-service firms. This would tally with the other justification usually offered by brokers at the full-service firms: "You're paying for the research." Maybe so, but you need to decide if it's worth the money.

With the emergence of the Internet, online investing has created a new generation of superdeep discount **online brokers,** whose commissions may be less than 10 percent of traditional brokerage commissions.

Financial Intermediaries

Other financial intermediaries from banks to fund groups to insurance companies have established brokerage business. Fidelity (www.fidelity.com) and other major fund groups offer cash management accounts. Comparable to Merrill's original CMA, they combine check-writing privileges with brokerage services, including, of course, the ability to purchase shares in the group's funds.

Large commercial banks such as Chase (www.chase.com) also have brokerage (and insurance) subsidiaries, allowing you to engage in one-stop shopping. And insurance companies are another point of entry to the system. With all this choice, there's bound to be some great deals out there. There will also be a continuation of the consolidation trend that has seen a decrease in the number of banks, insurance companies, and major brokerage firms. In sum, a smaller number of bigger firms offering a wider menu of financial products and services is the way things are headed. How far dare we extrapolate?

Direct Purchase

Financial services firms face fierce competition to survive. Not only must they compete against firms crossing over from related areas, but the very technological innovation that makes their businesses thrive can hurt them as well. For example, for many years it has been possible to bypass brokers entirely, buying stock directly from the issuer. Such direct investing programs are sometimes referred to as *dividend reinvestment programs* (DRIPs), because that is how they got started—as a way for existing stockholders to reinvest their cash dividends to buy more stock without a broker's involvement. That same technology has made it easier for a growing number of corporations to offer their shares directly to the public, without brokers or exchanges as intermediaries. Some of these programs charge no fees at all, justifying the new term **no-load stocks**. Others are beginning to charge small administrative fees that still compare favorably to the online brokers. One nice feature of many DRIPs is the extremely low minimums necessary to open an account. For a list of available no-load stocks, see www.investorguide.com/links-dir-dripslist.html.

Dividend reinvestment and payroll deduction programs make it easy to accumulate shares using **dollar cost averaging.** Further information on DRIPs is available from many sources, including www.dripinvestor.com.

no-load (fund, stock)
A fund or stock that is sold without a commission or sales charge.

dollar cost averaging
Technique for accumulating securities at lower risk by periodically purchasing equal dollar amounts of a security.

If It Sounds Too Good to Be True . . . Protecting Yourself from Stock Scams

A broker calls you out of the blue with a compelling pitch about a can't-miss investment. The broker will promise you the moon, or better, the next Microsoft—but only if you act quickly. Shares are cheap at $10 each. They're certain to go up 1,000 percent in no time at all . . .

The cold-calling broker is probably part of a multibillion dollar per year business in chop stocks. *Chop stocks* are stocks sold by crooked brokers colluding with equally crooked stock **promoters** associated with the sham companies. These promoters take "buy low, sell high" to an absurd—and illegal—extreme. Taking advantage of loopholes in SEC regulations, the promoters are able to acquire large blocks of stock for pennies a share. These shares are then sold to the **chop house** for a much higher price, say $12 per share. The chop house employs the cold caller who catches you in the middle of dinner with the "opportunity of a lifetime" (neglecting to mention that the only opportunity being offered is the wallet-emptying kind). Taken in, you buy 1,000 shares at $12.50 per share. Fifty cents isn't such a bad markup, you reason, for a thinly traded stock. Besides, you got a discount on the brokerage commission.

Chop stocks are characterized by enormous but cleverly disguised markups. They are the bad apples scattered among legitimate, thinly traded **microcap** companies (i.e., companies whose total market value is under $300 million). The low turnover (rate at which the stock is traded, a measure of its **liquidity**) makes it easier for the scamsters to manipulate the stock's price. In the case of chop stocks, the true value of the stock may be a big fat zero.

How can you protect yourself? The SEC, whose regulatory role includes protecting the investor against unscrupulous financial scamsters, has a very simple rule for investors to keep in mind: *Ask questions.* By asking the right questions before you invest, you can protect yourself against financial loss, bypassing products that are either inappropriate for you as an investor or products that serve no one's interest except the crook at the other end of the phone line.

Here's the SEC's list of questions you should ask about financial products before investing:

- Is this investment product registered with the SEC and my state securities agency?

- Does this investment match my investment goals? Why is this investment suitable for me?

- How will this investment make money? (Dividends? Interest? Capital gains?) Specifically, what must happen for this investment to increase in value? (For example, an increase in interest rates, real estate values, or market share?)

- What are the total fees to purchase, maintain, and sell this investment? After all the fees are paid, how much does this investment have to increase in value before I break even?

- How liquid is this investment? How easy would it be to sell if I needed my money right away?

- What are the specific risks associated with this investment? What is the maximum I could lose? (For example, what will be the effect of changing interest rates, economic recession, high competition, or stock market ups and downs?)

- How long has this company been in business? Is its management experienced? Has management been successful in the past? Have they ever made money for investors before?

- Is the company making money? How are they doing compared to their competitors?

- Where can I get more information about this investment? Can I get the latest reports filed by the company with the SEC: a prospectus, offering circular, or the latest annual report and financial statements?

Additional information is available from the National Fraud Information Center, a service of the National Consumer's League, at www.fraud.org.

A Note on Financial Planners

fee-based
Euphemism used by financial planners who earn commissions on the products they sell.

In their search for unbiased advice, many investors are turning to financial planners to occupy the void created when they dropped their full-service broker and got online with a discount firm. Ideally, a financial planner creates a well-thought-out, comprehensive financial plan customized for you or your family's unique circumstances. In actual practice, some plans may be geared more to selling you products that earn the planner a commission or other monetary or nonmonetary compensation.

Financial planners can be categorized as commission-based, **fee-based**, and **fee-only.** The unsuspecting investor could easily confuse fee-based planners with the less common fee-only variety. The fee-based planner can make commissions on top of the fees he or she charges for investment advice. The result? A potential conflict of interest between the planner, who would like to make a buck, and the customer, who would like to be sold a quality product at the lowest possible price.

fee-only   *Financial planners who promise not to accept any commissions from third parties.*

The term *financial planner* has no legal standing, nor is there any licensing requirement. Anyone who wants to call him- or herself a financial planner can do so. There are self-regulatory groups that set standards and offer certification programs. The best known of these certification programs is for the Certified Financial Planner (CFP) designation. If the planner has been certified by the National Association of Certified Financial Planners, www.cfp.net, he or she has promised to put the client's interest first.

Unfortunately, however, the potential for conflict of interest remains. The vast majority of planners, certified or not, get most of their compensation by selling products. Fee-only planners are few and far between; the vast majority of financial planners still receive compensation for selling products about which they also provide advice. Even some fee-only planners might get a commission here or there from a mutual fund distributor for selling you one of their no-load mutual funds. Please don't call it a commission, though. Instead, refer to it as an administrative fee or a distribution fee. It remains a reason for **caveat emptor.**

The National Association of Personal Financial Advisors (NAPFA), a 15-year-old organization of fee-only planners, has acknowledged the problem. To raise investor awareness, the organization has introduced a **fiduciary** oath for financial planners to sign, pledging them to put their clients' interests ahead of their own. You can contact the Association at 847-483-5400, info@napfa.org, www.napfa.org, or by mail: 3250 North Arlington Heights Road, Suite 109, Arlington Heights, IL 60004.

fiduciary *Someone who has the obligation to look after an investor's financial interests.*

Section Three
Mutual Funds and Investment Companies

MUTUAL FUNDS AND INVESTMENT COMPANIES

S hould you invest in mutual funds? If so, which ones? How should you go about buying them? When should you consider selling? To help you arrive at answers to these questions, we begin in Chapter Nine with a brief history and overview of the mutual fund industry, focusing on the United States. Chapters Ten and Eleven look at some of the advantages and disadvantages of investing in mutual funds. Chapter Twelve examines the major sources for information on funds. Finally, Chapter Thirteen looks at some related types of financial instruments.

Chapter 9

A HISTORY AND OVERVIEW OF THE MUTUAL FUND BUSINESS

Eighty-five years ago, the first modern mutual fund was born. In March of 1924, the Massachusetts Investors Trust was launched, beginning with $50,000 in assets invested in a 45-stock portfolio. That fund is still around today, managed by Massachusetts Financial Services (MFS). According to published data, a hypothetical $1,000 investment made on March 21, 1924, would have been worth approximately $1,000,000 on November 30, 2008 (dividends and capital gains reinvested at **net asset value**, or NAV). This represents an average annual compounded growth rate of slightly more than 8 percent.

Coming only five years later, the crash of 1929 and the ensuing Great Depression of the 1930s offered a less-than-hospitable climate for the growth of this fledgling industry. Even in this climate, however, the early growth of the fund industry was impressive. By 1940, instead of one fund there were nearly 70. Furthermore, from a total asset base of $50,000, the collective assets of the industry had grown 9,000-fold, to approximately $450 million. This period also witnessed the enactment of a series of laws for the regulation of the securities industry as a whole, forming the basic framework for the operation of the mutual fund industry as it exists today.

> Even before the creation of the Massachusetts Investors Trust, there were investment vehicles that can fairly be considered as ancestors of modern mutual funds. Though not as old as stocks and bonds, these diversified investment companies have been around for a lot longer than most people realize. What is now an enormous, multi *trillion*-dollar industry can trace its ancestry to The Foreign and Colonial Government Trust. This British investment company, created in 1868, possessed one of the key characteristics of a mutual fund: It allowed an individual investor to spread investment capital over many different securities and without needing vast sums of capital.

In the post–World War II period, the fund industry continued to grow, but at a slower rate. Rapid growth resumed with the deregulation of the brokerage business that began on May 1, 1975. A further impetus to growth stemmed from the inflation problems of the 1970s, as individuals withdrew their money from low-interest-paying bank accounts, and moved them into higher-interest-bearing money market funds. With the end of inflation and the birth of the bull market in the 1980s, investors began a major shift from short-term money market funds into equity and bond funds. All told, in the last 70 years or so, the industry has again recorded a 100-fold increase in the number of funds, and a 20,000-fold increase in total capital. Table 9–1 shows the growth of mutual fund assets under management, number of mutual fund shareholder accounts, and total number of funds from 1940–2008. Table 9–2 shows number of shareholder accounts by investment classification, for the years 1984–2007.

Table 9–1   U.S. Mutual Fund Industry Total Net Assets, Number of Funds, and Number of Shareholder Accounts *(end of year)*

Year	Total Net Assets *(billions of dollars)*	Number of Funds	Number of Shareholder Accounts* *(thousands)*
1940	$0.45	68	296
1945	1.28	73	498
1950	2.53	98	939
1955	7.84	125	2,085
1960	17.03	161	4,898
1965	35.22	170	6,709
1970	47.62	361	10,690
1971	55.05	392	10,901
1972	59.83	410	10,635
1973	46.52	421	10,331
1974	35.78	431	10,074
1975	45.87	426	9,876
1976	51.28	452	9,060
1977	48.94	477	8,693
1978	55.84	505	8,658
1979	94.51	526	9,790
1980	134.76	564	12,088
1981	241.37	665	17,499
1982	296.68	857	21,448
1983	292.99	1,026	24,605
1984	370.68	1,243	27,636
1985	495.39	1,528	34,098
1986	715.67	1,835	45,374
1987	769.17	2,312	53,717
1988	809.37	2,737	54,056
1989	980.67	2,935	57,560
1990	1,065.19	3,079	61,948
1991	1,393.19	3,403	68,332
1992	1,642.54	3,824	79,931
1993	2,069.96	4,534	94,015
1994	2,155.32	5,325	114,383
1995	2,811.29	5,725	131,219
1996	3,525.80	6,248	149,933
1997	4,468.20	6,684	170,299
1998	5,525.21	7,314	194,029
1999	6,846.34	7,791	226,212
2000	6,964.63	8,155	244,705
2001	6,974.91	8,305	248,701
2002	6,390.36	8,244	251,124
2003	7,414.40	8,126	260,698
2004	8,106.94	8,041	269,468
2005	8,904.82	7,975	275,479
2006	10,412.46	8,117	288,596
2007	12,021.03	8,024	292,624
2008	9,601.09	8,022	264,499

Source: Investment Company Institute

Note: Data for funds that invest primarily in other mutual funds were excluded from the series.

Number of shareholder accounts includes a mix of individual and omnibus accounts.

Table 9–2   U.S. Mutual Fund Industry Number of Shareholder Accounts* by Investment Classification *(thousands, end of year)*

Year	Equity Funds Capital Appreciation	Equity Funds World	Equity Funds Total Return	Hybrid Funds	Bond Funds Corporate	Bond Funds High Yield	Bond Funds World	Bond Funds Government	Bond Funds Strategic Income	Bond Funds State Muni	Bond Funds National Muni	Money Market Funds Taxable	Money Market Funds Tax-Exempt
1984	5,976	713	2,934	983	414	698	4	788	337	198	745	13,556	288
1985	6,736	806	3,519	1,323	485	1,073	6	3,279	418	381	1,139	14,435	499
1986	8,240	1,631	5,638	2,101	659	1,744	47	5,985	603	722	1,691	15,654	660
1987	10,557	2,171	7,644	2,732	708	1,974	156	6,666	694	874	1,866	16,833	842
1988	10,312	2,034	7,312	2,575	772	2,488	255	6,293	508	1,000	1,938	17,631	939
1989	10,172	2,062	8,114	2,727	810	2,409	237	5,847	584	1,147	2,138	20,173	1,141
1990	11,427	3,077	7,653	3,203	1,389	2,204	680	5,394	310	1,323	2,318	21,578	1,391
1991	13,628	3,478	8,542	3,620	1,678	1,992	1,306	5,846	432	1,631	2,624	21,863	1,693
1992	17,842	4,203	10,685	4,532	2,073	2,041	1,725	7,181	799	2,163	3,041	21,771	1,876
1993	22,003	7,122	13,430	6,741	2,463	2,373	1,878	7,226	977	2,579	3,639	21,587	1,998
1994	28,407	12,162	17,379	10,251	2,849	2,440	1,435	6,359	1,010	3,232	3,482	23,340	2,039
1995	35,758	13,195	20,387	10,926	3,160	2,816	1,283	6,395	1,132	2,621	3,409	27,859	2,278
1996	44,731	15,651	24,919	12,026	3,632	3,189	1,214	5,559	1,152	2,473	3,187	29,907	2,292
1997	53,101	17,912	30,666	12,856	3,722	3,756	1,116	4,918	1,344	2,289	2,995	32,961	2,663
1998	63,288	18,515	37,754	14,138	4,333	4,168	844	4,984	1,651	2,487	3,020	36,442	2,405
1999	83,170	21,833	42,388	14,252	4,760	4,110	783	4,871	1,448	2,228	2,754	41,177	2,438
2000	100,065	22,758	41,124	13,066	3,892	3,532	657	4,539	2,240	2,120	2,573	45,480	2,659
2001	99,973	22,036	43,639	14,257	4,813	3,605	632	5,120	2,822	2,044	2,524	44,415	2,821
2002	98,426	21,879	43,991	15,579	5,523	3,818	713	7,050	4,069	2,060	2,636	42,726	2,655
2003	102,534	23,941	47,585	17,672	5,529	4,780	907	7,025	5,111	1,841	2,559	38,412	2,802
2004	104,192	29,227	49,824	20,004	5,966	4,781	1,051	6,785	5,772	1,744	2,487	34,794	2,842
2005	101,886	35,318	50,788	21,206	6,369	4,623	1,371	6,404	6,487	1,713	2,476	34,033	2,805
2006	104,063	44,229	51,729	21,967	6,184	4,696	1,734	5,570	7,189	1,647	2,519	34,006	3,061
2007	103,269	52,720	51,592	22,327	6,217	4,698	2,152	5,199	7,879	1,580	2,508	35,359	3,465

Source: Investment Company Institute

Note: Data for funds that invest primarily in other mutual funds were excluded from the series.

*Number of shareholder accounts includes a mix of individual and omnibus accounts.

Acts of the SEC

The Securities and Exchange Commission (SEC) is an agency of the federal government. It was created by Congress as part of the Securities Exchange Act of 1934. Its initial purpose was to administer that law, as well as the Securities Act of 1933, which had been enforced by the Federal Trade Commission (FTC). These laws, passed at the height of the Great Depression, were intended to prevent the kind of abuses that had existed prior to the crash of 1929 and to help restore public confidence in the financial markets. Over the next 10 years, the SEC helped draft legislation that in large measure still governs the way securities markets operate in the United States.

IRA   *Individual retirement account.*

Despite impressive growth, the mutual fund industry has been relatively stagnant over the last decade. Partly, this is a natural result of a maturing industry. Partly, it is a side-effect of the secular bear market. And partly, it is a result of a major new source of competition: exchange traded funds (ETFs).

401(k)   *The most popular type of defined contribution pension plan.*

Open-End versus Closed-End Funds

The first investment funds offered to the public in the nineteenth century were sold by brokers and traded like ordinary stocks. This type of fund is today known as a *closed-end fund*. In contrast, most mutual funds in the United States are, like the Massachusetts Investors Trust, of the open-end variety. According to the Investment Company Institute (ICI), there are in 1998 approximately 8,000 open-end funds in the United States.

You may have seen a much higher estimate of the number of U.S. mutual funds. The reason? Many funds are offered with more than one class of shares. If all the separate classes of funds are counted, the total skyrockets to 22,000. It should be noted, however, that these are not really different portfolios, only different ways of packaging funds for marketing purposes. For example, one class of fund might carry an up-front sales charge, while another might have no initial charge, but a **contingent (deferred) sales charge** (i.e., a charge on sale of the fund that varies depending on how long you hold it).

In contrast, there are only 650 funds of the closed-end variety. Open-end funds tend to be larger as well. Total assets of the 8,000 funds are approximately $9 trillion, or an average of more than $1 billion per fund. In contrast, the total net asset value of U.S. closed-end funds is approximately $240 billion, and the average closed-end fund has only about one-third of the assets, or about $350 million.

The major difference between open- and closed-end funds is how shares are created and priced. With closed-end funds, the number of shares is fixed, resulting in market-related supply/demand forces that determine the price at any given time. Closed-end funds can therefore trade at a discount or a premium to the NAV. Often, funds that provide investors with a way to participate in a hot market are priced at a premium to NAV, whereas most closed-end funds trade at a modest discount. When the discount becomes significant, there is sometimes an effort on the part of the shareholders of the fund to convert it into an open-end mutual fund, an effort that can lead to a battle for control of the fund company.

In contrast, with open-end funds, buyers are issued new shares, while sellers' shares are "absorbed" by the fund company. Pricing is determined through calculation of the net asset value (see "Calculation of a Net Asset value for the Savvy Fund Investor"), a daily exercise that values individual shares by calculating the underlying assets of the fund, subtracting its liabilities, and dividing by the number of shares outstanding.

Index Funds

Index funds are funds that are designed to replicate an index. They are **passively managed** portfolios whose objective is to accurately track an index of stocks (or bonds) as closely as possible, at minimal cost. This distinguishes them from the larger universe of **actively managed** mutual fund portfolios. The securities in actively managed funds are chosen by portfolio managers in accordance with some investment analysis or strategy, and they are supposed to reflect the fund's objectives, such as current income and/or long-term capital appreciation.

Calculation of a Net Asset Value for the Savvy Fund Investor

How does a fund calculate its *net asset value (NAV)*? The calculation requires three inputs, as follows:

- Total fund assets
- Total fund liabilities
- Number of shares outstanding

$$NAV = \frac{\text{assets} - \text{liabilities}}{\text{number of shares}}$$

NAVs for many funds are printed in the newspaper every day. To get the NAV of a smaller fund, you may need to go online to a web site that carries fund information (e.g., www.nasdaq.com).

Load versus No-Load Funds

Some open-end funds are sold through brokers. These funds have sales charges and are known as *load funds*. The **load**, or sales charge, is set by the distributor of the fund and may depend on the dollar amount of shares purchased, prior share purchases, and the class of the share.

Frequently, load funds are offered with several different pricing structures. Technically, they are all separate funds, even though they are managed together. What distinguishes them is how and when investors are assessed the sales charge. One class of shares is typically priced with front-end load, while another class carries a back-end or deferred sales charge, which is

Opening a Closed-End Fund: A Double-Edged Sword for Unwary Investors

Frequently, closed-end funds trade at a discount to NAV. This has created an incentive for short-term investors—hedge funds, for example—to take a large position in a closed-end fund and then to attempt to convert it to an open-end fund.

Since open-end funds are priced at NAV, this can be a profitable strategy. There is no guarantee, however, that all investors will benefit from the conversion. In particular, long-term investors may find that expenses have increased, NAV has declined, and the need to raise cash to pay exiting investors has forced the fund to realize capital gains, thus presenting the remaining investors with a large tax bill. If you are in a closed-end fund, and there is an effort under way to convert it, you may find that you are better off selling before the conversion is completed.

waived if the investor stays in the fund for a minimum period, typically five years. Thus, investors who plan on staying with a fund for five or more years can avoid paying a sales charge by purchasing the back-end or contingent load version of the fund.

Chapter 10

ADVANTAGES OF MUTUAL FUNDS

Simplicity, Diversification, and Other Virtues

The enormous growth in the holdings of equity mutual funds has been accompanied by a decline in the direct ownership of stocks by individual investors. The average investor, it seems, has been voting with his or her wallet for mutual funds and against direct investment. In this chapter, we examine the reasons for this change in the way people invest, looking at the advantages that mutual funds offer individual investors. In the next chapter, we examine some of the costs and possible risks associated with mutual funds.

Simplicity

For individual investors who have neither the time nor the inclination to actively monitor a stock or bond portfolio, mutual funds have an obvious appeal. Just pick a good fund and let its manager do the work for you. This is perhaps the single most important factor driving the popularity of funds. Some surveys suggest that a majority of investors are skeptical of their own ability as stock pickers and are more inclined to believe that they can identify good fund managers.

On the other hand, some investors are skeptical about the existence of good fund managers or about their own ability to find them. For these investors, index mutual funds offer an approach that lets them participate in the performance of a broad market index such as Standard & Poor's 500 Index.

Diversification

As the old maxim says, "Don't put all your eggs in one basket." Many investors draw the inference that they should not invest all their money in a single stock or bond, but rather spread out their investments among a group of securities. However, it can be difficult for an individual investor to closely monitor more than a handful of individual stocks and still handle his or her other responsibilities. In these circumstances, it can be useful to hire someone who is a full-time participant in the markets. For many people, a mutual fund manager is the most obvious choice. Mutual funds offer varying degrees of diversification, depending on their stated **investment objective** (discussed in the next chapter) and on how the fund manager(s) translate that objective into a portfolio of securities.

investment objective
What an investor or portfolio manager hopes to accomplish.

Access to New Issues

Fund managers often have much better access to the best initial public offerings of companies and can benefit from an early run-up in the price of shares that may be difficult or impossible for the average investor to get on his or her own. This is an important point for investors who want to participate in such offerings, but it has little relevance for investors who want to be invested only in established company stocks or government bonds.

Diversification is interpreted by investors in a variety of ways. How many stocks should you own? How closely correlated should these stocks be to each other and to the market as a whole? What is the "market as a whole," anyway? Is it the entire global marketplace or the U.S. market? Is it the entire U.S. market (say, all stocks in the Wilshire 5000) or the S&P 500? A definition of the investment universe and strategic guidelines can help.

Economies of Scale

An equity fund with hundreds of millions of dollars under management is in a far better position than most individuals to conduct the organized research necessary for actively managed portfolios. And when it comes time to execute trades, mutual funds can benefit from the lower per-share trading costs associated with large portfolios. Furthermore, the cost of administrative work (confirming trades, tracking stock dividends, splits, etc.) is spread over a wide number of investors.

Dollar Cost Averaging

Dollar cost averaging (DCA) is a popular investment technique, employed by many mutual fund investors. It can be used to accumulate a large position in a fund (or other security) over a period of time, while reducing risk. Each month, you invest a fixed dollar amount, say $100, in the security. If the price is $10, you purchase 10 shares. If the price goes down to $5 next month, you buy 20 shares. If the price rises to $20, you buy only five shares. Over time, proponents of the strategy argue, it gives you better performance than if you bought all at once. Mutual funds and some direct stock purchase programs offer automatic DCA investment programs; many employers make it even easier by making it part of a payroll deduction program, often coupled with the firm's retirement savings program.

(Continued)

How good is dollar cost averaging as an investment strategy? This question is harder to answer than it seems. It depends on your criteria, and perhaps on your discipline as an investor. By itself DCA doesn't improve what market statisticians call your *expected return.* Expected return is a forecast of average future returns. It is not a return that you should expect in any other sense.

In fact, if the security you are purchasing is increasing in value, you would, on average, be better off putting all of your money in right at the beginning. On the other hand, you may not have a large sum available to invest right now; you may be reinvesting dividends or using payroll deduction to invest periodically. In this case, DCA makes a lot of sense.

What if the security doesn't increase in value, staying at roughly the same price or declining? If the price stays at roughly the same level, DCA has little obvious effect on return. And if the price is declining, DCA loses less money (again, on average) than would putting all your money in at once. All in all, it appears on first analysis that DCA lowers risk and return in equal amounts, making it suitable for investors who want to lower the riskiness of their investments and don't mind giving up some return.

Things are not quite so simple, however. There is a psychological, as well as a mathematical, component to investing. The study of how investors really act, taking into account how people think about the market and how they are swayed by emotions, is called *behavioral finance.* Some studies of actual investor behavior have shown that stocks and funds that individual investors buy underperform the market, while the stocks they sell tend to outperform the market. If this is so, DCA would actually improve the performance of the average investor by taking the investment timing decision out of his or her hands.

Note that some trading costs, such as those due to market impact, timing, and opportunity, are actually higher for larger portfolios. We look at these costs in the next chapter.

Professional Management

The evidence for professional management is mixed. The average mutual fund has frequently underperformed the S&P 500 index, the most widely used benchmark for performance comparison.

This seems like a big negative for professional management until we realize that the professionals are such a large part of the market that, on average, their performance should be about average—and a bit less than average after fees and expenses are taken into account (holding cash also may reduce returns). Finally, most of the time, underperforming the S&P 500 is not the greatest sin, either: That index has, over a long time horizon, delivered impressive growth, even after adjusting for inflation.

Indexing

For those who find low fees attractive, who have a long time horizon, and who don't mind "average" performance, indexing may be the answer—especially if the recent plunge in equity markets is followed by a period of average (or better) performance.

John Bogle, former chairman of the Vanguard Group of funds, has been the primary proponent of indexing. He has also been one of the leading critics of the mutual fund industry. He argues that index funds are a much better value than actively managed funds. Some, however, go still further, questioning whether even index funds are a good strategy for investors. In the next chapter, we see some of the reasons for this skepticism.

Chapter 11

DISADVANTAGES OF MUTUAL FUNDS

High Costs, Hidden Risks, and Loss of Control

N ot everyone is convinced that the advantages of mutual fund ownership outweigh their disadvantages. A commonly heard criticism is that the average fees and expenses of mutual funds are too high and that the whole pricing structure is more confusing than it could be. Indeed, sales charges, management fees, so-called **12b-1 fees** and other expenses all can eat into the performance of a mutual fund, significantly reducing shareholder returns.

Impact of One-Time Charges and Recurring Fees on Fund Performance

The impact of one-time charges can be significant. The most important charges of this type are sales charges. Aside from sales charges, some funds also

12b-1 fee *Fee charged by mutual fund distributors; used to compensate fund salespeople, although may also be used to defray marketing and advertising expenses.*

charge a penalty for early redemption of shares. This is intended to discourage **market timers** who tend to switch between funds frequently.

Sales charges can be applied at purchase or deferred until you sell the fund. Sometimes the deferred charge is contingent upon how long you hold the fund; then it is called a contingent sales charge. If you stay invested in the fund long enough, this charge can go to zero.

Consider two funds, one a **load** fund with an initial (front-end) sales charge of 3 percent, the other a no-load fund without any sales charge. Say you invested $1,000 in each of these funds, using your IRA. The load fund takes $30 right away, leaving you with $970 invested. Now let the money stay there for 20 years, with automatic **reinvestment** of dividends and capital gains distributions. Suppose that the average performance of each fund is 18 percent per year. At the end of 20 years, how much would you have in each fund? The answer may surprise you. The load fund would have grown to $26,571, while the no-load fund would be worth $27,393. The $30 charged to you 20 years ago has cost you more than $800 at retirement time. On the other hand, the difference would remain 3 percent of your portfolio's value.

Now let's look at recurring fees and expenses. While these tend to be small numbers, they hit you year in and year out, and can have a large cumulative effect on performance. There are several kinds:

- **Management fees** are the fees paid by the fund to its **advisor,** a separate legal entity but part of the same **mutual fund group**, or family. The advisor is paid for portfolio management and related services such as accounting and record keeping. These fees typically range from 0.25 to 1.5 percent, with index and bond funds tending to charge the least, and small-stock international funds the most. Sometimes, a fund will voluntarily reduce or waive its management fees, either because of poor performance or simply to enhance its performance for marketing purposes. While it may be nice to benefit from such largesse, it is not a good idea to count on it to last very long.

distributor   *Company that sells mutual funds directly to public or via brokers.*

- 12b-1 fees are paid by the fund to its **distributor**, another legal entity within the mutual fund group. These fees are mostly used to compensate fund salespeople, although they may also be used for marketing and advertising expenses incurred by the distributor. (The term *12b-1* refers to the section of the SEC code regulating these fees.) How high are these fees? The legal maximum is 1 percent of the fund's average net assets for the year, but most funds charge significantly less. Service fees to fund salespeople are capped at 0.25 percent of average fund assets per year. Not all funds charge 12b-1 fees.

- **Fund expenses** are costs that the fund pays for directly, including legal and administrative expenses. These tend to be higher, on a percentage basis, for small funds that lack the economy of scale to spread fixed costs over a larger financial base. Funds that participate in mutual fund supermarkets, such as Schwab One Source, are charged service fees for assets brought into the fund through the supermarket. Supermarkets typically receive about 25 **basis points**, or 0.25 percent, as a service fee. These fees are passed on to all shareholders, not just the ones who purchased the fund from a supermarket. For example, if 80 percent of the assets of your no-load fund came in through supermarkets, shareholders would be penalized by about 20 basis points—though they might not realize that the fund's higher expenses were eating into its performance.

basis point *One-hundredth of 1 percent.*

Recurring fees and expenses are added together to determine the **expense ratio** of a fund. The expense ratio is a measurement of the actual ongoing fees and expenses charged to shareholders by the fund. It does not include any sales charges or early-redemption fees.

How does the impact of recurring fees compare with one-time charges? What, for example, would be the impact of a half percentage point (0.5 percent, or 50 basis points) increase in the expense ratio on the performance of the no-load fund in the previous example? Its average performance would decline from 18 to 17.5 percent. The result? The $1,000 invested in the fund would now grow to only $25,163. The 50 basis points in annual expense cost you $2,230 over 20 years. Even though the difference in fees is much smaller than the sales charge, its cumulative effect is more than twice as great.

Where Does 12b-1 Money Go?

Most of this money typically goes to the *broker* or **financial planner** selling the fund. This provides him with a financial incentive to retain the assets for the mutual fund group, so that the advisor can go on earning his

(Continued)

management fee. Critics point out that there is a potential conflict of interest arising from this practice. Would the broker or financial planner who receives 12b-1 fees from Fund A be willing to recommend a superior fund that doesn't offer him these payments? Proponents of fee-only financial planning argue that investors are better off with planners who explicitly refuse to accept fees from anyone but the investor, eliminating potential conflicts of interest. To date, however, very few financial planners have foresworn these other sources of payment. Some describe themselves as fee-based planners, but this only means that they charge you a fee, not that they don't accept fees from other sources. See discussion of financial planners in Chapter Eight.

Hidden Cost of Brokerage

By now, you might think we have covered all the costs associated with investing through mutual funds. But there is another cost that is frequently overlooked: the cost the fund incurs when it buys and sells securities. You might think that these trading costs are already accounted for as part of the expense ratio. But they are not. Few people realize this. Brokerage costs do not figure at all in the calculation of a fund's expense ratio.

Indeed, it would be very difficult, if not impossible, to figure these costs accurately. Remember that the real cost of buying and selling securities goes well beyond what you are charged in commissions. It also includes things like dealer markup and spreads. It can be difficult to even estimate these costs. If commissions and other brokerage costs are not part of the fund's expense ratio, where do they go? Commissions are added to the price of securities when they are purchased and become part of the **cost basis** of those securities. When securities are sold, brokerage commissions are subtracted from the proceeds. Thus, the more a firm pays in commissions, the lower its performance will tend to be. You can get an idea of how much you are paying in commissions by checking the fund's annual report. Since 1995, funds have been required to disclose their average commission costs there.

While you're at it, you might want to check your fund's policy on **soft dollars.** Soft dollars are credits provided by brokers for the use of their services. These credits can then be used to purchase ancillary services, such as research, software, or financial data. But what if the "research" is primarily a vacation for the portfolio manager and his or her family? Critics contend that the complexity of soft dollar accounting makes it more susceptible to abuse. Proponents of soft dollars counter that they can be a good way to extend the purchasing power of the fund, helping it to buy needed research and other services at reasonable cost. Regulators have periodically attempted to restrict the use of soft dollars, as well as to publicize known abuses.

Figuring the Cost Basis: Why It Pays to Inherit Stock

Cost basis is the price used to figure capital gains. Ordinarily, this is just the price paid for an asset. When you purchase stock, the commission you pay to your broker is counted as part of the cost basis of the stock. Later, when you sell the stock, only your net proceeds are used in figuring capital gains. That way, you won't owe any tax on money that you paid to your broker.

Inherited property is an important exception to the method for figuring the cost basis. When you inherit stock (or other property), the basis is "stepped up" to the current market value (if available). If no market value is available, a current appraised value is used. This *stepping up of the basis* can provide very significant tax benefits for securities that have significantly appreciated from their original cost.

Here's an example of a soft dollar arrangement between a broker and a mutual fund. The fund buys 100,000 shares of IJK Corporation at $50 per share, paying a commission of 10 cents per share, or $10,000 in cash. The broker rebates half of this $10,000 payment, or $5,000, in soft dollar credits. The fund is now free to use those credits to purchase $5,000 in research, other portfolio management, or trading-related services from a third party who will accept that broker's soft dollars as payment. The third party redeems his or her soft dollars from the broker at a prenegotiated rate, let's say 60 cents on the dollar. The net effect is that the broker retains $7,000, the third party receives $3,000, and the fund gets both brokerage and other services.

Reasonable? Maybe. It seems like a good idea, however, to know what your fund's policy is, how its commission costs compare to other funds, and, if it uses soft dollars, what it is getting for its—no, for *your*—money. How can you get this information? Try calling the fund and asking them. While you're at it, you may as well request the long version of the prospectus, along with the "statement of additional information."

Beyond commissions, how do brokerage costs affect performance? While it may not be possible to answer this question definitively, it can't hurt to know how much trading your fund is doing. The higher the turnover of securities within a fund, the greater the impact on performance is likely to be. Recall that *turnover* is a measure of how many times the average share is bought or sold. For example, if the fund consisted of a round lot (100 shares) of each of the 30 stocks in the DJIA, and if the manager decided to sell everything during the course of the year, the turnover would be 100 percent. If the manager then used the proceeds to buy back those same 30 stocks in the same amounts, the turnover would be 200 percent. Several studies have shown that high-turnover funds tend to perform poorly compared to low-turnover funds. It is likely that brokerage costs account for most, if not all, of this disparity, although poor timing is also a possibility.

Another hidden trading-related cost results from the sheer size of some mutual funds. When they buy or sell large blocks of securities, they shift the balance of supply and demand in the market, raising their average cost on "buys" and lowering their average proceeds on "sells." Sometimes, it's better to be a small fish—you make much smaller waves when buying and selling shares. Thus, even though you probably pay a higher commission per share, there should be little if any loss due to your action in the market.

Your advantage as an individual stock trader is greatest with small, illiquid issues. So-called microcap stocks, stocks with a market value of less than $300 million, can be especially hard for fund managers to acquire and dispose of efficiently in the open market. On the other hand, as mentioned previously, fund managers often have much better access to IPOs and can benefit from an early run-up in the price of shares that may be difficult or impossible for the average investor to get into.

Some Hidden Risks of Fund Ownership

You may be paid in securities instead of cash. If the market crashes, a mutual fund can find itself without the cash (or credit) to pay all the shareholders lined up at the exit. In the worst case, funds may not pay cash but instead may pay investors "in kind," with securities that may be difficult to sell and whose ultimate market value may be substantially less than NAV calculations suggest.

Managers may stray from their stated strategies. All too frequently, the shareholders in a supposedly low-risk fund discover that the fund manager has imprudently invested in derivative securities whose risks are far greater than advertised. As a result, such funds sometimes sustain enormous losses.

Mutual fund management companies have a strong incentive to "manufacture performance" for a new fund coming to market. There are a number of ways they can do this, including what might be called **IPO juice** and clever use of **survivor bias.** The use of IPO juice involves seeding the fund with hot IPOs that are almost guaranteed to rise in price. New funds can be capitalized with as little as $100,000, so a few carefully chosen IPOs can give the fund a great performance record in the early going. And if performance isn't good enough for marketing purposes, the fund can be quietly closed down. By shutting down poor performers, fund groups can make the average performance of their funds look better than it really is. The **CFA Institute** has created a set of **Global Investment Performance Standards (GIPS)** that are intended to address this issue.

You will be subject to inherited tax basis. When you buy a stock, the price you paid for it establishes your cost for tax purposes. In contrast, when you buy a mutual fund, you join a pool of investors who share a common tax basis derived from the price the fund paid for the securities in its portfolio. For a top-performing fund, this can mean that you will get hit with capital gains taxes on shares that the mutual fund sells at a profit, even if you got little or none of the profit! In the worst case, you could see the NAV decline and have to pay taxes on top of a loss. For this reason, investors are warned against purchasing mutual funds with large capital gains toward the end of the year, just before most funds make their **capital gains distributions.** For example, if you bought a fund for $10 per share on November 1 and received a capital gains distribution of 50 cents in December, you could owe taxes on that distribution even though the fund's value did not increase after you bought it.

On the other hand, this will occasionally work in your favor. If you purchase a fund that has suffered significant losses, you may receive the tax benefit of those capital losses even though you didn't suffer them (but you may be taking a risk in buying a mutual fund with a poor performance record).

survivor bias
Distortion of average performance by excluding funds closed due to poor performance.

Same Fund, Different Performance

A fund's performance can be very different before and after taxes. This has led fund companies to create funds that modify their investment strategies to minimize taxes. Sounds good, but what if you invested in that fund for your 401(k) or other tax-deferred account? Then you are unlikely to get any benefit from the fund's tax strategy, but you may give up some performance. Wouldn't it be nice if funds were clearly divided into two groups, corresponding to the tax-deferral status of the investment?

You will have less control. This includes lack of ability to tailor your tax strategies. Even in the absence of cost-basis problems, ownership in a mutual fund may make it difficult or impossible to tailor your investment strategy to minimize your tax liability. Some fund managers, sensing a market opportunity, have made changes to their investment strategy to reduce the overall tax liability passed on to shareholders, but even this commendable innovation may not address an individual shareholder's timing issues with regard to taxes.

Chapter 12
SOURCES OF INFORMATION ON MUTUAL FUNDS

With about 8,000 funds being offered for sale in the United States, and some 50,000 globally, it is easy to get lost. Fortunately, there are some excellent sources of information and screening tools to help you find funds that may meet your investment objectives. Each of these sources has a slightly different approach to grouping funds into categories.

In this chapter, we look at the most important sources of information for the mutual fund industry: Investment Company Institute, Lipper Analytical Services, and Morningstar.

Investment Company Institute (ICI) is the association for the mutual fund industry, representing the vast majority of mutual funds and fund assets under management in the United States. In addition to its many publications, including the annual *Mutual Fund Fact Book,* ICI operates a very useful web site, www.ici.org, which provides a great deal of statistical information on trends in the fund industry.

Investment Company Institute Classification of Types of Funds

The ICI groups mutual funds into four broad classes: stock funds, bond and income funds, money market funds, and hybrids. The classes are further subdivided into a total of 33 categories of funds. Following is a brief description of the investment style of each of the 33 ICI categories.

Stock Funds

stock fund   *A mutual fund that invests primarily in stock.*

Stock funds include nine subcategories. The first four of these could be looked at as part of a spectrum, ranging from the near-total focus on capital gains of the aggressive growth fund to the near-total focus on income of the income equity fund. In between, growth focuses primarily on capital gains, while growth and income funds look for a balance between capital gains and income. The latter five subcategories are different in kind.

- *Aggressive growth* funds seek to maximize capital growth without any emphasis on current income. The aggressive label indicates a willingness to take on a significant degree of risk by investing in stocks that are either unknown or currently out of favor. Potential investments include IPOs, companies undergoing significant restructuring, or selected stocks within out-of-favor industries.

  In addition to the riskiness of the stocks that such funds invest in, aggressive growth funds will also tend to employ more aggressive investment strategies (e.g., higher turnover rates and/or increased use of leverage). Such strategies further augment both the potential for return and the riskiness of these funds.

- *Growth* funds are more risk-averse than their aggressive brethren; while they also de-emphasize current income, they tend to invest in mainstream companies with a track record.

  It is worth noting that sometimes "growth" is used as a contrast to "value" as an investment style, but ICI does not subscribe to this distinction. In fact, some of the "aggressive growth" funds are managed by value-oriented managers.

- *Growth and income* funds strive to benefit both from capital gains and current income. They tend to concentrate stock prices of companies that have risen and have an established history of paying dividends.

- *Income-equity* funds invest primarily in the stocks of companies that have good records for paying dividends.

- *International equity* funds are growth-oriented funds that invest primarily in stocks of companies domiciled outside of the United States.

- *Global equity* funds are growth-oriented funds that invest in stocks globally, including the United States. Examples:

- *Emerging market equity funds* participate in companies based in, or otherwise linked to, emerging markets such as the BRIC countries of Brazil, Russia, India, and China.

- *Regional equity* funds focus on a particular part of the world, for example, Asia, Europe, Latin America, or even specific countries.

- *Sector equity* funds aim for capital appreciation by investing in companies focused on specific industries or groupings of industries, such as financial services.

Bond and Income Funds

Bond and income funds include some subcategories that invest in both stocks and bonds and other subcategories that restrict themselves to fixed-income securities.

Strategic income funds strive to achieve a high level of income, investing in corporate and government bonds.

Government bond funds are divided into three subcategories: general funds, intermediate-term funds, and short-term funds. All invest at least 80 percent of their portfolios in U.S. government securities. General funds have no maturity restrictions, while intermediate-term funds have an average maturity between 5 and 10 years and short-term funds have a maturity of between 1 and 5 years (less than 1 year is considered a money market fund; see "Variable Annuities").

Mortgage-backed funds invest at least 80 percent of their portfolios in **mortgage-backed securities (MBS)**.

Global bond funds are divided into two further subcategories: general and short-term. Both invest in worldwide debt securities, with no more than 25 percent of their portfolio invested in U.S. companies. General funds have either no stated maturity or an average maturity greater than 5 years, whereas global short-term funds have an average maturity of between 1 and 5 years.

Corporate bond funds seek high income. They invest at least 80 percent of their portfolio in corporate bonds. They are subcategorized as "general" (no stated average maturity), short-term (1 to 5 year average maturity) or intermediate-term (5 to 10 year average maturity).

High-yield bond funds seek high income while accepting greater credit risk. They invest at least 80 percent of their portfolios in corporate bonds with lower credit ratings (Baa or lower Moody's rating/BBB or lower by S&P).

National municipal bonds strive to achieve income that is exempt from tax by the federal government. They do this by investing "predominately" in bonds issued by state and local governments whose income is exempt from federal taxation. They are further subcategorized as general funds or short-term funds.

State municipal bonds, long term, attempt to generate income that is exempt from both federal and state taxes. They do this by investing in bonds issued by a single state government. As in the case of national municipal bonds, they are subcategorized into general funds and short-term funds.

Hybrid Funds

Flexible portfolio funds strive for high total return; they can be invested in any combination of stocks, bonds, and short-term money market instruments, according to the portfolio managers' judgment of market conditions.

Balanced funds are funds that attempt to accomplish three goals: (1) provide current income; (2) provide long-term growth; and (3) invest conservatively in a fixed ratio of stocks (common and preferred) and bonds.

Income-mixed funds strive to achieve a high level of current income through a mix of stock and bond investments.

Asset allocation funds, like flexible portfolio funds, strive for high total return and invest in stock, bonds, and money-market instruments. However, they must "maintain a precise weighting" to the respective asset classes.

Money Market Funds

Taxable money market funds seek income with stability of the fund's net asset value, normally set at $1 per share. They accomplish this by investing in short-term, high-credit-quality money market instruments. There are two subcategories: (1) government funds, which invest primarily in U.S. government Treasury bills, other short-term U.S. government obligations and/or short-term obligations of U.S. government agencies or "instrumentalities"; (2) nongovernment funds, which invest in other money-market instruments, including certificates of deposit of large banks and commercial paper. *Tax-exempt money market (national)* funds invest in short-term municipal debt securities whose income is exempt from federal taxation.

Tax-exempt money market (state) funds invest in short-term municipal debt securities issued by a particular state whose income is exempt from federal and state taxation.

Variable Annuities

Take a mutual fund, wrap it up in an expensive insurance contract, and voilà, you have a typical **variable annuity**. The insurance part of the variable annuity confers tax-advantaged status to an otherwise taxable mutual fund. According to the Life Insurance Marketing and Research Association (LIMRA), about $156 billion of these heavily marketed investments were sold in 2008, down 15 percent from the previous year.

The tax status of variable annuities makes these products tempting to many investors. Unfortunately, that status is paid for with fees that are extremely high, on top of the fees that the underlying mutual fund charges. These fees are in addition to sales commissions that can take 7 percent of your investment on day one. For these reasons, *Forbes* magazine does not rate variable annuities; it considers most of them to be bad investments for 95 percent of investors. For further information on annuities, see "Annul the Annuity?" in the September 30, 2004 issue of *Forbes*. It is available at www.forbes.com.

Lipper Analytical Services

Lipper Analytical Services (www.lipperweb.com) provides detailed data on the global mutual fund industry. Many fund management companies, brokers, and financial publishers use Lipper's data and analytical capabilities in the course of business. Founded in 1973, Lipper was acquired in 1998 by Reuters. It began by providing analytical information to the independent directors of mutual funds to help them assess fund performance. Today it offers comprehensive information on over 37,500 funds all over the world. Collectively, these funds contain assets of nearly $7 trillion.

Forbes

Forbes offers a free web-based service, the 2009 Forbes Mutual Fund Guide (www.forbes.com/finance/funds). Drawing on the considerable data resources of Lipper Analytical Services, the Guide provides daily updates of the Lipper Indexes that serve as performance benchmarks, in-depth information on many thousands of mutual funds, their distributors, and managers. *Forbes* also puts out an annual mutual fund survey.

Morningstar

Morningstar provides a vast amount of free mutual fund and other financial data and research on its web site (www.morningstar.com). Information is grouped into categories including:

- Portfolio
- Stocks
- Options
- Funds
- ETFs
- Hedge Funds
- Markets
- Tools
- Personal Finance
- Discussion Forums

Premium service is available for $16.95 per month
There is also a site map, and a decent online glossary.

Chapter 13

ALTERNATIVE INVESTMENTS

Hedge Funds, Funds of Funds, and Other Alternative Investments

Beyond the world of mutual funds, there exists a parallel world of so-called "alternative investments." These include hedge funds, funds of funds, and other alternative products.

Hedge Funds

Hedge funds are usually structured as private investment partnerships that (as of April 2009) are exempt from many SEC regulations (as long as they abide by the rules and stay within the **safe harbor**). This appears likely to change as a result of the financial crisis of 2008.

From a U.S. perspective, there are two classes of hedge funds: **onshore** funds, which are located domestically, and **offshore** funds, which are domiciled outside of the United States. *Safe harbor* refers to limitations that investment companies must abide by in order to be exempt from most SEC regulation. These include restrictions on publicity and strict guidelines about the number and kind of investors they accept.

short sale   *Sale of securities not owned by the seller; used by investors anticipating a decline in the value of a security, or as a hedge.*

Hedge Funds or Hedged Funds? A Tangle of Terminology

The term *hedge fund* comes from the early use of these funds for *hedging* against a downturn in the markets by engaging in *short sales.* Today, paradoxically, many hedge funds do not engage in any hedging, but the term seems to be here to stay. Some advocate using the term *hedged fund* to describe the original type of fund; others have introduced *absolute return fund* to refer to the broader class of offshore and onshore hedge funds, allowing "hedge fund" to retain its original definition. Regulatory, technological, and economic changes have further confused the issue by blurring the distinction between hedge funds and the wider universe of mutual funds. For example, so-called 130/30 funds may be offered in a mutual fund format, even though they use some leverage and short-selling strategies traditionally associated with hedge funds.

Many domestic money managers offer both onshore and offshore hedge funds. The onshore fund is for sophisticated investors who, as U.S. nationals, are prohibited from investing in offshore funds. The offshore funds are for non-U.S. citizens (and tax-exempt domestic entities like pension funds, foundations, and endowments). The world of hedge funds is growing in importance. Over the last decade, it has become easier for **accredited investors** to find out about hedge funds.

Are You an Accredited Investor?

The lower threshold is liquid net worth of $1 million or income exceeding $200,000 for at least two consecutive years with the expectation that it will continue. There is also a new, more stringent requirement for funds that wish to accept more than the previous limit of 99 investors. These 3c-7 funds require a minimum net worth of $5 million.

Increasing numbers of accredited investors have decided that hedge funds offer benefits that mutual funds don't. Fighting back against this trend, mutual funds have become a bit more like hedge funds, striving for more flexibility in their investment strategies to counter the perception that hedge funds are simply better investment vehicles. This trend was facilitated by the end of a long-standing restriction on mutual funds, the **short-short rule**, which formerly prohibited mutual fund managers from engaging in aggressive short-term trading strategies without worrying about endangering the fund's **pass-through** tax status. Nonetheless, hedge funds remain far more flexible as investment vehicles, and this is unlikely to change soon. *A note of caution: As the much-publicized 2007–2008 collapse of many prominent hedge funds showed, the freedom that hedge funds have with regard to investment strategies often magnifies risk as well as return.*

Over the last decade, hedge funds increased in size and number as banks, mutual fund groups, and others launched hedge funds, trying to capture a piece of a very profitable business. In the case of mutual fund groups, these hedge funds frequently had investment objectives similar to those of their existing mutual funds. This raised the concern that managers might favor the hedge fund over the mutual fund when making investment decisions. Why would they? In addition to the 1 to 2 percent management fee, hedge fund managers typically also receive 20 percent of the profits of the hedge fund, as long as the fund is above its (or the investor's) **high-water mark.** In contrast, mutual funds generally do not charge performance fees.

This more lucrative fee structure could create a financial incentive to favor the hedge fund in executing investment strategies. It should be noted, however, that hedge funds are typically far smaller than their mutual fund brethren, not only in terms of legal limitations on the number of investors, but also because of **capacity constraints** on the strategies employed by many hedge fund managers.

Additional information about hedge funds is available from a number of sources:

- *Alpha Magazine* (212-224-3300, www.iimagazine.com/alpha) is published by Institutional Investor ("II"). II publishes a wide range of specialty newsletters for institutional investors, in addition to *Alpha Magazine* and its flagship publication, *Institutional Investor Magazine*. While many of these publications cost over $1,000 per year, a wide variety of free information is available on their website. www.iimagazine.com.

- The U.S. Offshore Funds Directory (212-371-5935, www.hedgefund-news.com) is an annual publication providing information on more than 1,200 offshore funds. Cost: $695.

- Lipper TASS Hedge Fund Data. (www.lipperweb.com) has data and research on hedge funds and related **alternative investments**. The company has a New York office (877-955-4773). The database includes information on more than 7,000 actively reporting hedge funds and CTAs and over 6,000 funds and CTAs that have either closed, liquidated, or just stopped reporting. Information on funds that have stopped reporting is important because it helps mitigate the problem of selection bias which arises when funds with better records report more frequently than do funds with poor records.

alternative investment
Investments intended to help diversify a traditional stock/bond portfolio, such as real estate, hedge funds, or commodities.

A Taxonomy of Hedge Fund Investment Strategies

The Credit Suisse/Tremont Hedge Index divides hedge fund investment strategies into 10 broad categories:

> *Convertible Arbitrage*
>
> *Dedicated Short-Bias*
>
> *Emerging Markets*
>
> *Equity Market Neutral*
>
> *Event Driven*
>
> *Fixed Income Arbitrage*
>
> *Global Macro*
>
> *Long/Short Equity*
>
> *Managed Futures*
>
> *Multi-Strategy*

(For additional information, see www.hedgeindex.com.)

Funds of Hedge Funds

asset allocation
Apportionment of a portfolio in various investment categories, especially stocks, bonds, cash.

A **fund of hedge funds (FoHF)** is an alternative investment vehicle that invests in other alternatives, generally hedge funds. The basic rationale for this is **asset allocation**. A manager of a FoHF decides on the sectors or types of funds that are most appealing, assigns weightings to those sectors, and looks for the best fund managers within each sector.

Critics of the fund of funds concept point out that they generate fees on top of fees and expenses on top of expenses. If you want asset allocation, you can get it without the extra layer of fees and without the extra layer of mystery about what the underlying investments are. Besides, why stop there? Why not create "funds of funds of funds," "funds of funds of funds of funds," and so on *ad infinitum*?

Proponents respond that no single fund company can afford to hire the very best managers in all markets, whereas a fund of funds has the freedom to compile a portfolio of the best managers in the world. There are, however, at least two assumptions hiding in that argument—namely, that the fund of funds manager can identify the best managers and that the FoHF's asset allocation will add value, not subtract it.

Other Alternatives

One of the biggest problems associated with hedge fund investing has been the lack of transparency into a fund's positions, strategies, and risks. An extreme example that came to light in late 2008 is perhaps the greatest financial fraud of all time, perpetrated by Bernie Madoff, and apparently facilitated by numerous intermediaries—wittingly and/or unwittingly. While Madoff never operated a hedge fund, billions of dollars were raised by hedge fund and fund of fund managers who offered *feeder funds*, funds that apparently served no purpose other than to collect fees and send the money to Bernie. The secrecy that still exists in the hedge fund industry can have no greater illustration than the realization that many hedge fund managers had never even heard of Madoff or knew what a feeder fund was until he surrendered to authorities in December 2008.

The problem of lack of transparency has been tackled in two ways: by hedge fund managers offering full position-level transparency in separately managed accounts that are owned by the investor; and by financial engineers who have developed hedge fund replication strategies that are intended to offer hedge-fund-like returns and use sophisticated mathematical and computer techniques to reverse engineer hedge fund strategies, and to attempt to replicate the returns using liquid instruments, especially futures contracts. Both of these approaches are in an early stage of development, but they are garnering significant attention from investors who wish to retain the diversification benefits of alternatives without paying the price of lack of transparency, liquidity, and control.

Section Four

Bonds and Other Fixed-Income Securities

BONDS AND OTHER FIXED-INCOME SECURITIES

Bonds and related *fixed-income securities* are essentially loans or IOUs issued by a wide range of borrowers, including governments and government agencies, public and private companies, and various financial intermediaries. The term *fixed income* derives from the constant, predictable nature of payments you receive. Depending on the terms of the security, specific amounts of money may be paid as *interest*. For non-interest-bearing securities, the money you receive is the difference between the security's purchase price, called its **original issue discount (OID)**, and its face value. *Face value* is the amount returned to you if you hold the bond until its maturity date.

To help you understand this complicated market, Chapter Fourteen examines the seven key elements that distinguish bonds from each other, and from the now familiar world of stocks. Having set out a conceptual framework in Chapter Fourteen, Chapter Fifteen gives an overview of the most important segments of the bond market. By the end of this section, you will have a clear understanding of who invests in these markets, how investments are made, and the major advantages and disadvantages of various fixed-income securities.

Chapter 14

SEVEN CHARACTERISTICS OF BONDS

In this chapter we create a conceptual framework to clarify how fixed-income securities differ from stocks and from each other. This framework is built around seven key factors that you need to understand in order to make sense of the world of bonds:

- The lifespan of bonds
- Interest versus discount
- Relationship of price to yield
- Four important yield measures
- Credit quality, ratings, and insurance
- Call and related features
- Fixed versus floating rates and currencies

The Lifespan of Bonds

Unlike stocks or mutual funds, almost all fixed-income securities have a pre-defined, limited lifespan. The beginning of that period is usually called the **issue date** (as with stocks). Unlike stocks, however, there is also a **maturity date**, the date on which the final payments from the issuer are supposed to be paid. Although stocks can be retired or merged out of existence, they do not have a predefined ending point. This is a key difference between stocks and (almost all) bonds.

LIBOR-plus   *Use of LIBOR as benchmark to define a floating interest rate (e.g., LIBOR + 2%).*

junk bond   *A bond of extremely low credit quality.*

A Bond by Any Other Name . . . A Note on Terminology

The bewildering variety and complexity of fixed-income securities is so great that the term *fixed* has a certain irony—*mixed* might be more appropriate. The income from many of these instruments is anything but fixed. There are adjustable rates, floating rates, and **LIBOR-plus** rates. In the global markets, fluctuating exchange rates impact the value of both interest and principal. **Junk bonds** have a high-risk element that can turn them into "nixed" income securities. And many securities come with complicated options or prepayment features built into them, making their future cash flow a subject for careful analysis by teams of mathematicians working with powerful banks of computers.

Sometimes people refer to bonds and other fixed-income instruments as *debt securities;* at other times, the term *credit instruments* is used. Adding to the potential confusion, although most fixed-income/debt/credit instruments trade in an enormous global over-the-counter (OTC) market, many U.S. corporate bonds trade on the New York *Stock* Exchange. (You might have thought that only stocks trade on a stock exchange; not true. In fact, two of the original five securities traded in the 1790s under the legendary *buttonwood tree* were government bonds.)

To keep it simple, just remember that bonds and other fixed-income securities may also be referred to as debt securities or sometimes credit instruments. Whenever it will help the flow of explanation, we'll just call them bonds.

Interest versus Discount

Some kinds of bonds are designed to pay interest; others are purchased at a discount from their face value, or redemption price. Most long-term bonds are of the former variety. Short-term **money market instruments** are sold at a discount. So are **zero-coupon bonds** and **strips**, which have maturities of up to 30 years.

money market instrument *Short-term debt obligations such as Treasury bills, certificates of deposit, and commercial paper.*

Perpetual Bonds

It is said that there is an exception to every rule. In the present instance, the rule is that all bonds have a maturity date; the exception is perpetual bonds. Perpetuals, like Peter Pan, never mature. Nor can they be redeemed by their issuer; they pay interest forever. They are also known as *annuity bonds*.

There is only one well-known example of perpetual bonds: the British consols. These were issued in the days when the sun never set on the British empire to help pay off other debt originally incurred during the Napoleonic Wars. Though we've never seen one, we've heard that consols are still around, as are proposals to issue perpetual U.S. Treasury bonds instead of constantly refunding debt as it matures. That proposal, whatever its merits, is a perpetual nonstarter.

The amount of interest that a bond pays as a percentage of its face value (also called **principal amount**) is called its **coupon**, or **coupon rate.** For example, a bond with an 8 percent coupon rate pays $8 for every $100 of face value. Individual bonds often come with a face value of $1,000; $5,000 is also a common amount.

Where Have All the Coupons Gone?

The term *coupon* comes from the originally almost universal practice of selling bonds with detachable coupons that could be presented to a paying agent on the coupon payment date. Such unregistered bonds were also known as *bearer bonds*, because the bearer's possession of the coupon was all that was necessary to secure payment. Coupon bonds are gradually disappearing, being replaced by registered book-entry bonds.

Relationship of Price to Yield

When the amount you pay for a newly issued bond is the same as its face value, you are said to have purchased it *at par*. But the price of bonds varies in response to changing levels of prevailing interest rates and other factors. If you pay less than par for a bond, it is called a **discount bond**. If you pay more, it is called a **premium bond.** For example, you might buy a $1,000-face-value bond with a 4 percent coupon for $800. Though the coupon rate is only 4 percent, you are getting more than 4 percent on your money. After all, you've only put in $800 and you're getting $40 per year in interest—that's 5 percent right there. In addition, you will get the full face value of $1,000 back if you hold the bond until maturity—that's a $200 bonus. To see how these factors are taken into account, we must turn to the subject of a bond's yield and the various ways to measure it.

Four Important Yield Measures

The exact definition and measurement of yield is a large and complex subject. Nonetheless, it is possible to get a grasp of the fundamentals by becoming familiar with four ways that yield is measured and quoted by banks, brokers, and in the financial press:

- Current yield
- Yield to maturity
- Yield to call
- Equivalent taxable yield

The **current yield** on a bond is simply its coupon divided by its purchase price. This is a more accurate gauge of your return than the coupon rate described previously, because current yield takes into account how much you actually paid, which could be more or less than par.

What it leaves out of the account, however, is the amount that you will receive if you hold the bond until its maturity date. For this, another measure is used—the yield to maturity. **Yield to maturity** adjusts your rate of return to reflect the difference between what you paid for the bond and what you will receive on the maturity date. It also adjusts for the exact timing of interest payments (typically, bonds pay interest semiannually).

What if you can't hold the bond to maturity? Sometimes, as we will see shortly in more detail, bonds are subject to **call provisions**—the issuer reserves the right to buy the bonds back from you on specific dates at a specific price. In those instances, you may want to know the **yield to call**, which adjusts your rate of return in a manner similar to the yield to maturity, replacing the maturity date with the **first call date**, and the principal amount with the **call price**, which is usually somewhat higher than par to compensate the bondholder for having the bond **called away**.

A final fundamental measure of yield derives from the need to compare tax-exempt municipals to other, taxable, bonds. This is the equivalent taxable yield. For example, starting with a yield of 6 percent on a municipal bond, someone whose marginal tax rate was 40 percent would need to earn 10 percent on a taxable corporate bond to get the same amount of money on an after-tax basis.

> **called away** *Said of an underlying asset exercised away from the call writer.*

Credit Quality, Ratings, and Insurance

So far, we have not discussed perhaps the most important reason people buy bonds: safety of principal. Some bonds, such as those issued by the U.S. Treasury, are generally considered paragons of safety. They have the highest credit rating of any securities in the world, though the financial crisis has highlighted potential long-term problems and led some to speculate that the U.S. dollar might lose its status as reserve currency of the global financial system. Independent credit-rating agencies, such as Moody's and Standard & Poor's, score the creditworthiness of issuers and also of specific bond issues. These agencies have been widely criticized for being slow to downgrade issuers and for the inherent conflict of interest stemming from the fact that the issuers pay for their ratings. Credit enhancement, in which an issuer or investor seeks to insure bonds against possible default, was very profitable for insurers like AIG, until the possibility of widespread defaults brought down the house, which turned out to be woefully undercapitalized.

Call and Related Features

Bonds with call provisions require additional vigilance on the part of investors. If you are the owner of a callable bond, what do you need to look out for? When a bond is trading at a discount, it is safe from being called. Interest rates are higher than when the bond was issued, and the issuer has no incentive to buy them back at par. The intrinsic value of the call is zero (see Chapter Sixteen). When the bond is trading at a premium, however, it will probably be called away at the earliest possible call date. The issuer really has no choice—it must act in the best interest of shareholders.

Some bonds come with what are called **sinking fund provisions.** These stipulate that, under certain conditions, the issuer must retire a certain portion of the bonds outstanding according to a fixed schedule. Which bondholders are affected is determined by lottery.

Occasionally, you may run across a **put bond** in the corporate bond market. Put bonds allow you to sell back the bond at par on certain date(s), offering some protection from a rising-interest-rate environment that would erode the market value of your bond. Alas, such protection is not free. Put bonds have lower yields than comparable bonds that do not offer this "insurance." Bonds with detachable **put options** are gaining in popularity (see Chapter Sixteen for a discussion of puts). The puts are usually purchased by the options trading desks of banks and brokerage firms, leaving the investor (usually an institutional money manager) with a plain old corporate bond.

Fixed versus Floating Rates and Foreign Currencies

Finally, we're back where we started, looking at the paradox of referring to bonds as "fixed-income securities" when there is so much that is variable about them—even their interest rates. Many issuers offer **floating-rate notes** that pay a variable interest rate, recalculated periodically to reflect changes in some benchmark rate. Typically, the benchmark is another interest rate of some kind, like the **prime rate** charged by major commercial banks on loans to their most creditworthy corporate clients, or the **London Interbank Offered Rate (LIBOR).**

As Time Goes By, Some Bonds Are More Durable than Others

Beyond knowing the maturity date of a fixed-income security, it is useful to understand the idea of duration. Recall that bond prices and interest rates have an inverse relationship: When one moves up, the other moves down. *Duration* is a measure of how sensitive a bond's price is to a small change in interest rates. Higher duration equals greater sensitivity. Even if two fixed-income securities mature on the same day, they may have very different cash-flow characteristics and may respond differently to changes in the overall level of interest rates. Putting aside for the moment such complications as callability, a fixed-income security that pays you back all at once on the maturity date is said to have a higher duration than one that pays periodic interest. And, all other things being equal, the higher the rate of interest, the lower the duration of the security.

But the benchmark does not need to be an interest rate. In 1997, the U.S. Treasury introduced **Treasury Inflation Protection Securities (TIPS)**, benchmarked to the U.S. Consumer Price Index. This means, in effect, that TIPS are denominated in **real dollars** (i.e., dollars adjusted for inflation), unlike the **nominal dollars** we still use to buy things at the grocery store. Foreign governments and corporations, of course, issue bonds in dozens of different currencies. The rate of return on these bonds depends on the currency of issue and the currency in which the bondholder does the analysis.

Chapter 15

HOW THE OTHER $30 TRILLION IS INVESTED

An Overview of the Bond Market

Some market analysts find little reason to invest in bonds. They point out that stocks have historically provided higher average returns and are therefore likely to be better long-term investments. For short-term needs, on the other hand, cash is just fine. And since many brokerage accounts are set up to pay interest on any cash in the account, there's no need to concern oneself with the nuances of short-term investments like Treasury bills and commercial paper. Concentrate on picking good stocks and stock mutual funds, they say, and the rest will take care of itself.

Thirty trillion dollars thinks differently. That, according to the Securities Industry and Financial Market Association (www.sifma.org), was the approximate value of the U.S. bond market as of June 30, 2008. This was more than double the total market value of all the stocks traded on the NYSE. Somebody obviously sees good reasons to allocate some of their assets to the bond market.

How is that $30 trillion divided? At first glance, Treasury securities would seem to make up about one-third, or approximately $10 trillion. According to the U.S. Bureau of the Public Debt, total public debt as of June 30, 2008, was $9.5 trillion. However, "only" $4.7 trillion is in marketable securities held by the public. What about the other $4.8 trillion? These are nonmarketable securities, mostly intragovernmental holdings, and they are not considered part of the bond market. Most of these securities represent money that the government has loaned to itself for various purposes. It also includes Savings Bonds and money loaned to state and local governments (nicknamed *SLUGs*).

So far, we've only identified $5 trillion out of the $30 trillion. Ten years ago, marketable treasury securities were the largest single component of the U.S. bond market. Today, they have been surpassed by the U.S. corporate bond market, with approximately $6.2 trillion outstanding. Even greater in size is the market for mortgage-backed securities (MBS), with $7.6 trillion.

Nearly $2.7 trillion more in municipal bonds brings the total for these four categories to about $21 trillion. The remaining $9 trillion is divided between the money market ($4 trillion), agency debt ($3 trillion), and other asset-backed securities ($2.5 trillion). (See Table 15–1.)

Treasuries

U.S. Treasury securities are public debt securities issued by the Treasury Department of the United States. They make up the most liquid part of the U.S. fixed-income market, with a turnover greater than the market for corporates, agencies, or munis (tax-exempt municipal bonds). In 2008, the Treasury market had average dollar trading volume in excess of $500 billion per day, dwarfing all markets except for the global currency markets, which are even larger. More than half of this trading takes place among **primary dealers**, banks authorized to buy and sell securities with the Federal Reserve Bank of New York.

According to the U.S. Department of the Treasury, about $300 billion of marketable Treasury securities are held directly by individuals. This is roughly 5 percent of the $5.8 trillion in outstanding marketable Treasuries. In comparison, the total amount of U.S. savings bonds outstanding is $194 billion, one-third less than the amount of marketable Treasuries in individual hands.

Table 15–1   Overview of Public and Private Debt Outstanding

	Amount ($ trillions)	Share of Market
Treasury (marketable securities held by public)	$4.7	15%
U.S. corporate bonds	6.2	20%
Mortgage-backed securities	7.6	25%
Municipal bonds	2.7	9%
Money markets	4.2	14%
Agency securities	3.1	10%
Other asset-backed	2.5	8%
Total bond market	30.8	100%

Sources: SIFMA, U.S. Department of the Treasury, Federal Agencies, Federal Reserve System, Bloomberg, Thomson Financial

Treasury securities are divided into three categories, depending on the length of time between date of issue and the maturity date. Securities with a maturity of between 10 and 30 years from issue date are called *Treasury bonds*. Securities with a maturity of more than 1 year but less than 10 years are called *Treasury notes*. Finally, securities with maturities ranging from 13 weeks to 1 year are called *Treasury bills* (or T-bills). Sometimes, however, Treasury securities are generically referred to as bonds.

Four Dimensions of Bond Risk

Traditionally, investors in bonds think about four kinds of risk to their investment: *credit risk, interest rate risk, exchange rate risk,* and *reinvestment risk.* Any of these risks can lower or even destroy the value of the bondholder's investment.

Credit risk refers to the possibility that the issuer's perceived creditworthiness may weaken, for reasons ranging from a general economic slowdown to an actual *default* on the part of the issuer. U.S. Treasury securities have the highest credit rating of any fixed-income security.

Interest rate risk results from fluctuations in the supply of, and demand for, Treasury and other fixed-income securities. When demand for bonds falls, the government (or any other issuer) has to offer higher yields to attract investors. But current bondholders don't see an increase in the amount of

(Continued)

default   *Failure to meet finncial obligations to a creditor.*

interest they are being paid. So what happens if you are holding a bond and interest rates go up? Nothing, unless you want to sell it. Now you are competing against new issues that pay greater interest. The only way you can attract a buyer is to lower the price of the bond you are trying to sell. This is why the market value of a bond falls when interest rates go up.

In general, interest rate risk is greater for longer maturities; also, it is greater for zero-coupon bonds than for coupon-paying bonds, and greater for premium bonds than for par or discount bonds.

Foreign investors have additional worries in the form of *exchange rate risk.* This can be a factor even if interest rates do not change in the currency in which a bond is denominated. If you are holding a foreign currency-denominated bond and the value of that currency falls relative to your home currency, you will receive smaller amounts of home currency after converting interest and principal payments.

Finally there is *reinvestment risk:* To understand it, recall that bond yields move in the opposite direction to bond prices. When the general level of yields increases, bondholders incur interest rate risk. But what if demand for bonds increases? The price of existing Treasury securities—those that have already been issued—increases. Because of this increased demand, the government doesn't need to offer as high a rate of interest on new Treasuries. This is good for existing bondholders, but only if they wish to sell their bonds at a profit. If, on the other hand, they hold the bonds until maturity, they will find (assuming that yields remain low) that they cannot get as good a yield as they did last time around.

---

gross federal debt
Federal debt, including interagency debt.

The federal government uses debt securities to finance its operations and to pay interest on the national debt. The national debt, or **gross federal debt,** which stood at approximately $10.7 trillion at the end of 2008, is the sum of all Treasury debt securities outstanding, whether 30-year bonds issued in the late 1980s or T-bills issued a few weeks ago.

In any given year, the difference between outlays and receipts is usually referred to as the **budget deficit,** although if receipts exceed outlays it is actually a **budget surplus** (shown as a negative deficit). (See Table 15–2.)

Table 15–2 Budget deficits versus gross federal debt

Year	Federal Deficit/Surplus(−) ($ billions)	Gross Federal Debt ($ millions)
1970	2.8	380,921
1975	53.2	541,925
1980	73.8	909,050
1985	212.3	1,817,521
1990	221.2	3,206,564
1995	163.9	4,921,018
2000	−236.2	5,628,700
2005	318.3	7,905,300
2008	454.8*	10,699,805

Sources: U.S. Treasury Department, Bureau of the Public Debt, and Office of Management and Budget

*Estimate.

One of the most important decisions faced by buyers of Treasury bonds is how long a maturity date to choose. The **maturity date** is simply the date on which the bond comes due and the **face value** of the bond is given to you. If you purchased the bond at **par value**, the face value is simply the amount you paid. If you paid less than par, the bond is said to have been trading at a *discount*. If you paid more than par, it was trading at a *premium*.

face value   *The amount of money due on a bond's maturity date; also called principal amount.*

Typically, the longer you lend out your money, the higher the interest rate you receive. But there are times when the reverse is true—at those times, you get higher interest rates for bonds with shorter maturities.

Using a Seesaw to Envision the Relationship between Price, Yield, and Maturity

As we have previously explained, the price and yield of fixed-income securities move in opposite directions. This is not merely a tendency or a correlation; it is simply a matter of how yield is defined. The relationship between yield and time to maturity is another matter. Here we can identify two tendencies:

• Yields of bonds with more time to maturity are usually higher. The graph showing the relationship between yield and time to maturity is called a *yield curve*. Its normal condition is to have a positive slope, although that

(Continued)

slope can be fairly small. When its slope is positive but small, it is referred to as flat. When its slope is negative, it is referred to as inverted. This is considered abnormal.

* The sensitivity of a bond's price (and yield) to a change in the overall level of interest rates is called its *duration*. In general, the longer the time to maturity, the greater its duration.

The relationship between price and yield can be envisioned as a seesaw, with prices on one side and yields on the other side. Longer maturities tend to be farther out on the seesaw, making them more sensitive to changes in the overall interest rate environment. The farther out you sit on the seesaw, the more you move when the seesaw moves. (See Figure 15–1.)

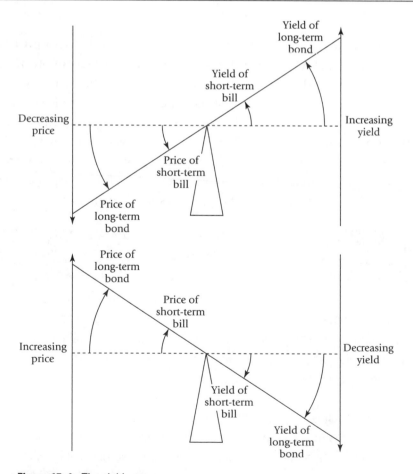

Figure 15–1. The yield seesaw.

Bond investors must decide the length of time they would like to put their money out on loan. A complementary decision is faced by issuers of bonds: How far out should they set the maturity date of the bonds they issue? Of course, forces of supply and demand come into play here. For example, if investors want more long-term debt than is readily available, they will bid up the price of such bonds, making them more attractive for issuers and thus eventually balancing the forces of supply and demand. The existence of a wide variety of maturity dates, each with its own **yield** and effective rate can be depicted in a graph of yields versus maturities. This graph, called the **yield curve**, provides a valuable reference point for understanding how yield varies with maturity.

Though yield curves can be drawn for any set of bonds of comparable quality, the most commonly depicted yield curve is the one for Treasury securities. Each day, as the yields of different Treasury bonds fluctuate in response to market forces of supply and demand, the yield curve changes its shape. Daily financial papers will often show the Treasury yield curve as it existed at yesterday's market close, and one or two earlier curves, perhaps one week ago and one year ago.

Yield curve data can also be obtained on a same-day basis from a variety of Internet resources, including www.bloomberg.com and www .cnnfn.com.

Over time, a yield curve can undergo dramatic changes in shape, reflecting significant changes in market sentiment, especially related to inflationary expectations. The three basic shapes of the yield curve are steep and upward-sloping, flat, and inverted. (See Figure 15–2.)

A steep and upward-sloping yield curve reflects an environment in which bond investors demand significantly more compensation for longer-term debt, reflecting concern that inflation may be on the increase.

Upward-sloping yield curves, whether or not they are considered steep, are also referred to as **positive yield curves**, because of the positive slope of the straight line that most nearly approximates the curve.

In recent years the yield curve has been nearly flat. A flat yield curve suggests an economic climate in which there is relatively little fear of inflation, and the government is able to obtain longer-term financing for roughly the same rate as for short-term financing like T-bills.

The term *inverted* suggests an abnormal situation, and inverted yield curves have been relatively uncommon. They typically occur in response to

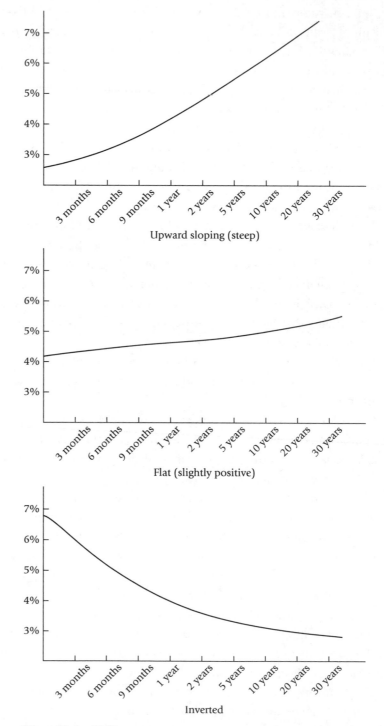

Figure 15–2.   Yield curves.

tight monetary policy on the part of the Fed, which is able to influence the market's short-term rates by raising (or lowering) the **discount rate**, or by changing its target **Fed funds rate.** Higher short-term rates are a traditional means of cooling off an overheated economy, either to prevent inflation from increasing or to bring about an actual decrease in its rate.

> **discount rate**   Rate charged by the Federal Reserve on loans to member banks.

Some analysts believe that a positive yield curve is normal, reflecting investors' need to be compensated for the greater risk of a longer-term investment. This viewpoint is understandable, given the inflationary experience of the past several decades. Under deflationary market conditions, however, it would be desirable to be able to lock in a rate for as long as possible, so it may be wiser to keep an open mind on this subject.

Two Ways to Buy Treasuries: From a Broker/Dealer or Direct

Most brokers and many banks will be happy to sell you Treasury bonds, notes, or bills for a modest commission. Bills, notes, and bonds are sold in amounts beginning at $1,000.

There is a way to buy Treasuries without paying any commissions. Federal Reserve Banks and the Bureau of the Public Debt (www.publicdebt. treas.gov) offer what is called **Treasury Direct.** Using Treasury Direct, you can arrange for your T-bills to be automatically reinvested when they mature. (See Table 15–3.)

Savings Bonds

What about savings bonds? There's a $5,000 per person per year limit for EE bonds, and a separate $5,000 limit for I bonds. For as little as $25, you can buy savings bonds, which can be purchased at many banks or even through a payroll deduction plan. EE Savings bonds, like other Treasury instruments, offer guaranteed rates of return if held until maturity. But they also offer the added protection of a guaranteed rate if held for a minimum of five years. This can be of value if interest rates move up sharply, sending the price of other long-term bonds sharply lower. EE Savings bonds have a built-in floor that adds protection to your capital investment. Of course, you pay for this protection in the form of a somewhat lower yield. The new I bonds are modeled after TIPS, to which we now turn. (See Table 15–4 for a comparison of EE and I bonds.)

Table 15–3   Federal Reserve Offices

Office	Address	Telephone	Web Site
Board of Governors	20th and Constitution Ave. NW Washington, DC 20551	(202) 452-3000	www.federalreserve.gov
Atlanta	1000 Peachtree Street NE Atlanta, GA 30309 (branches in Birmingham, Jacksonville, Miami, Nashville, New Orleans)	(404) 498-8500	www.frbatlanta.org
Boston	600 Atlantic Avenue Boston, MA 02210 (branch in Windsor Locks, CT)	(617) 973-3000	www.bos.frb.org
Chicago	230 S. LaSalle St., Chicago, IL 60604 (branches in Des Moines, Detroit, Indianapolis, Milwaukee)	(312) 322–5322	www.chicagofed.org
Cleveland	1455 E. Sixth St., PO Box 6387 Cleveland, OH 44101 (branches in Cincinnati, Columbus, Pittsburgh)	(216) 579-2000	www.clevelandfed.org
Dallas	2200 N. Pearl St., PO Box 655906 Dallas, TX 75201 (branches in El Paso, Houston, San Antonio)	(214)922-6000	www.dallasfed.org
Kansas City	925 Grand Blvd., Federal Reserve Sta. Kansas City, MO 64106 (branches in Denver, Oklahoma City, Omaha)	(816) 881-2000	www.kc.frb.org
Minneapolis	90 Hennepin Ave. Minneapolis, MN 55401–1804 (branch in Helena, MT)	(612) 204-5000	woodrow.minneapolisfed.us
New York	33 Liberty St., Federal Reserve Bank of New York New York, NY 10045 (branch in Buffalo, NY)	(212) 720-5000	www.ny.frb.org
Philadelphia	10 Independence Mall Philadelphia, PA 19106-1574	(215) 574-6000	www.philadelphiafed.org
Richmond	701 E. Byrd St., PO Box 27622 Richmond, VA 23261 (branches in Baltimore; Charlotte)	(804) 697-8000	www.richmondfed.org
St. Louis	411 Locust St., PO Box 442 St. Louis, MO 63166 (branches in Little Rock, Louisville, Memphis)	(314) 444-8444	www.stls.frb.org
San Francisco	101 Market St., PO Box 7702 San Francisco, CA 94120-7702 (branches in Los Angeles, Portland, Salt Lake City, Seattle)	(415) 974-3341	www.frbsf.org

Table 15–4   What's the Difference between EE Bonds and I Bonds?

	EE Bond	I Bond
Features	Issued at 50 percent of face value (a $100 EE Bond costs $50)	Issued at face value (a $100 I Bond costs $100)
	Offered in eight denominations ($50, $75, $100, $200, $500, $1,000, $5,000, and $10,000)	Initially offered in six denominations ($50, $75, $100, $500, $1,000, and $5,000). Two additional denominations became available in May 1999 ($200 and $10,000).
	$5,000 (face value) annual purchase limit per person	$5,000 annual purchase limit per Social Security number
Interest	Calculated as 90 percent of 6-month averages of 5-year Treasury Securities yields	Calculated as an earning of a fixed rate of return and a semi-annual inflation rate based on **CPI-U**
	Rates announced every May 1 and November 1	Rate Announcement: Same as EE
	Guaranteed to reach face value within 20 years	No guaranteed level of earnings
	Increases in value monthly and compound semiannually. Interest is paid when the bond is redeemed.	Generally increases in value monthly and interest compounds semiannually (except in periods of deflation when the bond value could remain unchanged). Interest is paid when the bond is redeemed.
	Earn interest for up to 30 years	Life span: Same as EE
Cashing	Can be redeemed after first 6 months	Same as EE
	A 3-month interest penalty applies to bonds redeemed during the first 5 years	Same as EE
	Financial institution reports interest earnings (difference between redemption value and purchase price) on IRS form 1099-INT. Savings bonds are exempt from state and local income taxes.	Same as EE
	Eligible for tax benefits upon redemption when used for qualified education expenses	Same as EE

Source: Bureau of the Public Debt

Inflation-Indexed Bonds

Since the mid-1990s, the U.S. Treasury has offered bonds whose interest and principal repayments are linked to a measure of consumer inflation. Treasury Inflation Protection Securities (TIPS) are designed to protect the bondholder against a loss of purchasing power due to inflation.

Corporates

Corporate bonds are securities representing debt obligations of U.S. corporations. After MBS, corporate bonds represent the second-largest segment of the U.S. bond market, with over $6 trillion in market value outstanding. Issuance of MBS and corporate bonds has surged in the last decade, unseating Treasuries from the spot at the top of the market value charts. Nonetheless, in terms of **liquidity**, Treasuries remain preeminent: the trading volume of corporate bonds (and MBS) remains far smaller than for Treasuries, and is likely to remain so, because there are thousands of different issuers of corporate bonds (and because of the complexities of MBS).

Corporate bonds offer greater returns than Treasuries. They are issued by a wide variety of U.S. corporations, including utilities, transportation companies, industrial companies, financial companies, and conglomerates. High-quality corporate bonds offer dependability of income and safety of principal. In addition, it is possible to diversify your holdings among many issuers while retaining marketability. Corporate bonds are available with a wide variety of terms. Maturity dates range from a few days to 100 years; interest earned can be fixed or floating. **Zero-coupon bonds** allow you to get all your money at maturity.

zero-coupon bond
Bond purchased at discount, paying par at maturity.

There is no free lunch in the financial markets. The greater returns of corporate bonds are accompanied by varying degrees of additional risk. In contrast to Treasuries, which are considered the most creditworthy of all securities, corporate bonds vary from AAA ratings all the way down to bonds that are in default. Another risk posed by many corporate bonds is the chance that they will be called if interest rates decline. This increases your reinvestment risk, because you may get back your principal before the maturity date and find that the yield you can get in the current market is substantially lower than what you were receiving. On the other hand, if you want to sell early, there is less liquidity in this market than in the market for treasuries. This means that it will cost you more to sell: Spreads are higher.

Foreign Bonds: Yankees and Beyond

Many foreign governments (and corporations) issue dollar-denominated bonds as a means of attracting investors who prefer a U.S. dollar-based investment. Collectively, these bonds are referred to as **Yankee bonds**. Unlike foreign currency bonds, they have no direct exchange rate risk, although a dramatic move in exchange rates might alter the credit rating of a Yankee issue, affecting its market value or, in the worst case, even leading to default. Other countries also have markets for foreign bonds denominated in their home currency. For example, the yen-denominated bonds issued by foreigners are referred to as **Samurai bonds**. In contrast to Yankees and Samurais, in which a foreign issuer sells bonds in a local currency, the **Euromarket** refers to the issuance of foreign bonds in foreign currencies. The lion's share of this market is for dollar-denominated bonds, so-called **Eurodollars**.

Mortgage-Backed Securities and Other Asset-Backed Securities

Fueled by and fueling the boom/bubble in housing, issuance of mortgage-backed securities (MBS) surged during the decade leading up to the financial crisis of 2007–2008, making MBS the largest single category of debt outstanding in the United States. During the boom years, MBS were generally considered safe and liquid investments. In the aftermath of the financial crisis of 2007-2008, many investors exited this market causing great uncertainty about price, value, and liquidity.

MBS represent the lion's share of all **asset-backed securities** (ABS). ABS are debt securities that are backed or "collateralized" by a pool of assets expected to generate cashflows. Besides mortgages, ABS may be backed by auto loans, credit card receivables, student loans, and so on.

ABS may be subdivided into several subcategories, including:

- Agency MBS (Government National Mortgage Association (GNMA or "Ginnie Mae"), Federal National Mortgage Association (FNMA or "Fannie Mae"), Federal Home Loan Mortgage Corporation (FHLMC or "Freddie Mac"). The financial crisis caused both FNMA and FHLMC to become insolvent.

- Non-agency MBS are issued by private companies including banks and other financial institutions. With the bailout of banks by the U.S. government, this distinction has become somewhat harder to make.

- Other ABS, i.e., debt backed by pools of assets other than mortgages.

With disappearing demand for new issues and loss estimates over $1 trillion (U.S), the relative size of the ABS market is likely to revert toward earlier levels.

Municipals

marginal income tax rate   *Highest tax rate paid by an investor (i.e., tax paid on last dollar earned).*

Tax-exempt municipal bonds (**munis**) have a long history of use by individuals in a high tax bracket. In the days when **marginal income tax rates** went as high as 90 percent, these bonds were an especially good way to generate additional current income. Lower taxes have been a boon to the stock market, making bonds less attractive on a relative basis. Lower tax rates have also meant that there is less reason to invest in munis, driving their yields closer to the yields on taxable instruments. Even though the decline in marginal rates (and the existence of the alternative minimum tax) has weakened their advantages over taxable investments, munis retain many adherents.

The name *municipal* is actually somewhat misleading; munis are bonds issued by many governmental entities, including states, cities, counties, and their agencies. They are put to many uses, from highways and hospitals to prisons and schools. Munis are interest-bearing loans, just like corporate bonds and Treasuries. As the owner of a muni, you are entitled to regular interest payments as well as the return of your principal on the bond's maturity date. Most, but not all, munis are exempt from federal tax on the interest income they generate. Those that are not exempt from federal taxes are called **taxable munis**, even though they still offer state and local tax exemptions. We will focus on the larger and more important tax-exempt market.

Though it is the smallest of the four major markets in terms of market value outstanding, munis are still an enormous market, with more than $1.3 trillion outstanding. In addition, it remains of great importance to individual investors. This can be inferred from the fact that fully one-third of munis are held directly by individuals. This roughly $450 billion in municipals is more than double the amount of marketable Treasury securities directly held by individuals. Clearly, individual investors are attracted to munis.

Another third is owned by mutual funds, including tax-exempt money market funds and closed-end funds. This means that roughly two-thirds of the market value is fairly directly controlled by individual investors. The final third is spread among insurance companies, commercial banks, trusts, and others.

One of the major selling points of munis is that for many investors, they provide a higher **equivalent taxable yield** than taxable bonds. This is the yield after adjusting for taxes. As an example, let's compare a high-quality corporate bond paying 8 percent to a muni paying 6 percent. Which will put more money in your pocket after taxes? There is no universal answer to this question—it depends on where you live and your marginal tax rate for federal, state, and local taxes. If your marginal federal rate is above 25 percent, then you will keep more money with the muni—even without considering state or local taxes. If you can buy a muni that is double or triple exempt, you can do even better. (See Table 15–5.)

While all "tax-exempt" munis are free of federal taxes on income, state taxation rules vary for how individuals and corporations are taxed. Each state has its own rules to determine which munis are **double exempt**, and to whom this double exemption applies. Double exempt means that income from such munis is not subject to state income tax (as well as being exempt from federal income tax). For example, munis are not taxable for Utah residents, even if the bonds are issued by another state. On the other hand, Utah corporations are subject to tax on muni interest income, even for State of Utah bonds. A state-by-state guide for individuals and corporations is published by Commerce Clearing House.

equivalent taxable yield *The yield on a taxable bond that provides equal income to a particular municipal bond investor.*

Table 15–5 Equivalent Yields for Various Taxable Yields and Marginal Tax Rates

Taxable Yield	Marginal Tax Rate				
	20%	25%	30%	35%	40%
4%	3.2%	3%	2.8%	2.6%	2.4%
5%	4%	3.75%	3.5%	3.25%	3%
6%	4.8%	4.5%	4.2%	3.9%	3.6%
7%	5.6%	5.25%	4.9%	4.55%	4.2%
8%	6.4%	6%	5.6%	5.2%	4.8%
9%	7.2%	6.75%	6.3%	5.85%	5.4%
10%	8%	7.5%	7%	6.5%	6%

Until the credit crisis, many muni bonds were insured against default. In 2007 and 2008, it became apparent that the so-called monoline insurers had entered unrelated risky businesses that made their own credit-worthiness questionable at best. This led to a re-thinking of the vale of bond insurance that is just beginning.

Many issuers of munis, like corporate issuers, give themselves the right to redeem all or part of the issue before maturity. These call provisions are a way for the issuer to take advantage of falling interest rates by **refunding** the bonds with a new, lower interest-bearing issue. Of course, if your bonds are called, you are unlikely to be able to reinvest the proceeds to receive the same rate at the same credit quality. This is your reinvestment risk. In contrast to noncallable bonds, callable bonds should offer you something to compensate you for your reinvestment risk. That something can be a **call premium.**

An important point about tax-exempt bonds: The exemption applies only to interest income (or in the case of discount instruments, to the portion of capital appreciation that is equivalent to interest). Capital gains are still taxable. Taxable capital gains can occur if you sell a muni whose price has increased due to a decline in interest rates, tax rate changes, or an improvement in credit quality.

Money Market

Another market adversely affected by the financial crisis, money market funds were hit with losses following the September 2008 bankruptcy of Lehman Brothers. The Reserve Primary Fund, the oldest money market fund in the United States, "broke the buck." This means that they sustained losses large enough so that the sponsoring firm was unwilling or unable to make up the difference, resulting in a loss of capital for shareholders. As the "raison d'etre" of money market funds is safety of principal, this was a true crisis for the global financial system, requiring dramatic action to prevent a run on the "shadow banking system." The U.S. Treasury defused the problem by guaranteeing the assets of more than $3 trillion in money market funds against a loss of up to $50 billion. This "temporary guarantee program" only covers shareholders up to the amount invested as of September 19, 2008. Initially set to end on April 30, 2009, the program has been extended through September 18, 2009. Updates to this information should be accessible at www.treas.gov.

Summary

Bonds offer many important advantages. High credit-quality bonds offer safety of principal and interest, while providing some diversification from stock market investments. Also, in contrast to stocks, bonds give you the ability to precisely match expected future liabilities. For this reason, insurance companies and pension funds make extensive use of bonds in their portfolios.

On the other hand, bonds are not without disadvantages. In general, they are harder to buy and sell. Outside of the Treasury market, they can bear a high markup. In addition, the bond market is not very transparent, especially to individuals. It can be hard to figure out your true cost of buying and selling. For these reasons, many individuals decide to hold bonds indirectly, in the form of mutual fund investments. It is important to understand, however, that such indirect holdings do not offer certainty of principal and interest income. Bond funds do not have a maturity date; bond fund shares are actually shares of stock in an investment company that buys bonds. The value of these shares fluctuates with the market forces that raise and lower bond prices and interest rates like a seesaw.

The financial crisis has added further uncertainties to bonds, especially bonds that are not backed by the "full faith and credit" of the U.S. government. Eventually, a new financial order will emerge from the ashes of the old. Bonds and the markets they trade in will be changed in many ways, but they are highly likely to remain an essential part of the new system.

Options, Futures, and Other Derivatives

OPTIONS, FUTURES, AND OTHER DERIVATIVES

Engines of Financial Innovation

Options and futures are examples of *derivative* securities, that is, securities that derive their value from the value of another security, underlying asset, or benchmark. There are two basic types of options. *Call options* (calls) are securities that give the holder the right but not the obligation to buy some underlying asset at a predefined price during a specific period of time. *Put options* (puts) are securities that give their owner the right, but again, not the obligation to sell an underlying asset at a predefined price during a specific period of time. Futures are exchange-traded, standardized contracts for the future delivery either of an *actual* (physical) commodity or for cash settlement based on future values of some financial security or index. Other examples of derivatives include **forward** contracts or agreements, and swaps. Forwards are similar to futures, except that they are privately negotiated, over-the-counter transactions, and therefore are not marked to market. Swaps are complex trades between financial institutions or other sophisticated investors. There are many types of swaps, including interest-rate swaps, currency swaps, and equity swaps.

The term *derivative* came into widespread use in the mid-1980s (previously, financial analysts talked about "synthetics"). The concept of linking the value of a security to an underlying asset, however, is a very old one—you could say that it is the basic idea of securities. In a broad sense, all bonds, stocks, and mutual funds are derivatives. They derive their value from underlying assets: in the case of secured bonds, specific corporate assets such as a building; for unsecured bonds and stocks, a claim on general corporate assets; and for mutual funds, a claim on the securities that make up the funds' portfolios.

No one uses the word *derivative* in this way, nor are we suggesting that you should do so. We are merely pointing out that though the term is new, and though a great deal of creativity and ingenuity have gone into creating new derivative securities, these securities are part of a tradition of innovation going back to the beginning of financial markets.

In this section, we will provide an overview of the world of options, futures, and other derivatives. In Chapter Sixteen, we focus on options, describing what they are, who uses them, and why. Chapter Seventeen introduces you to the world of futures, highlighting how they are used and explaining their special risks. Finally, in Chapter Eighteen, we will give a brief introduction to some of the other creative uses of derivative products, which are gradually making their way from the world of institutional high finance and onto a computer screen in your home.

Chapter 16
OPTIONS

You may recall from our discussion of bonds a basic distinction between bonds and stocks. While stocks have no built-in maturity date, almost all bonds do. What about options? In one way, they resemble bonds, having a predefined ending point. The nature of that ending point, however, is very different. That difference can be summed up as follows: Bonds mature; options expire.

The ending value of an option is not fixed in advance. It is linked to the value of an **underlying asset.** For example, a **call** option on IJK Corporation common stock is linked to the value of the stock as follows: Suppose that on January 2, 2010, you purchase a call option giving you the right to purchase 100 shares of IJK at $50 per share on any trading day until March 16, 2010, the **expiration** day. What is the option worth to you on March 16? If IJK stock is trading at more than $50 per share, the option has value. Let's say the current market price is $55. Theoretically, you could exercise your option (i.e., buy the 100 shares of IJK at $50 per share). You would have paid $5,000 for $5,500 worth of stock. (We are ignoring, for the moment, the cost of these transactions.) Thus the theoretical value of this option is $500.

On the other hand, if IJK is trading at less than $50 at the end of the March 16 trading day, it has no value. Exercising such an option would be pointless; it would be cheaper to buy the shares directly.

underlying asset
The asset an option holder has the right to buy (call) or sell (put).

Similar considerations apply to the other basic kind of option, a put. The difference between calls and puts is simply this: Whereas a call gives you the right to buy something, a put gives you the right to sell something. In contrast to a call, the value of a put increases as the price of the underlying asset falls. For example, if you had purchased a put on IJK with an exercise price of $50, it would have a positive intrinsic value when the stock *declined* below $50 per share. Otherwise, its intrinsic value would be zero. Beyond this fundamental difference, calls and puts are quite similar: Each has a well-defined linkage to an underlying asset, an exercise price, and an expiration date.

After the expiration day, an option is worthless. Unlike a bond, which can be redeemed for its face value long after its maturity date, options that are neither sold nor exercised lose all value after expiration. (Of course, a bond should be redeemed as soon as possible so that it can be reinvested and continue to earn interest.) Other things being equal, options lose value as the expiration date approaches. For this reason, it is often said that options are a "wasting asset."

But what is the value of an option before the last trading day? Let's imagine that it is March 2, 2010; we have two weeks to go before a call option expires, and IJK stock is at $50 per share. There is no point in exercising this option now; it confers no advantage compared with just selling it in the open market. However, it appears that there is a reasonable chance that IJK will go above $50 per share sometime in the next two weeks. The option has value because sometime within the next two weeks, IJK's stock price may go above $50 per share. Remember, we are ignoring transaction costs, and we haven't yet considered how much you paid for the option.

The Ins and Outs of Options

When an option can be exercised for a profit, it is **in-the-money**; otherwise, it is **out-of-the-money**. A call option whose underlying asset price is higher than the exercise price of the call is in-the-money. Similarly, a put option whose underlying asset price is lower than the exercise price of the put is in-the-money. In either case, a holder of the option can make money by simultaneously exercising the option and either selling the underlying asset (if the option is a call) or buying the underlying asset (if the option is a put).

(Continued)

Usually, when options are characterized in this way, transaction costs are not taken into account. If transaction costs are included, some in-the-money options cost more to exercise than they are worth. Even if that weren't so, it is seldom necessary to exercise an exchange-traded option. It is easier, and almost always more profitable, just to sell it. Even out-of-the-money options can be sold before expiration, because they have time value even though they have no intrinsic value.

Exchange-Traded Options

Calls and puts usually exist in tandem for underlying assets, striking prices, and expiration dates. However, market participants tend to favor calls in some circumstances and puts in other circumstances. Frequently, for example, after a long bull market in a stock, index, or commodity, you may see the volume of puts being traded on that underlying asset begin to increase. The total number of options contracts created between buyers and sellers, known as the **open interest**, may also increase. Nervous investors buy puts as a form of insurance against a sudden market panic. Speculators also buy puts, albeit for a different reason: They use puts to bet on a market downturn.

Other investors, or market makers, who do not expect an imminent change in the market, sell these puts and pocket the premium. What is true for stocks and bonds is also true for options—for every buyer there is also a seller. In the options world, the seller is frequently described as a *writer,* and the price he or she receives by selling you a call or a put is described as a *premium*. The insurance language is not accidental. Many investors buy options as a form of financial insurance.

Options create a link between a buyer and a seller that persists for the life of the option. For this reason, an option transaction is sometimes described as a **zero-sum game** with two players. This means that one player's winnings are exactly offset by the other player's losses. This contrasts with stock investments, in which there is no finite time span in which the players' wins and losses cancel out. (Someone selling you a stock might have made a profit or a loss, depending only on its current price and the price at which he or she bought it. Your subsequent profit or loss bears no direct connection to the previous owner's investment performance.)

Looked at in another way, however, options provide value to both buyer and seller, even though one of them has lost money. The value comes from reduction of risk, or more generally, improved correlation between assets and liabilities. This type of transaction, in which both parties may benefit, is the major justification for a whole range of derivatives known as **swaps.** We will discuss swaps in Chapter Eighteen.

swap *A two-party transaction involving securities, currencies, commodities, or other assets in conformance to a precise set of rules called a* **swap agreement.**

If a call writer owns the underlying asset, then he has written a **covered call.** Though he may have to deliver the underlying asset, his risk is limited because he already owns that asset. The underlying asset is said to have been called away from him.

In contrast, a call that is written by someone who does not own the underlying asset is referred to as a **naked call.** Brokers are required to restrict this type of options trading strategy to investors who are able to engage in riskier investments. If the price of the underlying asset increases, a naked call writer has potentially unlimited losses. He can lose his shirt—maybe that's why the call is "naked."

Listed versus OTC Options

How options are regulated depends on the underlying asset:

- Exchange-traded options on stocks and stock indexes are regulated by the SEC.

- Options on exchange-traded futures are regulated by the Commodities Futures Trading Commission (CFTC).

- Over-the-counter options, offered primarily by major banks (and potentially very complex instruments), may come under the regulatory purview of either of those agencies, but may also be scrutinized by the Federal Reserve, the Office of the Comptroller of the Currency, and a trade association set up by the banks themselves, the International Swaps and Derivatives Association (ISDA).

Depending on the terms of the options contract, a call writer may be responsible for delivering the actual underlying asset, unless the terms call for **cash settlement**, in which case the buyer receives the net value of his or her option, equal to the difference between the market value and the striking price of the underlying asset, less brokerage commissions. For example, index options are settled in cash because it would be too burdensome to deliver each of the stocks underlying the index.

Combination Strategies

The following five combination strategies involve options and underlying assets.

Buy Stock and Buy Put

This strategy is typically used to protect an existing position in the underlying asset against a decline in value while retaining all of its upside potential. Investors who are nervous about a short-term decline that can erode the value of an asset can use a put to provide protection.

Let's look at an example. Say that you own 1,000 shares of IJK Corporation, which is trading at $144, and you are nervous that the price is going to drop in the short term. But you don't want to sell the stock outright—you just want short-term protection. What can you do? You can buy 10 "IJK 140" puts. Each of these puts gives you the right to sell 100 shares of IJK at $140 per share (up until expiration), protecting you against a sharp decline in the price of IJK.

Notice that the "insurance" doesn't actually kick in until IJK goes below 140. This is somewhat like having a deductible on your insurance policy. There is an important difference to keep in mind. Insurance coverage is governed by the contract between you and the insurance company. The "insurance" obtained through purchase and sale of exchange-traded options is subject to market forces and may offer more or less protection than the theoretical value of the option. On the other hand, the fact that you can exercise an option that is in the money does provide you with a hedge that goes beyond the market's forces of supply and demand.

Buy Stock and Sell Call

This is called a **buy-write** investment strategy. A different investor may not feel the need to insure the underlying asset, but wants to extract additional income from that asset. This can be done by writing a call against the asset you own. Remember that when you write a call, you are selling someone the right to buy something from you and receiving an amount of money known as the option's *premium*. Since you own the underlying asset, it is a covered call, and as explained previously, your risk is limited to having the underlying asset "called away" from you, in which case you receive the striking price for your asset. The further "out of the money" the call when it is written, the less likely it is to be called away from you over the life of the option. On the other hand, if the underlying asset is very volatile or is subjected to an unexpected event, the option may be exercised. But this is what the writer receives a premium for—if there were no chance of exercise, the option would have no potential value to any (rational) buyer.

Buy Stock, Buy Put, and Sell Call

One can combine the two previous strategies, in effect paying for put "insurance" with the premium earned from writing the call. It may appear from the payout diagram in Figure 16–1 that the asset is becoming more and more like cash, and indeed, careful analysis of costs is warranted to make sure that someone besides the broker can make money from this strategy. This strategy is the basis for a relationship between the price of puts and calls known as **put-call parity**. This relationship, based on arbitrage, allows you to derive the price of a put if you know the price of a call with the same strike price and expiration date. Likewise, you can derive the price of a call from the corresponding price of a put. Put-call parity is a useful means for comparing relative value of calls and puts, and it can also be used as a gauge of market **sentiment**.

put-call parity
Relationship between prices of puts and calls allowing you to derive a fair price for one if you know a fair price for the other—as long as they have the same strike price and expiration date.

Straddles and Strangles

Straddles and strangles are two related options strategies for benefiting from an increase in the volatility of the underlying asset. Each involves the simultaneous purchase of a put and a call on the same underlying asset. A **straddle** consists of a combination of put and call options with the same strike price, usually close to the current market value. The options should also share the same time to expiration. A **strangle**, in contrast, consists of a call and a put option with different strike prices, each option being out of the money.

Straddles are more expensive positions to initiate, but may show a profit for a smaller move in the underlying asset than would be required by a strangle. Part of the reason for this has to do with the so-called **delta** of the option (see Options and the "Greeks").

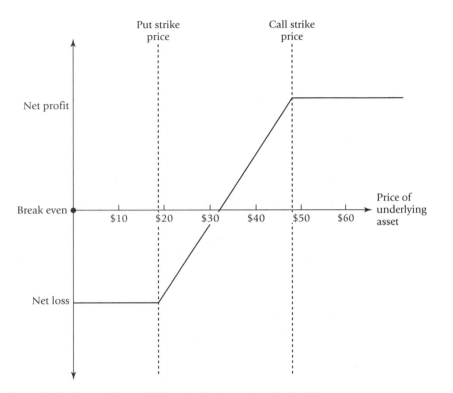

Figure 16–1. Payout diagram for buy stock, buy put, and sell call.

Calendar Spreads

Calendar spreads are options positions spread out over time, usually to bet on a shift in the relationship between near-term options and those with longer to run, based on changes in the value of the underlying asset. For example, a trader may feel that the near-term price of an option is "rich" relative to an option with a later expiration date. The trader could sell the near-term option and buy the option with the longer expiration date, making a profit if the price of the near-term option declines relative to the price of the long-dated option. On the other hand, this can be a risky trade, especially if the trader does not own the underlying asset (i.e., if he or she is writing a naked call).

Determining the Value of an Option

Intuitively, it seems that if the clock hasn't run out, the option still has some value. That value comes from the chance that the underlying asset's value will increase enough to make the option worth exercising before the expiration date. This situation is described by saying that the option has a **time value**, but no intrinsic value, because it is not currently worth exercising.

What if IJK Corporation stock were to increase to $52 per share, with one week left to expiration? The option would then have an intrinsic value of $2 per share, and it would also have some time value (i.e., another week remaining in which it could increase in price).

But the underlying price may also decrease. How can you figure out what this option is really worth? This was an unsolved problem until 1973, when Fischer Black and Myron Scholes introduced their famous **Black-Scholes option pricing model** containing a formula, based on several restrictive assumptions, for determining the fair value of an option. One of those assumptions was that the option could be exercised only on the day of expiration (**European style**) rather than at any time up to expiration (i.e., **American style**). Later that year, Robert Merton extended the theory. In 1997, Merton and Scholes shared a Nobel Prize in Economics for their pioneering work in options pricing theory. (Unfortunately, Fischer Black had already passed away and so could not share in the award.)

Trading options with the help of their formula in the 1970s was like shooting fish in a barrel. Only a few savvy investors understood how to price options. They could spot big mispricings and make lots of money. Eventually, the rest of the street caught on. Now a version of the Black-Scholes options program comes built into many software packages—and can even be found on good calculators. To get a feel for what goes into the formula, recall from our previous example that we needed to know the following:

- The current price of the underlying asset
- The exercise price of the option
- How much time remains until expiration

In addition to these three numbers, Black and Scholes identified two other important factors:

- The volatility of the underlying asset—how much its price tends to fluctuate
- The **risk-free rate**—how much your money can earn when put into the safest possible investment, a Treasury bill

Armed with these five factors and the program, you can determine the theoretical fair value of a stock option—in other words, what it should cost. With that number in hand, it seems, you will always know whether a stock option is fairly valued, a bargain, or expensive. Almost, but not quite. There is a little problem with one of the numbers you need to provide for the program to do its work. That number is the *volatility*, the jumpiness or tendency for the stock's price to fluctuate. What the formula wants you to tell it is how volatile the stock's price is right now—its instantaneous volatility. But you can only estimate that number. At best, you can guess what the stock's volatility was at different times in the past—its **historical volatility**—and assume that there is some predictability to its future volatility. What you wind up doing is estimating the future volatility from your guess of its historical volatility.

Why do you need to guess about a historical number? The problem is choosing an appropriate time frame for calculating the historical volatility. Should we look back a year? Six months? Three months? What if the stock was very volatile last week, but fairly inactive for months previously? Which are the relevant numbers? There's no way to know for sure. In any event, investors tend to use rules of thumb to choose what they believe to be a relevant period of historical volatility. Six months seems to work here, nine months there.

Options and the "Greeks"

Options pricing theory helps us to understand how the value of an option should change when one of the factors determining an option's price changes. If you spend much time with options, you will soon run across references to the **Greeks.** This is shorthand for a set of Greek letters used in formulas to calculate the **sensitivity** of an option's value to small changes in one of those factors (e.g., time to expiration, price of underlying asset, interest rates). The five "Greeks" are as follows:

- Delta (δ) is the sensitivity of an option's price to a change in the value of the underlying asset, all other things remaining constant.

- Gamma (γ) is the sensitivity of an option's price to a change in the option's delta, all other things remaining constant.

(Continued)

sensitivity *Measure of the degree of responsiveness of some financial variable to a small change in some market condition. In mathematical terms, a partial derivative or partial difference.*

- Rho (ρ) is the sensitivity of an option's price to a change in the risk-free interest rate, all other things remaining constant.

- Theta (θ) is the sensitivity of an option's price to a change in the time to expiration, all other things remaining constant.

- Vega (a mnemonic for volatility, not a Greek letter) is the sensitivity of an option's price to a change in volatility, all other things being equal.

There's another approach to the problem, which sort of comes at it backward. Instead of solving for the theoretical fair value price, you simply set it equal to the market price of the option. Then you plug in all the other numbers and solve for the volatility. Now you can solve the Black-Scholes formula for volatility, the only remaining unknown. The answer you get is called the **implied volatility.** It is the volatility implied by the price the market has put on the option.

Implied volatility can be used in many different ways. Like prices and volumes, it can be charted to show its month-by-month, day-by-day, or even moment-by-moment changes. These changes can be graphed for technical analysis or subjected to a variety of statistical tests.

One basic way of using implied volatility is to compare the value of different options on the same underlying asset. For example, a stock such as IBM has over 100 different exchange-traded options at any given time. How can one stock generate so many options? Consider that exchange-traded options may have, say, a dozen different strike prices and five expiration dates. For each of these combinations, there can be both a call and a put being traded. Thus,

$$12 \text{ strike prices} \times 5 \text{ expiration dates} \times 2 \text{ call/put} = 120 \text{ different options}$$

Each of these options has a market price, but how much are they really worth? You can use the Black-Scholes formula to calculate the theoretical value of these options, but as we explained previously, this requires estimating the volatility of the underlying asset. On the other hand, you can get a feel for the relative value of these options by calculating their implied volatility. This can be a useful way of pricing options that trade infrequently. First, you get the implied volatility, using a liquid option on the stock or other underlying asset. Then you use that volatility to come up with a "quasi-market price," which you can think of as the price the option might have if it were more actively traded.

Remember, this method doesn't tell you what any of the options are worth in absolute terms, but only how the market is pricing them against each other. For example, you might find that the put options have a lower implied volatility than the calls, or that certain out-of-the-money options have a significantly higher implied volatility than their in-the-money brethren.

Another approach taken by traders compares implied volatility with historical volatility numbers. For example, if the 180-day historical volatility of a stock is 15 percent, and its implied volatility (as calculated from its most liquid option) is only 10 percent, these traders might reason that "volatility is cheap," because the stock's implied volatility is lower than at least one estimate of its current volatility. Theoretically, volatility and price should rise and fall together. Therefore, either the future volatility of the stock should diminish, bringing it into line with the option's price, or else the price of the option should increase, reflecting the market's current volatility. Traders can put on positions to exploit either or both of these possibilities.

Finally, implied volatility can be used as a benchmark to identify the market's idea of the relevant historical volatility (e.g., 90-day versus 180-day). Some go one step further, interpreting implied volatility as the market's forecast of the future volatility of the stock.

All of this information can be incorporated into options trading strategies. We'd like to remind you, however, that successful options trading requires a combination of skill, access to good information, and ability to execute trades at a reasonable cost. A little luck doesn't hurt, either.

Chapter 17

FUTURES

utures have a long history. For centuries, producers and traders of goods have agreed on prices long in advance of the delivery, or even the production, of the goods being offered for sale. Indeed, without such forward commitments, the large trading networks of a modern economy would be difficult if not impossible. Markets for trading of standardized contracts in futures evolved as a means to lower the costs and risks of trade, both to the producer and consumer of goods, by transferring that risk to a financial intermediary willing and able to accept that risk in exchange for some compensation.

A Seller's Need to Hedge . . .

To see how the need for futures arose, consider the case of a farmer who grows soybeans. Many factors influence the income he can derive from selling his beans at market. How large his crop is depends on many local conditions, including weather, soil, the quality of the seeds, loss due to harmful insects and other pests, and effectiveness of insecticides. All other things being equal, the more beans he produces, the more money he will receive when it comes time to sell. It is, however, quite unlikely that local conditions alone determine the value of the farmer's crop. Shortages, oversupplies, and shifts in demand can all have a major impact on the price he receives, making it very difficult for him to keep his farm financially healthy. If, on the other hand, he could lock in a future price for his soybeans sufficiently far in advance, he would have a less volatile asset—cash—with which to meet his liabilities.

Example of Seller Hedging with Futures

Let's say a farmer expects to have one million bushels of soybeans to sell. He can proceed in one of several ways. The most obvious is to wait until the beans are harvested and then deliver them to a local elevator, selling them at whatever market price prevails at that time. But this leaves him open to the risk that the price of soybeans will fall when he is ready to sell. One alternative is to enter into a forward contract, locking in a cash price for the soybeans before they are sold. The other alternative is to sell an appropriate number of soybean futures contracts before the harvest, thereby locking in a sales price.

Either of these alternatives will protect his **gross profit margin (GPM)**— even though the soybeans themselves won't be sold for another two months. The futures market approach offers more flexibility, but also more risk, than the forward contract. The flexibility comes from the existence of an active market in soybean futures. The risk derives from the difference between the type and the location of the beans specified by the standard futures contract and the beans that the farmer is selling. It is called **basis risk**.

Most likely the soybean futures will be sold at the Chicago Board of Trade (CBOT, now part of the CME Group), where soybean futures have been traded since the 1930s. At the CBOT, each soybean contract is for 5,000 bushels of number 2 yellow soybeans. There are six separate contracts per year, expiring in alternate months: January, March, May, July, September, and November.

basis risk   *Risk deriving from variations in type and quality between a marketable commodity and the specific commodity described in a standard futures contract.*

Some Buyers Need to Hedge, Too

Further up the food chain, a food processor consumes prodigious amounts of soybeans in the manufacture of soybean oil and meal. Market forces constantly change the relationship between the price of the processor's raw material (soybeans) and its finished product (oil and meal). If the price of soybeans soars, the food processor may find its GPM shrinking dangerously. This can be avoided by a combination of buying futures in the raw material and selling futures in the finished product. Soybean oil and meal contracts have been traded on the CBOT for nearly 50 years. Together, the three contracts (soybeans, soybean oil, and soybean meal) are referred to as the **soybean complex**.

Speculation or Insurance? Maybe a Little of Both

So it is evident that there are occasions when it makes sense for buyers and sellers to hedge their price risks by contracting for future sale, through forwards or futures contracts. When sufficient numbers of buyers and sellers have an interest in hedging, futures markets emerge as places for buyers and sellers to meet. As in other markets, the broker's role is to facilitate market liquidity.

What is the relationship between prices in the **spot market** and the futures market? Putting aside possible differences in contract terms, how prices in the spot market for a commodity relate to prices in the futures market will depend on many factors, including supply and demand forces in these markets, liquidity, financial forecasts, and importantly, **arbitrage** possibilities arising from differences in costs of maintaining positions in these markets. These costs include insurance and storage costs until **delivery** is taken on a physical commodity; margin costs for leveraged positions; and opportunity costs for capital tied up in a commodity (unless it can be used as collateral for other investments).

arbitrage *Buying and selling of equivalent investments to take advantage of mispricings in different markets.*

Actuals versus Cash-Settled Contracts

Futures may be classified by the way in which the contracts are settled at expiration. Futures contracts in a physical commodity are settled by the actual delivery of the underlying good, whether it is gold bars or pork bellies. "Delivery" does not necessarily mean that the goods physically change hands; *ownership* of the goods is what changes.

Cash-settled contracts do not involve any change in ownership of the underlying asset. Instead, the value of the asset is calculated by predetermined rules, and the contract is concluded with a cash payment. This is the way that **index futures** are settled. These futures' value is linked to an index such as the S&P 500 or the S&P **Goldman Sachs Commodity Index (S&P GSCI)**. While it would be theoretically possible to "deliver" such an index, in practical terms, cash settlement makes far more sense.

What Is Triple Witching Friday?

Sometimes, around a particularly volatile day in the markets, you may hear about **triple witching Friday**. This is a day on which three related contracts expire: index options, index futures, and options on the index futures. Triple witching Friday occurs four times a year, on the third Friday of March, June, September, and December.

Margin and Collateral

Futures contracts, like many stocks, can be purchased on margin. In the case of futures, however, the amount of initial margin can be very low, often as low as 10 percent. The result is that a small initial investment is often said to "control" a large position. The word *control* may be inappropriate, however. Each day the position is marked to market, meaning that its current value is determined and any loss in the large position is subtracted from the value of your net position. Over time, even modest price movements can precipitate a margin call, the broker's demand for additional funds to bring the ratio of funds left in the account back over the minimum threshold. In fact, a sudden price move could precipitate a margin call at any time. Failure on the part of the customer to come up with the required margin allows, and in some cases requires, the broker to close out the position, erasing any assets you had in the account and potentially leaving you with a liability for costs incurred by the broker.

An Example of Marking to Market

Let's say you purchase a single soybean futures contract on the CBOT. The cost of the contract is the price of soybeans, say $6.50 per bushel, times the number of the bushels in a contract, 5,000:

(Continued)

Total cost: $6.50 × 5,000 = $32,500

Do you have to come up with $32,500? Not at all. What you need is only a small percentage of the full cost—namely, the cost times the **initial margin requirement**. Let's say the broker sets an initial margin requirement of 10 percent. That means you must deposit $3,250 into the margin account you have set up with that broker. The rest of the money is a loan from the broker, on which you pay interest.

Each day, the broker determines the value of your futures position. Let's say that soybeans increase in price by 10 percent. The contract is now worth $35,750. Your position, however, has done even better. You put up only $3,250, but now you have a position worth $6,500. You have doubled your money.

Now let's assume that the market declines to the point that your position is worth less than, say, 5 percent of the total value of the contract. This triggers a maintenance margin call from your broker. You must come up with additional money immediately or face being closed out—having the position sold by the broker in order to protect the money he or she loaned you. In the worst case, by the time the broker sells out your position, the contract is worth less than the loan, in which case you've lost your entire investment and owe the broker the difference between the amount realized on the sale and amount he or she loaned you—plus interest and commissions.

For these reasons, many individual investors avoid the futures markets entirely. For those who wish to participate in these markets, caution is advisable. One way for individuals to participate is through managed (futures) accounts. These are investment partnerships that trade futures, primarily for institutions and high-net-worth individuals. Such accounts, like the underlying futures, are usually highly leveraged investments, offering high potential returns—with high levels of risk.

Chapter 18
OTHER DERIVATIVES

I n the previous two chapters we have explored how options and futures work. Though exchange-traded options and futures have many uses for hedgers, speculators, and sophisticated investors, they are only the beginning in the world of derivatives. In fact, the private, over-the-counter (OTC) market in derivatives is far larger than the exchange markets.

The OTC market is almost exclusively an institutional market, although individuals may make use of it through "retail foreign exchange brokers" and/or market makers. There have been many instances of fraud in this lightly regulated market: caveat emptor! That is why it is described as private, in distinction to the very public world of over-the-counter Nasdaq stocks. The OTC derivatives market is used to execute strategies that would be impractical or unwieldy in the public, exchange-based futures and options markets.

The prime example of a private OTC market is the foreign exchange (FOREX) market. The FOREX market is not strictly speaking a securities market, nor is it exclusively a derivatives market. Rather, it is the global market for currencies. It includes a spot market, in which currencies are traded for immediate delivery. These are not considered derivative transactions. It also includes forward exchange transactions, in which two parties agree to trade currencies at a later date (or dates) at the **forward rate**, a currency **exchange rate** determined today. These are like currency futures except with much more flexible terms and no standard marking to market. Individual contracts may require occasional or periodic cash transfers similar to margin calls. The combined spot and forward currency markets are larger than any single securities market, far bigger in terms of dollar volume than even the market for U.S. government securities. The current estimated trading volume exceeds $3 trillion per day, according to the Bank for International Settlements (www.bis.org).

Most of this foreign exchange trading is purely financial in nature; only a small part of it is associated with actual trade in goods and services. Spot and forward markets exist for all the major commodities. By far the largest of these is the international oil market. Then there are OTC markets in all kinds of securities, ranging from indexes to hybrid securities that may combine features of stocks, bonds, commodities, or indexes. The general rule of thumb is this: If somebody (typically a large corporation or institutional investor) has a reason to buy it, and someone else (typically a bank or brokerage firm) can figure out a profitable way to sell it, an OTC derivative will be created. Today we even have derivatives for catastrophic insurance losses, the cost of electricity, pollution rights, and the credit-worthiness (default risk) of a borrower—known as credit default swaps or simply, CDSs.

Swaps are another major dimension of the derivatives world. The word *swap* originally was used in the management of bond portfolios to refer to a market strategy employed by an individual bond trader in the market. These strategies were collectively referred to as *bond swaps*. Today, however, the word *swap* has evolved to mean a two-party transaction involving securities, currencies, commodities, or other assets in conformance to a precise set of rules called a **swap agreement.** The earliest swap agreements involved currencies and interest rates. Today, in addition to currency swaps, interest rate swaps and CDSs, there are also equity swaps and even **swaptions**, which combine the features of swap agreements with options.

In the first decade of the 21st century, CDSs emerged as an important alternative means of trading credit risk. CDSs grew from a small corner of the OTC derivative market to become the dominant way of trading credit. Instead of buying and selling bonds or bank debt, investors (or managers acting on their behalf) were now able to buy and sell contracts designed to protect against an "event of default" by an issuer of such debt. As a largely unregulated OTC market, CDSs grew to the point that the total notional (face value of contract) outstanding was far greater than the underlying value of the debt! More important, although CDSs possess many of the characteristics of an insurance contract, they were not regulated in this way. As a result, "writers of protection", i.e., sellers of credit insurance, were not required to demonstrate to a regulator that they had adequate reserves to pay their counterparties in the event that one or more issuers defaulted. In particular, insurance giant AIG had written far too much insurance, leading to a liquidity crisis in September of 2008 that required a multi-billion dollar **bailout** by the Federal Reserve, which became the majority owner of AIG.

As a result of the financial crisis, a new regulatory regime emphasizing transparency, standardized contracts, and centralized clearing, is likely to emerge. Such developments may further blur the distinctions between OTC institutional markets and exchange-based markets for the broad investing public.

While the initial thrust of so-called **financial engineering** innovations has taken place in an institutional, OTC setting, more and more of this innovation is finding its way to the public markets and individual investors. *Financial engineering* refers to the development of sophisticated financial products using derivatives and based on mathematical and computer models. The financial crisis has cast a harsh light on financial engineering, though it seems that much of what went wrong has less to do with math and models and more to do with lack of transparency and greed run amok.

Exchange-traded index funds, such as **SPDRs** (ticker symbol SPY) and **DIAMONDs** (ticker symbol DIA) are examples of what has become a mass market in exchange-traded derivatives. ETFs represent a substantial percentage of total trading volume on exchanges like the NYSE.

SPDRs (S&P 500 Depository Receipts) were the first and are still the most popular exchange-traded derivative contract. Developed by the American Stock Exchange, SPDRs are designed to track the performance of the S&P 500 Index. Unlike Vanguard S&P 500 index fund, SPDRs can be bought and sold on a market at prices that reflect the intraday movements in the underlying index. Vanguard's index funds and open-end mutual funds that track indexes are priced only once a day. As no-load funds, they are bought and sold at their net asset value (NAV).

DIAMONDs are an exchange-traded derivative designed to track the Dow Jones Industrial Average. Trading in these derivatives is currently less than 10 percent of the trading in SPDRs.

SPDRs *S&P 500 Depository Receipts, an exchange-traded index product developed and traded by the American Stock Exchange (AMEX).*

DIAMOND *An index fund based on the Dow Jones Industrial Average, traded on the American Stock Exchange.*

WEBS (World Equity Benchmark Shares) *Index funds based on Morgan Stanley Capital International Equity Indexes.*

Beyond these plain-vanilla products are a variety of structured products that embed optionlike protection into an index contract. An example of this type of derivative is Merrill Lynch's **MITT (Market Index Term Trust)**. MITTs combine index investing with a bondlike guarantee of principal. They are traded on the NYSE and are aimed at a broad range of individual investors.

For well-heeled investors, **MPDs (Market Participation Deposits)** offer features comparable to MITTs, but in larger size. MPDs are sold by private banking divisions of major financial institutions. Typically, customers must open seven-figure accounts with the bank.

An important word of caution about ETFs and structured products: they may contain hidden counterparty risk. In the case of ETFs, it is important to ascertain how they are getting exposure to the underlying assets. Do they own them directly, or are they engaged in a swap with a counterparty who may default? Likewise, "bondlike" returns of structured products implies bondlike default risk. Caveat emptor.

In looking at these early entrants into the burgeoning market of derivatives for everybody, we are reminded of what Alvin Toffler described nearly 30 years ago in *The Third Wave:* an age of mass customization. The proliferation of all these new forms of securities is frequently bewildering and sometimes frightening. It should be remembered, however, that used properly, they allow investors to tailor their investment strategy to match their own unique needs and goals.

Section Six
Summing Up Risk and Return

SUMMING UP RISK AND RETURN

In the preceding sections we have learned a great deal about financial investments and their markets. No guide to the markets would be complete, however, unless it addresses how to evaluate investment results. Though this is a large and complex topic, it boils down to an understanding of how investment results (referred to as *investment returns* or *performance*) are measured and reported, both in absolute terms and after adjusting for risk.

Chapter Nineteen provides an introduction to the ways that performance is calculated and to the standards used by investment managers for presentation of performance results to clients and prospects. Chapter Twenty introduces the concept of investment risk and explains some of the ways it can be measured, or at least estimated. It concludes with some guidelines for applying an understanding of risk to the investment process. Finally, in Chapter Twenty-one, we take a step back to the larger context of the financial markets, offering some final thoughts.

Chapter 19

HOW WELL ARE MY INVESTMENTS DOING?

Measuring Investment Results

here are many ways to measure the results of your investing activities. You may have heard about the high **performance** of a particular mutual fund, or that a certain stock has a good **return on equity (ROE)** or **return on investment (ROI).** All of these have some bearing on the measurement of investment results. But right now, we are more concerned with a more personal aspect of return: How can you calculate the return on your money?

Figuring out the return on your money can be a difficult and time-consuming task. Most of the difficulty is of the grunt-work variety. You may have to track down all the pieces of paper that tell what happened when. Some of the difficulties are interesting and can lead to a deeper understanding of the investment process.

> **performance** *Measure of return as proportion of original investment, or measure of investment performance in an average period.*

We will begin by giving you an overview of what goes into calculating the rate of return on a single security and on a portfolio. We will explain how the different ways of thinking about averages affect the measurement of investment results. Building on the simplest concept of return, we illustrate how time and cash flows in and out of an investment portfolio factor into measurements of performance. This will lead into a comparison of time-weighted and money-weighted measures of return. Finally, we explain how these two very different measures are used in the reporting of investment performance. As the saying goes, knowledge is power. And that is probably why you are reading this book.

The Basics of Return

Starting with some amount of hypothetical capital, the simplest measure of return is just the change in dollar value: "How much did I make (or lose)?" At a gut level, this is what we all want to know when we turn to the financial pages or open the envelope containing a statement from our broker.

At the most elementary level, **return** is simply the profit or loss on an investment. If you bought 200 shares of IBM at $100 per share and sold them for $106, your gross return is

$$(\$106 - \$100) \times 200 = \$1,200$$

This $1,200 return was earned on an investment of $20,000. The percentage return is

$$\frac{\$1,200}{\$20,000} = 0.06 = 6\%$$

Many people, when they see a "%" sign, automatically assume that it refers to a rate. But this is not so. We haven't yet mentioned how long the stock was held. Adding to the potential for confusion, the word *return* is often used as shorthand for a rate of return, usually an annual percentage. If we assume that the shares were held for exactly one year, then the **annual rate of return** is exactly 0.06, or 6 percent. This number takes into account how quickly the return was earned. It is expressed as a return for some unit of time, most often a year. Other frequently used time periods include quarterly, monthly, weekly (seven-day), and even daily rates of return.

By convention, they are usually expressed as percentages, but remember that they need not be.

Rates for longer time periods are also frequently quoted by mutual funds: 2-year, 5-year, and even 10-year rates of return. Frequently, these numbers are **annualized** to represent how a fund or other investment did in an average year of the 2, 5, or 10 years in question.

An Example of How to Calculate Return and Monthly Rate of Return for a Two-Stock Portfolio

Let's say you have a two-stock portfolio with no cash, just 100 shares of XYZ Corporation and 200 shares of ABC Corporation. Say XYZ's closing price last month was $75 per share and ABC's was $55 per share. Last month's total portfolio value was $18,500 = ($75 × 100) + ($55 × 200).

Annualizing Rates of Return and the Meaning of Average

Annualizing is a way of converting a rate of return with a period of either less than a year or more than a year into a number that represents its hypothetical return for a year. If the rate you start with is for less than a year—say it's a monthly return—then annualizing tells you what the return would be if it continued to grow at the same rate for exactly a year. If the rate you start with is for a period greater than a year, then annualizing shrinks the time period to a year, giving you an idea of what the portfolio earned in an average year of the full period.

In a way, it's unfortunate that both of these conversions are called *annualizing,* because they are very different. In the first case, you are **extrapolating,** or stretching, from a shorter period to a year, while in the latter case, you are **interpolating,** or shrinking, from a longer period to a year. As we will soon see, there are also two fundamentally different ways to shrink or stretch rates of return—arithmetic and geometric averaging.

We explained that annualizing a return of longer than one year provides you with a measure of the rate of return for an average year of the period. This raises an important question: Just what is meant by an average year? Sometimes, when people speak about averages, they have in mind the

(Continued)

commonest, most frequent value of something. Statisticians call this type of average the **mode**. Other times, people think of the average as the value that sits halfway between the thing with the highest value and the thing with the lowest value. Statisticians refer to this type of average as the **median**. Usually, however, when people think about averages, they have in mind what the statisticians call an **arithmetic mean**. To get an arithmetic mean of a set of prices, you just add up all the prices and divide by the number of prices.

Your current month's statement arrives from your broker. How did you do? It shows that XYZ's closing price has advanced to $85 per share, a nice move for a month, while ABC is off a little, down to $53 per share. Nothing else happened Your portfolio is now worth

$$\$19,000 = (\$85 \times 100) + (\$53 \times 200)$$

This is a gross return or profit of $600. (This is a so-called paper profit, or unrealized gain.)

Rounded to the nearest hundredth of a percent, or basis point, your monthly rate of return is

$$\frac{600}{18,500} = 3.24\%$$

We are unlikely to be content with just knowing the monthly return of our account. We'd like to know how this month's return compares to returns in previous periods for this portfolio and to previous and current returns of other investments. We'd also like to make projections of how much the portfolio might be worth in the future at various rates of growth.

Avoiding a Common Pitfall

Remember to use consistent numbers when doing your calculations. End of month ÷ end of previous month is a good way to figure out a monthly return, but end of month ÷ beginning of month is bad. Why? You're not using a full month of data; you're leaving out any price movement from the end of the previous month to the beginning (**opening price**) of the current month. This could be a significant source of error.

It is most important when comparing rates of return of an investment over different time periods, or when comparing rates for different portfolios, to make sure that they are stated on a comparable basis. Obviously, it would make no sense to compare a monthly return with an annual return. One of the numbers needs to be adjusted in some way to account for the difference in time periods. By convention, returns are frequently annualized to make a common basis for comparing investment results obtained over differing time periods.

If we are to accurately compare rates of return for different investments, we must take into account the time units or periods of the different investments' rates of return. Periods can be of any length. Typical measurement periods include daily, seven-day, monthly, month-to-date, quarterly, quarter-to-date, annual, year-to-date, 2-year, 3-year, 5-year, 10-year, 20-year, and **since inception.**

__since inception__
Measure of investment performance since a fund opened.

How Not to Compare Fund Performance

Some rates of return are described as *since inception*. This refers to the lifetime performance of a fund or other security. Sometimes these numbers are annualized; sometimes they are not. Since different securities have been around for different periods of time, it would be a serious mistake to compare their unannualized lifetime returns. Even if they are annualized, the comparison is often not very meaningful, because it ignores the effects of the environment in which those results were obtained.

Annualized Returns: Arithmetic (Simple) or Geometric (Compound)?

Whether you start with a period shorter or longer than a year, there are two ways to annualize a rate of return. The simpler way is to calculate an arithmetic mean return, also called a **simple return.** Arithmetic means are useful, but they are not good at representing rates of growth. For this we need a different kind of number, a **geometric mean.** Geometric means take into account the effect of **compounding,** or exponential growth. Compounding occurs when you get money (e.g., interest or dividends) from an investment and put it back into the portfolio, letting it grow alongside the original investment. Over time, the effects of exponential growth can dwarf the value of the original investment, so it is very important to understand the difference between arithmetic mean returns, also known as simple returns, and geometric returns, also known as **time-weighted returns.**

Example of an Arithmetic Return Calculation

To calculate an arithmetic rate of return, all you need is the starting and ending values for the period, although a good calculator wouldn't hurt. Let's say that we're reviewing a monthly statement from a broker. At the beginning of the month, the portfolio had a value of $10,000. At month's end, the portfolio was worth $10,200. Divide the ending value by the starting value:

$$\frac{\$10,200}{\$10,000} = 1.02$$

This means that the portfolio is now 1.02 times larger than it was one month ago. Expressed as a percentage, it is 102 percent. This means that it has grown by 2 percent during the month. Of course, the portfolio's value could have been higher or lower during the month, but right now our only concern is with the beginning and ending points.

In the current example, we can annualize the arithmetic return of a 2 percent monthly increase simply by multiplying 2 percent times 12 to get 24 percent for the year. Nice and simple, but potentially misleading. It does not take into account the money that is being generated by the portfolio each month, which could be reinvested in something, perhaps earning the same rate of return as the initial capital investment. *Arithmetic returns assume that you earn nothing on this interim money, while geometric returns assume that you earn the same rate of return on this new money as on the initial investment.* The former accurately describes certain kinds of investment situations, where one has no opportunity to reinvest new money. The latter accurately describes a more typical situation in the world of no-load mutual funds, where money being reinvested into the account from interest or dividends gets pretty much the same treatment as money already in the account. Taxes may make a difference—distributions in taxable accounts are treated as income or capital gains. In general, you cannot know what return will

Table 19–1   How a Net Loss Can Look Like a Gain (key numbers in boldface)

Beginning Value	Arithmetic Return	Ending Value	Average Arithmetic Return from Inception	Net Change from Inception
Year 1 $100	80%	$180	80%	80%
Year 2 $180	−50%	$90	**15%**	**−10%**

be available on the cash that comes into your portfolio—this is known as *reinvestment risk*, which will be described in the next chapter.

Beyond the frequently inaccurate assumption of no return on intra-period earnings, there is an even more serious problem with arithmetic returns: They can lead you to believe that you are up 15 percent per year for two years, when in fact you have lost 10 percent of your money. How? Let's say you start with $100 and earn 80 percent in the first year. At the end of the first year, you have $180. In the second year, however, you lose 50 percent, going down to $90. Even though you've lost 10 percent of your money, the arithmetic mean annual return for the two-year period is 15%. (See Table 19–1.)

Example of a Geometric Return Calculation

When interest or dividends are reinvested, a geometric return should be calculated. A good calculator or financial software is indispensable for working with geometric returns.

With arithmetic returns, you might need to do only a single multiplication or division. In contrast, geometric returns are combined by multiplying **return relatives.** A return relative is simply the ratio of the current end-of-period value of the portfolio, security, or index to its previous end-of-period value.

Working on a Geometric Chain Gang

If, for example, your rate of return for a given month was 2 percent, the return relative would be 102 percent or 1.02. To annualize, we raise 1.02 to the twelfth power:

$$1.02^{12} = 1.02 \times 1.02 \times 1.02 \times 1.02 \times 1.02 \times 1.02 \times 1.02 \times 1.02 \times 1.02 \times 1.02$$
$$\times 1.02 \times 1.02$$
$$= 1.2682 \text{ (to the nearest basis point)}$$

You can annualize a monthly rate using return relatives. If the monthly rate of increase is 0.02, or 2 percent, the return relative is 1.02, or 102 percent. Multiply 1.02 together 12 times (1.02^{12}). This repeated multiplication is sometimes referred to as a *geometric chain.*

A point worth remembering: You must always remember to subtract 1 after annualizing a return relative to get back to a percentage change (what you're subtracting is the starting value, which is always 1, or 100 percent). So you raise 1.02 to the twelfth power, subtract 1, and you get 26.82 percent. This is the geometric return, also known as the **effective annual rate of return.** Note that it is 2.82 percent larger than the arithmetic return of 24 percent. The extra 2.82 percent comes from the compounding of returns.

Sometimes you may want to calculate your effective annual return from starting and ending values separated by some number of years. This is easy to do—with a decent calculator. For example, consider an investment that, after eight years, is worth $20,000. Its value at the beginning of the eight-year period was $8,000. To figure the compound annualized (i.e., geometric) rate of return, just take the endpoint value of $20,000 and divide by the starting value of $8,000 to get the return relative of 2.5 for the whole eight-year period. Instead of multiplying this number eight times, you need to find the number that multiplied by itself eight times equals 2.5—in other words, you must take the eighth root of 2.5. This is approximately 1.1214, the *annualized* return relative. To get the annual return, you still need to subtract 1: giving 0.1214, or in percentage terms, 12.14%, your annualized geometric rate of return.

effective rate (effective annual rate of return)
Yield to maturity.

Rule of 72

There is a nice shortcut for figuring how long it takes money to double at various rates of return (its usual use is for working with compound interest, but it works just as well for working with any return calculation). It is called the **rule of 72.** To figure the approximate doubling time of an annual rate of return, just divide 72 by that rate, leaving off the percent. For example, the calculation for a 6 percent annual return would be

$$\frac{72}{6} = 12 \text{(years)}$$

(Continued)

You can check that result by raising 1.06 to the twelfth power (or if you don't have that kind of calculator, just multiply 1.06 12 times). The answer is (approximately) 2.012, which for most purposes is a very good approximation. Don't use the rule of 72 for calculations that must be precise or for rates of return less than 2 percent or greater than 24 percent.

A Practical Hint for Calculating Effective Annual Rate of Return

How, exactly, do you calculate the eighth root of 2.5? Even good calculators don't have a special eighth-root button. In this particular example, even a cheap calculator can do the job, because you can get an eighth root by taking the square root three times in a row, which is nice for this example and for other examples in which the number of periods is a power of two. But it won't help with three years, five years, and so forth.

On a good calculator or a spreadsheet, you just use the exponent key (or function), y^x. When you want an eighth root, you are raising 2.5 to the one-eighth power. Expressed as a decimal number, one-eighth is 0.125. So you would need to calculate $2.5^{.125}$. On a good calculator, you would just input 2.5 [function key(s) for y^x].125. And on a spreadsheet? Depending on which spreadsheet program you use, you would simply enter 2.5^.125 or 2.5**.125 into a spreadsheet cell.

Remember—to get the annual return, you must subtract 1.

From the preceding examples, you can readily see why it is so important to know whether a given rate of return was calculated on an arithmetic or geometric basis. We have seen that an arithmetic rate of return can grossly mislead an investor into thinking that he or she is making money when in fact the portfolio's value is standing still or, worse, rapidly diminishing. Geometric returns are far more accurate in evaluating past performance. For this reason the CFA Institute insists, in its widely adopted Global Investment Performance Standards (GIPS®), that investment managers (e.g., mutual fund portfolio managers) use geometric returns. While geometric returns are more difficult to calculate than arithmetic returns, they give you a much more reliable idea of what the portfolio is actually doing. Even geometric returns, however, must be used carefully, especially when extrapolating from a short period to a much longer time frame (see the discussion of extrapolation risk in Chapter Twenty).

Time-Weighted Returns versus Money-Weighted Returns

If we want to know how well our investments did in an average period of time, we calculate what is known as a **time-weighted rate of return**. If, however, we care about what happened to an average dollar or other unit of money, we calculate a dollar or **money-weighted rate of return**.

The King and the Wizard: A Tale of Chess and Geometric Returns

Perhaps the oldest story illustrating the hazards of projecting geometric returns too far into the future concerns a king and the wizard who invented chess. The king, thrilled by the wizard's invention, offers to grant any wish the wizard might have. The wizard, who we can infer was a crafty sort, says that all he would like is a single grain of rice for the first square of the chessboard, two grains for the second square, four grains for the third, and so on, each succeeding square to be paid for with twice as many grains of rice as its predecessor until all 64 squares have been accounted for. The king, apparently not familiar with the fecundity of geometric progressions, quickly grants this wish, muttering to himself in some versions of the story about what a good deal he has gotten from this silly wizard! He calls for his servants to bring forth the required number of grains. For the first 10 squares, 2,047 grains of rice are counted out—about a bowl's worth. For the next 10 squares, more than 1,000 times as much rice is counted out. Each succeeding square requires more rice than all the previous squares combined. Eventually, it becomes clear to the king that the whole kingdom's supply of rice is inadequate. (In fact, the total number of grains of rice necessary to fulfill this

(Continued)

contract equals 2^{64} minus 1, which is more than 18,000,000,000,000,000,000 [18 quintillion] grains of rice!)

At this point in the story, the king reneges on the deal. Some say he opted instead to execute the sly wizard as punishment for his overabundant cleverness. This tale can serve as a warning against extrapolating geometric returns too far out into the future. They always look great on paper, but continued long enough, other factors (e.g., the world's supply of rice, the king's patience) run out and further growth prospects evaporate. So the next time your broker, insurance salesperson, or financial consultant tells you about the wonders of compound interest, you can tell them that you are well aware of the wonders—and the dangers—of excessive reliance upon exponential growth curves.

Neither of these approaches tells the full story. In general, the time-weighted approach gives a more accurate measure of an investment manager's skill. In contrast, the money-weighted approach provides more information about the actual accumulation of money in a portfolio. It also provides a formula for aggregating multiple portfolios run by the same investment manager, so it can be used to safeguard against selective presentation of performance results.

An example should help explain things. Suppose that at the beginning of the year you had $100,000 in your brokerage account in the form of 2,000 shares of the DEF company, trading at $50 per share. After six months, DEF has risen in price to $55, and you decide to buy an additional 2,000 shares with money transferred from another account. You now have 4,000 shares, whose current market value is $220,000 and whose cost to you was $210,000 (for simplicity, we will ignore transaction costs). In the second half of the year, the price of DEF rises to $66 per share, with a market value of $264,000. What is your rate of return?

Time-weighted return: From the standpoint of time, the second half-year period has twice the rate of return of the first half-year period:

$$\text{TWR (first 6 months)} = \frac{55}{50} - 1 = 1.1 - 1 = 10\%$$

$$\text{TWR (second 6 months)} = \frac{66}{55} = 1.2 - 1 = 20\%$$

The total increase for the period is

$$\frac{66}{50} - 1 = 32\%$$

This tallies with the product of the two six-month periods:

$$(1.1 \times 1.2) - 1 = 32\%$$

Linking the periods in this way is referred to as forming a geometric chain. For this reason, the time-weighted return is sometimes called a *geometric chain time-weighted rate of return*.

Notice that there is an extra 2 percent, compared with the arithmetic sum of 10% + 20%. This extra 2 percent comes from the compounding effect—in the second half of the year, you are getting 20 percent not just on the original 100 percent, but also on the 10 percent you made in the first half.

If you are wondering how a time-weighted return takes into account the effect of money being added to or subtracted from the portfolio, the answer is that it doesn't. It ignores the effect of deposits and withdrawals completely. All it "cares" about is the effect of time. While this is fine for understanding how well a stock or mutual fund is performing, it ignores what for some purposes is more important to you, namely, understanding how an average unit of money that you invest in the stock or fund has performed. To see the combined effect of the stock or fund manager's performance with the timing of your deposits and/or withdrawals, we must look at money-weighted returns.

Money-weighted return: If you hadn't put in additional money at midyear, you would have 32 percent more money at year-end than at the beginning. In fact, you invested only $100,000 at the beginning of the year, putting in another $110,000 at midyear. So you had a total cost of $210,000, but not all of this money was invested for the full year. There are a number of ways to figure out the return on an average dollar invested. One way is to subdivide the year into the two six-month periods. In the first six months, you earned 10 percent on $100,000. In the second six months, you earned 20 percent on $220,000. This second period counts, or weighs, 2.2 times as much as the first period in figuring the return on an average dollar.

$$\frac{(2.2 \times 20\%) + 10\%}{1 + 2.2} = \frac{54}{3.2} = 16.875\%$$

This number represents the (arithmetic) average return on a dollar in a six-month period. It needs to be annualized to get the money-weighted return for the full year.

To get a more accurate picture of the return on an average dollar, financial analysts calculate an **internal rate of return.** The idea is to find the rate of return that equates two sets of cash flows. For a simple example, let's find the rate of return that makes $1,000 increase to $4,000 in 12 years. By the rule of 72, we know that money invested at 12 percent doubles roughly every six years. Investing for 12 years at 12 percent would quadruple your money. Therefore, 12 percent is the internal rate of return that equates $1,000 today with $4,000 twelve years hence.

internal rate of return
A measure of return on investment that takes into account both the timing and the amounts of individual cash flows.

In working this simple example, we've snuck in another key concept used by financial analysts: **present value.** What is the present value of a future cash flow? That depends on the rate of return used in the calculation. In the preceding example, the present value of $4,000 received 12 years from now is $1,000 if we assume a 12 percent rate of return. If we assume a lower rate of return, say 6 percent, then the present value would increase to $2,000, reflecting the fact that you need more money at the starting point if your rate of growth is smaller.

The standard way of calculating investment performance is to use time-weighted rates of return for individual portfolios. Money weighting is used, but not for calculating investment manager performance. The reason? Investment managers seldom have control over the timing of cash inflows and outflows. Since they are beyond the manager's control, it would make little sense to credit or penalize the manager for their occurrence.

Nevertheless, inflows and outflows of cash do impact a manager's strategy and, indirectly at least, his or her performance. Usually, they act as a drag on performance. Cash tends to come into the portfolios of top-performing managers. While management companies love to accumulate assets, the fast accumulation of cash in a portfolio can make it extraordinarily difficult for a manager to maintain a particular strategy. The manager might want to take some profits, but is already "awash in cash" and struggling to find investments that meet his or her objective. Likewise, when a fund manager is doing poorly, investors rush to the exits, forcing the manager to sell at a time when it might make more sense to buy.

Despite its limitations, time weighting is the best available way to measure an investment manager's performance. But this doesn't mean that money weighting has no role to play. In fact, it has an important role in keeping performance reporting fair and accurate. Money weighting is the standard way that investment managers are supposed to aggregate collections of portfolios with similar investment goals. These standards are intended to prevent a manager from selectively highlighting a few small portfolios with good time-weighted returns while hiding poor performance in other portfolios.

Complicating Factors

In real life things are seldom as simple as the idealized examples of this chapter. Most brokerage accounts consist of more than just two securities and have some spare cash lying around. Trades may occur, accounts may be assessed fees or interest charges for stocks purchased on margin, securities may undergo any of a number of capital events during the month, and cash may be deposited into and/or withdrawn from the account at different times during the month.

Let's look at each of these complicating factors in turn:

- *Multiple securities and spare cash.* Multiple securities present no special problem, just a few more multiplications and additions to calculate end-of-previous-month and end-of-current-month values. Similarly, cash in the account presents no intrinsic difficulty. For purposes of calculating return, it can be regarded as just another security. The cash may sit idle, in which case it neither adds to nor subtracts from the account return (but can impact its rate of return). Or it may be swept into a **money market account**, leaving you with slightly more cash at the end of the month than at the beginning. In that case, it makes a small but positive contribution to your return, though it can still lower your rate of return if your securities are doing well. In rising markets, excess cash is frequently frowned upon by investors, most of whom try to stay **fully invested.** On the other hand, in nervous markets, investors are sometimes encouraged to be **selective** or **defensive** and to **raise cash.**

fully invested
A portfolio that has used (almost) all of its cash to buy securities or other assets.

- *Trades may occur.* Assuming for the moment that no new cash or securities enter or leave the account, trading that takes place within the account will produce a calculation similar to our simple example, although perhaps lacking its symmetry. If, for example, we had sold half of the 200-share position in ABC Corporation sometime during the month for $54 per share, we would have an end-of-month account value that was $100 higher than given in the example.

- *Accounts may be assessed fees or margin interest charges.* Such fees lower both the return and the rate of return. The impact of explicit fees on return is easy to measure. In contrast, there are the hidden trading costs we discussed in Chapter Eight, such as bid/asked spread, dealer markup, and payment for order flow, all of which can impact your return without showing up on your statement.

- *Securities may undergo any of a number of capital events.* Stock is subject to splits, reverse splits, dividends, rights offerings, mergers, and spin-offs; bonds can offer interest income or return of principal (either at maturity or at call date); bonds can also default in payment of either interest, principal, or both; mutual funds have dividend distributions and capital gains distributions.

- *Cash or securities may be deposited into and/or withdrawn from the account.* This is a tough one, from a calculation standpoint. When money comes into or leaves an account, you have a brand-new ball game. Previously, you had a unique starting point or base amount from which to calculate return. But each time you add or subtract money from the account, you create a new base amount from which return is to be judged. This is where money-weighted returns can be useful.

Calculation of raw investment performance tells you how much an investment made or lost, but does not provide a context for evaluating that investment in the light of your unique risk profile. Such an evaluation requires an understanding of how risk relates to performance, the subject of our next chapter.

Chapter 20

COMING TO GRIPS WITH THE MANY DIMENSIONS OF RISK

We begin with a definition of investment risk, illustrated with an example. Then we explain the key concept of market risk and some of the ways it is measured. Next, we offer an overview of some of the other kinds of risks faced by investors, ranging from those that can be quantified to those that are more subjective. Finally, we present a perspective on risk that strives to balance complementary risks against each other.

A Definition of Investment Risk

If there are many ways to measure an investment's rate of return, there are even more measures of investment risk. The complexity embodied in the idea of risk means that it cannot be adequately captured by any single measurement or number. Nevertheless, there is an underlying unity that links the different kinds of investment risk:

Risk is the chance that your investment goals will not be realized in the time frame you specify.

Notice that the definition says *goals*, and not merely *results*. Unfortunately, investors are not always clear on what their goals are. Furthermore, an investor's goals can, and frequently do, change in response to the following:

- Changes in the investor's financial situation
- Changes in the investment climate
- Changes in the economy

The Relativity of Risk

Recognition that risk is relative to an investor's goals, time horizon, and other constraints helps avoid confusion in thinking about risk. An example further illustrates the point. Let's say you are deciding how to invest $100,000. You have the following three goals:

A1 To at least double your money in the next six years

A2 To keep up with a broad market index, like the S&P 500, never falling below its rate of return as measured quarterly

A3 To never be down more than 10 percent in any given calendar year

What's missing from this example? An explicit statement of the investor's time horizon and other constraints. The first goal suggests that the horizon is six years, perhaps the date of some anticipated future liability such as a child's education or expenses associated with retirement. The other goals are shorter term, reflecting the investor's desire not to fall behind a broad measure of average stock market performance and also not to lose a significant amount of money in a short time frame.

How achievable these goals are, singly or in combination, is not certain. From our definition of risk, it is apparent that there are three separate risk factors:

- Your average annual rate of return may be inadequate to double your money in six years. (Recalling the rule of 72, you would need to average about 12 percent.)

- Quarterly rate of return might fall below the benchmark in one or more of the 24 quarters of the investment period.

- Calendar year return could be worse than −10 percent at some point during one of the calendar years of the investment period.

To illustrate the dependency of risk on the investor's goals, we now consider an alternative set of goals for the same $100,000 investment, this time with an investment horizon of 18 years:

B1. To grow to a minimum value of $800,000 by the end of the 18th year

B2. To grow at least 6 percent per year, net, after taxes, expenses, and consumer price inflation

B3. No calendar year return worse than −15 percent in inflation-adjusted dollars

It should be apparent that the risks associated with this second set of goals are different from the risks associated with the first set of goals. Some observations:

- Goals A1 and B1 each establish a minimum average rate of return for the investment, calculated from the end of the period. In fact, each works out to the same target return number, except that goal B is for a more distant time horizon.

- Goals A2 and B2 each establish an intermediate benchmark, but on very different terms. While A focuses on tracking an investment index, B selects a measure of potential future liabilities against which to measure success or failure.

- Finally, A3 and B3 each establish absolute worst-case limits, figured annually, but they differ in the way they establish a standard of value over time.

In the preceding examples, we gave no indication of the relative importance of the separate goals, lending credence to the assumption that they should be given equal weight. In general, different investors may give more or less importance to particular goals. Different weightings of, for example, short-term versus long-term goals, may have important consequences for the design of an investment strategy.

Having established a working definition of risk and illustrated the relativity of risk to an investor's goals, we are now in a position to analyze one of the most fundamental investment risks: market risk.

What Is Market Risk?

Some measures of investment risk define it in terms of any deviation from an anticipated result, whether positive or negative. For example, volatility, the most frequently used measurement of **market risk**, counts positive deviations as well as negative deviations in attempting to quantify the riskiness of an investment. A stock that moved up faster than anticipated would have a higher risk rating than a stock that performed poorly but closer to expectation. This may seem like an odd way to define risk, but it is probably the single most widely accepted measure of market risk, and it works well under many circumstances. It is widely used because it is (relatively) easy to calculate, and the problem cited doesn't arise too often. Investments that are volatile to the upside are volatile to the downside as well—for the most part.

When most people think about market risk, they think about stock market crashes, like the infamous **Black Monday** crash that sent the Dow Jones Industrial Average down by over 20 percent in a single day. Others, taking a longer-term view, think of market risk as the chance of encountering a bear market, which by one definition is a decline of at least 20 percent from a market's high (see Chapter Five, "Of Bulls and Bears"). At this point, you might be tempted to ask, "Whose perspective on market risk is valid?" The answer, as we have already seen, is that they both are. *Market risk, like all forms of investment risk, is relative to the investor's time horizon, goals, and constraints.* An investor who plans to be in the market for 12 months will tend to have a very different idea of market risk than an investor who is in for 20 years.

modern portfolio theory (MPT) *The standard theory for building an optimally efficient market portfolio. Alternative theories are sometimes referred to as* post-modern portfolio theory (PMPT)

Not only is market risk linked to the investor's time frame, goals, and limits, the very concept of market risk has evolved in response to changes in the markets themselves and to changing risk measurement techniques. As recently as the 1950s, stocks were deemed risky investments by the majority of institutional investors, who largely avoided them in favor of bonds. Only gradually did new ideas, notably the **modern portfolio theory (MPT)** of Harry Markowitz and the Capital Asset Pricing Model of William Sharpe, combined with the fading memory of the Great Depression and the great postwar boom of the 1950s and 1960s, convince professional money managers that stocks were an appropriate part of an institutional portfolio.

Part of the justification for investing in stocks came from Markowitz's and Sharpe's mathematical analysis of the role of diversification in building long-term returns. In addition, it was argued that the greater potential returns of stocks justified their greater risk. Many analysts began looking at individual stocks in terms of their **beta coefficient**, a number indicating the degree to which a stock's price moves in relation to changes in the overall market. Though beta still has its adherents, it has gradually surrendered pride of place to volatility, a measure of a stock's (or other security's) tendency to undergo fluctuations in its rate of return.

beta (beta coefficient)
Correlation of a stock with an index such as the S&P 500.

"It Will Fluctuate"

J.P. Morgan's fabled three-word answer to the anxious investor who wanted to know what the market would do next contains within it a hint of the importance of volatility to markets. Market price levels fluctuate. The price of individual securities that comprise markets fluctuate. We have already seen, in Chapter Sixteen, the importance of the volatility of prices to the valuation of options.

Now we are learning about the importance of another related fluctuation. *Rates of return, which are calculated at least in part from price movements, also fluctuate.* It is the fluctuation in rates of return, not in prices alone, that is the primary means used to define volatility. It is not the only means, however. The concept of volatility actually shows up in at least three ways in the markets: as historical volatility, as forecasted future volatility, and as implied volatility.

These three faces of volatility reflect three different ways in which market risk is measured and used. The first, *historical volatility*, is the most fundamental. For any particular time frame and group of investments, a unique historical volatility can be calculated. For example, you can calculate the 200-day historical volatility of IBM common stock based on daily return data (derived from closing prices, adjusted for dividends, splits, etc.). This is a well-defined number. So, however, is the 10-year historical volatility of IBM common stock based on monthly return data (derived from month-end prices with the same adjustments). These numbers would be useful in studies of the historical relationship between risk and return for **large-cap stocks.**

A problem with historical return volatility arises when someone attempts to use it to forecast future return volatility. We have already encountered this problem with price volatility: How do you go about figuring out which historical volatility, if any, is a useful predictor for the forecast period? The solution requires a **model** of the relationship between historical and future volatility. This model can be so simple that the person using it isn't even aware of the model's existence, or it can be an elaborate mathematical/statistical construct implemented on a computer. Either approach may yield good results; neither can be guaranteed to work. This is an example of **model risk,** which will be discussed later in this chapter.

model *Set of mathematical formulas or computer programs representing a part of the world; a set of computer programs designed to simulate some aspect of the financial markets.*

Finally, *implied volatility* is also a model-derived measure of the riskiness of an investment. In the case of price volatility, the model is an options pricing model. Here, however, implied volatility, like future volatility, may be derived from a theoretical model of the investment portfolio. It is subject to the same type of model risk already mentioned.

Other Kinds of Investment Risk: From the Quantifiable to the Subjective

Some market analysts reserve the use of the word *risk* for quantifiable uncertainties. For them, other uncertainties are just . . . uncertain. We understand their desire to emphasize quantifiable measures, but we take a broader view of risk that encompasses a whole spectrum of quantifiability and subjective judgment. We do this because it is apparent that any risk has a combination of quantifiable and subjective components. We do not think it wise to draw an arbitrary line, in the process increasing the risk that something difficult to quantify is overlooked.

That said, we begin our survey of other investment risks with those (relatively) easy to quantify. These include reinvestment risk/rollover risk, credit risk, inflation/deflation/currency/exchange rate risk, country/sector/asset mix risk, catastrophic risk, and liquidity risk.

Reinvestment/rollover risk arises most obviously in the world of bonds and other fixed-income securities. Bonds are often chosen for the reliability of their payment of interest and principal. Reinvestment risk is the chance that you won't be able to get a comparable interest rate when seeking to reinvest either interest and/or principal. The term *rollover risk* refers to the reinvestment of principal.

Of course, there are other risks that can affect bondholders. Bond issuers may suffer financial reverses, leading to credit downgrades or even default and bankruptcy. These possibilities make credit risk one of the great fears of bondholders.

For a long time, U.S. investors were most worried about **inflation risk**, as oil price shocks and expansive monetary policies combined to erode the purchasing power of the U.S. dollar.

More recently, **deflation risk** has become more of a concern to the public, as global labor markets and ever more powerful information technologies have combined to lower the cost of a broad spectrum of goods and services. The danger of deflation is its tendency to depress economic activity.

Each of the two preceding risks can be looked at as special cases of **currency risk**, another dimension of which is exchange rate risk. All of these involve the financial loss that can result when a currency deviates from its expected value. For bondholders and stockholders, changes in interest rates and currency exchange rates can have major impact on their portfolios.

Consideration of currency risk leads us naturally to the related concept of **country risk**, which arises when the economy of a particular country suffers a setback impacting its financial markets. Japan is a recent example of country risk. Sector risk is conceptually similar, except that industries instead of countries are affected. The gold mining industry can serve as an example of industry risk. Both of these risks can be thought of as special cases of asset-mix risk, which also includes decisions about which broad categories of assets to invest in (e.g., bonds versus stocks).

Catastrophic risk includes disasters of human origin (e.g., 9/11, Bhopal, and Three Mile Island) and natural disasters (e.g., Florida's recurrent hurricanes and the episodic earthquakes of the Pacific Rim). Such catastrophes can have major economic fallout beyond the immediate damage and suffering they cause. Then there is the much less noted but cumulatively enormous damage of catastrophes whose effects are local: building fires, burst water pipes, and run-of-the-mill accidents that collectively far outweigh the headline-grabbing disasters in economic impact.

Liquidity risk is something of a misnomer—it should probably be called *illiquidity* risk—the hazard that demand for a company's shares or other securities will dry up, leaving investors with no one to sell to.

Having briefly mentioned a number of moderately quantifiable risks, we now describe some that are more difficult to quantify. Ironically, several of these risks involve the potential misuse of mathematical models.

Model risk occurs whenever there is a discrepancy between how a model defines and/or measures a real-world phenomenon and the thing in itself. An example of model risk is the recent controversy over whether inflation is being measured correctly. There are two special subclasses of model risk. **Extrapolation risk** arises whenever we wrongly assume that the past can be reliably used as a guidepost to the future. **Interpolation risk** is a subtler, time-related risk, which comes from wrongly assuming that by drawing a straight line from the past to the present, we can accurately calculate intervening values. An obvious problem with this approach to data analysis is that it ignores cyclical phenomena like the weather. If it is dark outside now, and was dark outside 24 hours ago, it would not be advisable to assume that it was dark, say, 12 hours ago. And yet this is the equivalent of what many people do.

Benchmark risk is another kind of model risk. It occurs when an incorrect index or other proxy is chosen as a reference point for a portfolio. Benchmarking compares the increase in a portfolio to an appropriate *reference portfolio*, or index. The index may or may not be an actual portfolio that is traded. If it is or can be traded, it is sometimes referred to as an investable index.

Tax risk can arise from a change in tax rates or a reclassification of the tax status of an investment (or an investor). The byzantine complexity of the tax code can make it much harder to compare the attractiveness of different investments. Consider, for example, a choice between two investments:

- Investment A is a high-quality corporate bond paying 7 percent.
- Investment B is a triple-tax-exempt municipal bond paying 4.5 percent.

Assume, for the sake of simplicity, that maturity, quality, and call provisions are equal. Which of these investments is better for you? Well, it depends on your current tax rate, and it may depend on your legal residence. But it also depends on your future marginal tax rate, which depends not only on your future earnings but on possible changes to state and national tax laws.

Tax risk can be seen as a special case of **regulatory risk**, which derives from changes in the regulatory environment that impact the profitability of a company or industry. Sometimes, it is the failure to change regulations to keep up with new economic or technological realities that leads to trouble (jobs moving overseas, capital flight, etc.).

Political risk develops when governments undergo change, whether evolutionary and peaceful or revolutionary and violent. **Accounting risk** refers to the possibility that the accounts of a company do not reflect its real business situation, whether by error (of omission or commission) or by design. **Operational risk** encompasses all the problems that can arise in the day-to-day operations of a business, including errors (of omission and commission) and malicious acts such as fraud and theft. Death of a key executive can be considered as an operational risk, although some would classify it as a catastrophic type of risk.

"Of Cotton Futures, Black Swans, and Uncertainty": An Important Special Risk

In 1962, a then little-known (but now famous) mathematician named Benoit Mandelbrot discovered something funny about cotton futures prices. He realized that they were subject to more dramatic changes than would be expected by conventional finance theory. He proposed mathematical models for cotton and other markets in which such jumps would be expected, in contrast to the orthodox "Gaussian" view in which large moves should be extremely rare.

In 2004, he wrote (along with Richard Hudson) a book called ***The Misbehavior of Markets***, in which he challenged regulators to devote 5 percent of the $400-plus million Wall Street settlement money to basic research in the structure of financial markets with a particular emphasis on understanding the dynamics of major financial disasters. His challenge was ignored.

It took Nassim Taleb's talents as a writer and polemicist to bring Mandelbrot's ideas the attention they deserved. In his book ***The Black Swan***, Taleb forcefully argues that Wall Street habitually underestimates the likelihood of unexpected rare events, events that Taleb refers to as "Black Swans."

This idea has caught the popular imagination, especially in the aftermath of 2008, even though many would argue that the collapse of the market was inevitable and that to label it a "Black Swan" is simplistic. An emerging view of financial markets begins by acknowledging the role of uncertainty in periodically upsetting our established view of things. Uncertainty can come from a "black swan"; it can also come from a bubble's bursting; or from the actions of regulators trying to clean up the mess. It is a cardinal mistake to over-rely on "black swans" or any other "theory of everything." It is better to admit that our knowledge is surrounded by a cloud of unknowing, which every so often descends on us like a thick London fog.

Balancing Risk and Return

Having provided some perspective on both risk and return, we are now in a better position to understand the interaction between these two concepts. A basic guidepost to the risk-return relationship states the greater the return an investment promises, the greater the risk it holds—and conversely, the riskier an investment is, the greater the return investors must be offered to compensate them for taking on that risk. While this principle holds good on average and in the long run, there are many important exceptions to consider. These exceptions arise from hidden assumptions about investor behavior, most notably, the assumptions that all investors have equal access to information and that all investors make rationally optimal decisions on the basis of the knowledge they do have. Both assumptions are clearly false at least some of the time. Investors do not always have equal access to information. Furthermore, different investors respond to new information in different ways and at different speeds. Finally, even when a given investor is in possession of all relevant information about a stock or other investment option, he or she may not act in a way that economists would consider rational or optimal.

> A view of your market risk, Riskgrades (www.riskgrades.com), is a free service developed by RiskMetrics, a leading vendor of risk management systems.

How can an investor set about trying to balance risk and return? There is no universally accepted formula or simple rule for this. Instead, each investor needs to consider his or her unique financial situation. First, determine as best you can your present financial assets and liabilities. It is important to recognize that even at this stage—before looking to the future—there can be significant uncertainties about how to value your assets and liabilities.

What Is Alpha, and Would You Like Some?

Some investment professionals describe their work as a search for positive alpha. **Alpha** is defined as the difference between an investment's actual expected return and the expected return that modern portfolio theory says it should have. Investments with positive alpha are said to be *underpriced*. Investments with negative alpha are said to be *overpriced*.

(Continued)

Unfortunately, the search for alpha is complicated by three sources of noise that can lead the unwary astray: luck, hidden risk, and fraud. A manager who is lucky may appear to be a good source of alpha, but outperformance that arises from luck is likely to be fleeting. Worse are the instances where managers generate outperformance by (consciously or unconsciously) making risky bets that are likely to work for a while, until they fail dramatically. Short-term incentives at banks and hedge funds led to a dramatic increase in levels of hidden risk and are likely responsible for the financial crisis of the last few years. Finally, there are still too many bad actors in the investment business who try to get away with anything they can, and whose recent crimes are likely to keep the courts busy for years to come

Fortunately, finding real positive alpha, based on skill rather than luck, hidden risk, or fraud, though it may be rewarding for professionals who are judged against their peers, is neither necessary nor sufficient for most investors. Indeed, identifying small mispricings may be more effort than it is worth, especially after transaction costs are taken into account. What's more, it can distract from the important task of estimating and planning for future liabilities.

In some cases, a range of values gives a more accurate depiction of reality than does a single number, which offers only the illusion of precision. For example, an inactively traded stock is hard to price accurately; its value is only an educated guess. In such cases, it may be prudent to set its value to a small fraction of what analysis says it should be worth. Sometimes, however, this approach can be costly. Biasing your estimates of value can distort the overall picture of your portfolio and lead to bad investment decisions. On the liability side, a mortgage that can be refinanced is not a simple investment: Its *current* value depends on *future* changes in interest rates and the availability of credit.

Shifting our focus from the present to the future, we are confronted with an exponential increase in possibilities. This complexity arises from the need for and interaction of three financial forecasts:

- Future personal earnings
- Future performance of investments
- Future liabilities

Let's face it, even the most rigorous analysis of investment alternatives cannot guarantee a good result in the face of so much uncertainty. Why? Because of the uncertain relationship between future earnings, investments, and liabilities that each investor must try to understand. Risk is the dark side of opportunity. It is often said that there is no opportunity without risk. Even so, some opportunities are better than others. Some risks are more worth bearing than others.

An important consequence of the relativity of risk explained in the previous chapter is that performance standards do not attempt to compare unrelated investments by adjusting for risk. Instead, the standards limit themselves to comparing similar investments with each other, trying to ensure that comparisons are relevant, meaningful, and fair. Organizations that have created performance standards, such as the CFA Institute, tend to focus on the return component of performance.

This leaves investors with some difficult tasks—estimating their likely future assets and liabilities, developing a reasonable set of financial objectives, and trying to identify and avoid the risks that matter most to them. Good financial planners can help; unfortunately, all too many planners are narrowly trained in a particular product area. Furthermore, most planners do not have the proper degree of detachment from the products they are hired to evaluate. Finally, many lack an understanding of the risk/return relationship. Fortunately, the increased sophistication and information access of individual investors is likely to force financial planners to better serve their clients.

Chapter 21

A CRESCENDO OF CHANGE

Markets and the New Millennium

I n this book we have provided a broad overview of the financial markets, encompassing the amazing variety of stocks, funds, bonds, derivatives (including futures and options), and their markets. We have also presented a framework for analyzing investment results, both in absolute terms and after adjusting for risk. In this concluding chapter, we offer some closing thoughts on the state of the markets, which we would characterize as in a period of profound uncertainty in the aftermath of a decades-long boom that ended in a big bust.

Again, We Ask, What Is a Market?

We began this book by examining the factors that go into making a market and looking at their historical development. We suggested that markets require at least three parties—that without the involvement of a third person, a crucial aspect is missing: the ability to take your business elsewhere.

Financial markets have changed decisively since the days of the button-wood tree. Today we have global markets that require no person-to-person contact between buyer and seller, not even through the intermediation of brokers. Markets can no longer be localized to the floor of an exchange, or even to electronically linked exchange floors such as at the Pacific Stock Exchange. Markets have moved into **cyberspace**, by which we mean not only the World Wide Web but the rest of the Internet, intranets, extranets, and virtual private networks. This is the culmination of a trend that began more than 100 years ago, when the invention of the ticker brought telegraphy to the markets. And let's not forget to mention POTS (plain old telephone service), whose introduction vastly broadened the scope of exchange-based markets, first within cities and regions and then, with the introduction of long-distance service, nationally and globally. It is also worth remembering that most of the Internet sits piggyback on top of the telephone network.

Only in the last few years, however, have computers become powerful enough, and cheap enough, to combine more or less seamlessly with communication networks. This combination has enabled new types of markets in which new types of products are traded according to new rules and regulations. And all of these changes have created new types of market participants.

In the last decade, a proliferation of online discount brokers has made professional trading capabilities available to individual investors. Until now, much of this innovation has been at the periphery. But we are rapidly approaching a critical point in the evolution of financial markets. With the creation of new forms of trading, specialists and other open-outcry stalwarts are increasingly marginalized: the era of electronic markets is upon us.

Dynamic orders, derivatives, technology, and globalization have reshaped the financial markets. The speed with which this transformation has taken place has created and destroyed fortunes. In response, market participants are being challenged to rethink and reinvent the way they operate. Some investors are embracing new technologies that give them access to the markets like never before. Many others, frightened by the uncertainty rampant in today's financial system, have grown wary of anything that sounds new or complicated. Intermediaries, whether brokers, exchanges, advisors, or financial planners, are learning to adapt to this brave new world. Issuers, too, are becoming more directly involved in the markets, putting yet more pressure on intermediaries to add value.

Where is it all leading? Unlike fiction, the world has no humanly imaginable end. It continues to change; it continues to evolve. The financial markets exemplify this process of unfolding newness. No one can predict the exact form of future financial markets. On the other hand, the knowledge and tools you have acquired while reading this book have provided you with an excellent guide to what may come.

Mark Twain is said to have remarked, "History does not repeat, but it rhymes." Eventually, perhaps, intelligent agents will wander the World Wide Web, in search of counterparties to a trade, recapitulating in cyberspace the dumb-barter rituals of millennia long gone.

Glossary

A

account agreement   Contract between broker and customer.

accounting risk   Risk arising from accounting practices, errors, or fraud.

accredited investor   An individual with sufficiently high net worth to invest in more speculative types of securities, such as hedge funds and similar unregulated investments.

accumulate   Analyst recommendation to acquire shares of a stock; not as positive as **buy**, more positive than **hold.**

actively managed   Portfolio created according to some decision-making process and intended to outperform a **benchmark**, not simply mirror it.

actual   A physical commodity, such as gold or soybeans.

advance-decline (A-D)   Ratio of stocks going up to those going down, a technical indicator.

advisor (adviser)   Person or entity who is compensated for investment advice or portfolio management.

alpha   Measure of the attractiveness of an investment or the degree to which a security or portfolio is under- or overpriced. Positive alpha values are good; negative values are bad.

alternative investment   Investments intended to help diversify a traditional stock/bond portfolio, such as real estate, hedge funds, or commodities.

American Depository Receipt (ADR)   Security traded on a U.S. exchange that is equivalent to a foreign stock.

American style   Option that can be exercised on any day through expiration. (Compare to **European style.**)

analyst   Market professional who studies companies within a particular industry.

annual rate of return   Standardized measure of an investment's rate of growth.

annualized   Stated as an annual rate of return.

arbitrage Buying and selling of equivalent investments to take advantage of mispricings in different markets.

arithmetic mean Simple numerical average of a set of numbers. (Compare to **geometric mean.**)

articles of incorporation Legal document creating a corporation.

ascending tops Bullish technical indicator showing a series of new highs.

asking price Price at which a seller offers to sell a security.

asset Something that has economic value to someone.

asset allocation Apportionment of a portfolio in various investment categories, especially stocks, bonds, and cash.

asset-backed securities (ABS) Securities backed by a specific set of assets, which are referred to as underlying assets.

Association for Investment Management Research (AIMR) See **CFA Institute.**

authorized shares/stock Number of shares a corporation is allowed to issue, per the articles of incorporation.

average life Average amount of time before maturity of bonds in a portfolio.

B

bailout Saving a company from bankruptcy through loans, guarantees, or other forms of capital.

balance sheet Statement of a corporation's assets and liabilities.

bankruptcy Inability of a corporation or individual to meet financial obligations.

barter Exchange of goods and/or services for other goods and/or services.

basis point One-hundredth of 1 percent.

basis risk Risk deriving from variations in type and quality between a marketable commodity and the specific commodity described in a standard futures contract.

bear market A pronounced downturn in a market.

bearer bond Unregistered bonds with detachable coupons.

behavioral finance Theory of the psychology of investor behavior.

benchmark A performance standard used for valuation purposes.

benchmark risk Risk of selecting an inappropriate benchmark or of failing to match its return.

beta (beta coefficient)   Correlation of a stock with an index such as the S&P 500.

bid   What a buyer is willing to pay for a security.

Black Monday   October 19, 1987, the day of the second great stock market crash of the twentieth century.

Black Tuesday   See **Wall Street Crash of 1929.**

Black-Scholes option pricing model   Theoretical framework for determining value of financial options.

black swan   A rare, largely unexpected event, with negative consequences.

blue chip   Stock of a large-capitalization, financially sound corporation.

board of directors   Individuals elected by shareholders to oversee corporate management.

bond   Long-term debt securities issued by governments and corporations; also used generically to refer to debt of any maturity.

book entry   Proof of securities ownership recorded on an issuer's books, in contrast to issuance of certificates.

book value   Value of a corporation or corporate asset according to accounting conventions.

breakout   Technical indicator of an increase in a security's price range.

budget deficit   Cash-flow problem of a company or a government requiring additional financing.

budget surplus   Excess cash that may be available to a company (or a government) for investing, paying **dividends,** or cutting taxes.

bull market   Market characterized by a pronounced upswing in price level.

bullish   Having a positive view of a market or security.

Buttonwood Agreement (buttonwood tree)   Agreement in 1792, leading to the creation of the New York Stock Exchange.

buy   Analyst recommendation to buy shares in stock. More positive than **accumulate,** less positive than **strong buy.**

buy side   Institutional money managers who buy securities from underwriters and broker/dealers; the buy side includes banks, insurance companies, mutual funds, pension funds, and hedge funds.

buy-write   Investment strategy combining purchase of an asset with sale of a call option on that asset.

buying climax   A frenzy of buying; technical indicator for the end of a rally or bull market.

C

call   An option to buy an asset at a certain price up until (or on) the expiration date.

call market   Market in which individual stocks are traded periodically rather than continuously.

call premium   Price paid or received for a call option.

call price   Price paid for a callable bond when its **call provision** is exercised.

call provision   Right retained by some bond issuers to redeem a bond before maturity.

called away   Said of an underlying asset exercised away from the call writer.

capacity constraint   Size limit for a portfolio investment strategy.

capital   Surplus goods and/or money used to create more goods and/or money.

capital appreciation   See **capital gain.**

capital assets   Long-term assets of a business, consisting of fixed assets (land, buildings, machinery, furniture, etc.) and securities held for over six months.

capital event   A change in the capital structure of a firm resulting from a stock split, corporate merger, spin-off, or similar activity.

capital gain   Increase in the market value of an asset.

capital gains distribution   Distribution of capital gains to investors in a mutual fund.

capital stock   Common stock, or common and preferred stock.

capitalization-weighted   An index whose parts are weighted according to their total **market capitalization.**

cash settlement   Futures contract settled in cash rather than by delivery of **actual** commodity.

catastrophic risk   Financial risk arising from man-made or natural disasters.

caveat emptor   "Let the buyer beware."

CDO   See **collateralized debt obligation.**

CDS   See **credit default swap.**

CFA   Certified financial analyst, a profession credential for investment research specialists on Wall Street.

CFA Institute Professional organization of certified financial analysts, formerly known as Association for Investment Management Research (AIMR).

cheap Underpriced security. (Compare to **rich.**)

chop house An unscrupulous brokerage firm that sells worthless **chop stocks.**

chop stock Worthless stock whose price has been manipulated for use in financial scams.

churning Illegal buying and selling of stocks by a broker for the sole purpose of generating commissions.

classified stock Stock that is divided into classes with different rights.

close(d) corporation Privately held corporation.

closed-end A mutual fund or other investment company with a limited number of shares, often traded in a market.

closed out Forced sale of a portfolio whose value has fallen below a minimum level.

closely held Public corporation controlled by a few shareholders.

collateral Assets that can be used to secure a loan or margin account.

collateralized debt obligation (CDO) A kind of financial instrument that is issued by a special purpose entity (sometimes also referred to as a CDO) and backed ("collateralized") by other financial instruments such as bonds (CBO), mortgages (CMO), or bank loans (CLO).

commission A charge associated with a transaction. Commissions may be set by law or regulation, or they may be negotiable between parties.

Committee on Uniform Security Identification Procedure (CUSIP) A nine-character identification code for North American securities. ISIN is the international equivalent.

common stock Security representing a claim to a portion of the corporation's assets, frequently with voting rights and eligibility to receive dividends.

compounding Earning money by periodic reinvestment of previously earned money.

contingent (deferred) sales charge Sales charge imposed by mutual fund when shares are held less than a minimum number of years.

continuous trading Market in which stocks may trade at any time between the open and close of the market, in contrast to a **call market**, in which stock trades take place periodically.

control stock   A block of stock ownership sufficient to determine outcome of voting in a corporation.

convertible   Bond that may be converted into stock.

corporate bond   Securities representing debt obligations of U.S. corporations.

correction   Term used by technical analysts to describe certain price declines.

cost basis   Amount paid for a security.

country risk   Risk factors unique to investments in a particular country.

coupon (coupon rate)   Percentage of face value of a bond paid annually as interest.

covered call   A call whose writer owns the underlying asset.

CPI-U   A measure of inflation, standing for Consumer Price Index-Urban. Used in calculating value of Treasury Inflation Protection Securities (TIPS).

crash of 1929   Stock market crash, October 29, 1929.

crash of 1987   Stock market crash, October 19, 1987.

credit default swap (CDS)   An agreement in which one party receives a premium for guaranteeing against a default by some other party. Until 2009, the market for CDS was entirely an OTC market with very little transparency.

credit risk   Risk that the borrower will default.

creditor   Lender or bondholder.

creditor hierarchy   Priority of claims in bankruptcy.

critical point   In the theory of complex systems, the point at which a new phenomenon emerges; for example, the emergence of money in systems based on barter.

cumulative voting   Alternative system of shareholder voting that strengthens representation of minority shareholders by allowing them to vote all their shares for a single director.

currency risk   Investment risk due to fluctuations in exchange rates (sometimes extended to include inflation risk).

current yield   Coupon divided by purchase price of a bond, usually expressed as a percentage.

customer accounts   For **SIPC insurance** purposes, brokerage accounts that are owned in different ways (e.g., individually versus jointly with a spouse) are insurable separately up to the full amount provided by law.

cyberspace   The virtual world of computer networks.

D

day order   Buy/sell instructions valid only on the day they are made.

dealer   A firm that sells securities from inventory.

defensive   Investment posture focusing on risk more than on return.

deflation risk   Financial and investment risks arising from widespread shortage of cash and cash equivalents.

delisted   Removal of a stock from an exchange for failure to meet continuing **listing requirements.**

delivery   Transfer of ownership of a commodity as a form of settlement. (Compare to **cash settlement.**)

delta   Sensitivity of an option's price to a small shift in the price of the underlying asset.

depreciation   Lowering of the value of an asset on a corporation's books.

derivative   A security that derives its value from the value of another security, **underlying asset,** or **benchmark.**

descending tops   Bearish technical indicator.

DIAMOND   An index fund based on the Dow Jones Industrial Average, traded on the American Stock Exchange.

diluted   Earnings estimate that takes into account options, convertible debt, and other forms of noncommon stock.

dip   Technical analyst's description of a certain type of price decline.

direct IPO   Initial public offering of a security without the involvement of an underwriter.

director   See **board of directors.**

discount bond (instrument)   A bond or other fixed-income security sold at a discount to face value.

discount broker   Broker offering lower commission costs but fewer services than a **full-service broker.**

discount rate   Rate charged by the Federal Reserve on loans to member banks.

discounted cash flow (DCF) analysis   Analysis of present value of future cash flows.

distributor   Company that sells mutual funds directly to public or via brokers.

diversification   Investing in a broad range of securities to lower risk and/ or enhance return.

dividend   Portion of corporate earnings distributed to shareholders by vote of **board of directors**.

dividend discount model (DDM)   Financial model that analyzes a stock's value in terms of future dividends.

dividend reinvestment program (DRIP)   A way to use **dividend** payments to automatically purchase more shares of a company's stock directly from the company, hence without paying a broker's commission.

DJIA   See **Dow Jones Industrial Average.**

dollar cost averaging   Technique for accumulating securities at lower risk by periodically purchasing equal dollar amounts of a security.

double auction   Simultaneous buying and selling.

double bottom   Bullish technical indicator.

double exempt   Municipal bond whose income is exempt from federal and state taxes.

double top   Bearish technical indicator.

Dow Jones Industrial Average (DJIA)   An index of 30 of the most important, **large-cap stocks** (excluding transportation and utility stocks) traded on the New York Stock Exchange.

DRIP   See **dividend reinvestment program.**

duration   A measure of a bond price's sensitivity to a small change in prevailing interest rates.

dynamic order   A new type of buy or sell order capable of adjusting to evolving market conditions; for example, trading using a **preference profile.**

E

earnings estimate (earnings forecast)   Analysts' predictions of future corporate profitability.

earnings per share (EPS)   Measure of a stock's profitability, either historically (trailing EPS) or prospectively (forecast EPS).

EDGAR project   SEC's system for Electronic Data Gathering, Analysis, and Retrieval of corporate filings.

effective rate (effective annual rate of return)   Yield to maturity.

electronic communications network (ECN)   A term for electronic trading systems that operate without the need for human intermediaries or a physical trading floor.

Elliott Wave   Technical analysis theory of stock market based on Fibonacci numbers.

enhanced indexing   Strategy for outperforming index funds using mathematical models.

EPS   See **earnings per share.**

equivalent taxable yield   The yield on a taxable bond that provides equal income to a particular municipal bond investor.

ETF   **See exchange-traded fund**

Eurodollars   Term for dollars held in foreign banks, mainly in Europe.

Euromarket   Market for bonds outside of the issuer's home country.

Euronext   A European stock exchange; the European side of the NYSE Euronext merger.

European style   Option that can be exercised only on the expiration date.

exchange   A market with significant organizational structure for trading financial instruments and/or commodities.

exchange rate   Rate at which one currency can be bought with another currency.

exchange-traded fund (ETF)   **A fund that trades on a stock exchange**

ex-dividend   No longer eligible for a dividend, because dividend has been announced and payment date scheduled.

ex-dividend date (ex date)   Date that a stock goes **ex-dividend.**

execution   Implementation of a customer order to buy or sell.

exercise   Use by an option holder of the right to buy or sell the underlying asset.

expense ratio   Measure of the costs borne by a mutual fund shareholder.

expiration   Date after which an option loses all value.

exponential weighting   Way of adjusting data to give more importance to more recent measurements.

extrapolating   Making a prediction based on a sample.

extrapolation risk   Risk that the pattern detected in the sample will not continue as expected.

F

face value   The amount of money due on a bond's maturity date; also called **principal amount.**

FASB   See **Financial Accounting Standards Board.**

Fed funds rate   Rate member banks charge each other; the Fed sets a "target" rate.

Federal Home Loan Mortgage Corporation (Freddie Mac)   U.S. government-sponsored, publicly owned corporation, traded on NYSE, that sells **mortgage-backed securities.**

Federal National Mortgage Association (Fannie Mae)   U.S. government-sponsored, publicly owned corporation, traded on NYSE, that sells **mortgage-backed securities.**

Federal Reserve Board   Governing board of the Federal Reserve System, which serves as the central bank of the United States.

fee-based   Euphemism used by financial planners who earn commissions on the products they sell.

fee-only   Financial planners who promise not to accept any commissions from third parties.

Fibonacci number   Element of an infinite sequence that begins 0, 1, 1, 2, 3, 5, 8, and so on. Third and higher numbers are equal to the sum of previous two numbers. Used by some technical analysts who subscribe to the **Elliott Wave** theory.

fiduciary   Someone who has the obligation to look after an investor's financial interests.

Financial Accounting Standards Board (FASB)   Independent self-regulatory body for accounting standards.

financial analyst   See **analyst.**

financial engineering   Creation of financial products, especially derivatives, using math and models.

Financial Industry Regulatory Authority (FINRA)   A "SRO" or self-regulatory organization that helps the SEC discharge its regulatory responsibilities. It is the successor to two previous SROs that operated independently: the NASD and the regulatory arm of the NYSE.

financial market model   A mathematical model of a financial market.

financial planner   Someone who offers to help investors develop an investment plan.

financial ratio   A number, such as earnings per share, used by financial analysts to evaluate a company.

first call date   Earliest date on which a bond can be redeemed by its issuer.

fixed-income securities   Generic term for securities that are essentially standardized IOUs issued by governments and corporations. Also called *debt securities.*

flag   Technical analyst's chart indicating a consolidation within an ongoing uptrend or downtrend.

float   Publicly available stock in a corporation.

floating-rate note   A bond with an interest rate that varies according to some benchmark.

floor broker   A broker who works on the floor of an exchange.

footnotes to financial statement   Explanations of financial details that do not appear on the balance sheet or **P&L.**

forward   A private contract for a future transaction at a currently agreed-upon price.

forward rate   Currency exchange rate for a transaction to be completed at a later date.

401(k)   The most popular type of defined contribution pension plan.

free float   The publicly tradable portion of a company's shares or **market capitalization.**

full-service broker   Broker who offers research and other services, but may charge high commissions.

fully collateralized   A futures contract or account that is 100 percent backed by eligible securities (such as T-bills).

fully hedged   A portfolio that is (theoretically, at least) protected against shifts in the market, interest rates, or other identified risks.

fully invested   A portfolio that has used (almost) all of its cash to buy securities or other assets.

fully valued   A security with a market price as high as, or higher than, a financial analyst believes to be warranted based on **fundamental analysis.**

fund expenses   Management fees and other costs of running a mutual fund.

fund family   A group of mutual funds managed by the same advisor and sold by the same distributor. Also known as a *fund group* or *complex.*

fund of (hedge) funds (FOHF)   An alternative investment that invests in other alternative investment vehicles, typically hedge funds

fundamental analysis   A method for determining the **intrinsic value** of companies.

futures (contract)   Exchange-traded, standardized contracts for the future delivery of an **actual** commodity or for **cash settlement** based on future values of some financial security or index.

G

GAAP   See **generally accepted accounting principles.**

gap   A type of technical chart showing a sudden shift in price, volume, or other variable.

G.A.R.P.   Stands for Global Association of Risk Professionals.

generally accepted accounting principles   Standard accounting practices for analysis and presentation of financial statements and other financial data.

geometric mean   Proportional mean or average value.

geometric return   A time-weighted rate of return.

Goldman Sachs Commodity Index (GSCI)   See **S&P Goldman Sachs Commodity Index.**

good-till-canceled (GTC) order   Order that continues in force until filled or canceled.

Government National Mortgage Association (Ginnie Mae)   Government-sponsored enterprise that issues mortgage-backed securities.

Great Depression   Period of economic stagnation between the crash of '29 and World War II.

Greeks   Numbers representing the sensitivity of an option's price to small changes in certain factors, including price of underlying asset, interest rates, volatility, and time to expiration.

gross federal debt   Federal debt, including interagency debt.

gross profit margin (GPM)   Profit margin based on the cost of raw materials.

growth   An investment approach that strives to identify growth stocks.

growth stock   Stock of a company with growing earnings and/or sales.

H

head and shoulders   A type of technical chart.

hedge fund   An unregulated private investment company available only to qualified investors; or a fund located **offshore.** Originally, the term referred to funds that engaged in **hedging.**

hedging   Purchase or sale of securities to offset an existing securities position. See **fully hedged.**

hidden liquidity Desire to trade that is held back for fear of moving the market.

high-water mark Provision in a hedge fund contract that requires the fund manager to make up any losses before receiving incentive fees.

historical volatility A measure of the historical tendency of a stock's price (or return) to fluctuate.

hold Usually the weakest recommendation an analyst will give a stock. Sometimes, a euphemism for "sell."

horizontal price movement Technical chart.

hostile takeover Purchase of a company by another company, an investor, or a group of investors against the wishes of the company's existing managers and/or board.

hurdle rate A minimum acceptable rate of return for a project or business venture.

hybrid market A market that allows for a choice between automated electronic trading and traditional brokers or specialists.

I

implied volatility A measure of the current tendency of a stock's price to fluctuate, inferred from the price of its most liquid option.

in-the-money An option whose exercise price is better than the market price of the underlying asset.

index A list of stocks, bonds, or other securities whose prices are combined to create a single number that represents the value of its constituents. See **price-weighted, capitalization-weighted.**

index fund A fund designed to track the value of a financial index.

index futures Futures contracts whose values are related to financial indexes.

indicator A measurable financial or economic variable used to analyze securities, markets, and economies.

inflation risk The risk that inflation will erode the value of an investment.

initial margin requirement The minimum proportion of an investment's cost that you must pay.

initial public offering (IPO) First offering of a company's stock to the public.

Instinet An electronic market for institutional investors and brokers.

institutional   Representing a corporation, government, or other organization.

intelligent agent   A computer program that can search for and retrieve information and engage in transactions, such as buying and selling securities, without human intervention.

interest   Money paid to an investor in consideration for a loan of principal.

interest rate risk   The risk that an investment will respond unfavorably to a change in interest rates.

internal rate of return   A measure of return on investment that takes into account both the timing and the amounts of individual cash flows.

internalization   Filling an order to buy stock from a firm's own inventory.

interpolating   Plugging in estimates of in-between values of data based on sample data.

interpolation risk   Risk that in-between values of data will not conform to the pattern of sample data.

interview with management   Part of an analyst's evaluation of a company.

intrinsic value   A measure of the true value of an asset, as opposed to its current market price.

invest   Put capital to use in a productive enterprise.

investment objective   What an investor or portfolio manager hopes to accomplish.

IPO   See **initial public offering.**

IPO juice   Use of IPOs to artificially inflate a fund's performance.

IRA   Individual retirement account.

issue date   The date on which a security is available to be sold.

issued shares   Amount of a security that has been sold.

issuers   The corporate or governmental entities issuing particular securities.

J

junk bond   A bond of extremely low credit quality.

K

Kondratieff Wave   A hypothetical roughly 60-year economic activity cycle.

L

large-cap stocks   Stocks with a total market value greater than $10 billion.

leverage   Magnification of investment gains or losses (e.g., by using debt or options).

liabilities   Financial obligations.

LIBOR   See **London Interbank Offered Rate.**

LIBOR-plus   Use of LIBOR as benchmark to define a floating interest rate (e.g., LIBOR +2%).

limit order   Order to buy or sell stock at the **limit price** or better.

limit price   A price point that triggers a **limit order.** For a purchase, the limit price is the most you will pay; for a sale, it is the minimum you will accept.

liquidation   Sale of a bankrupt company's assets.

liquidity   Presence of buyers and sellers for a security.

liquidity risk   The chance that there won't be buyers or sellers.

listing requirements   Minimum standards set by an exchange for the right to be traded.

load   Sales charge of a mutual fund, expressed as percent; funds with sales charges are *load funds.*

London Interbank Offered Rate (LIBOR)   Interest rate that major international banks dealing in **Eurodollars** charge each other.

M

majority shareholder   Owner of more than 50 percent of the voting shares of a corporation.

managed (futures) account   A professionally managed individual portfolio of futures.

management fee   Fee for portfolio management services, typically a percentage of assets under management, assessed daily for mutual funds, quarterly for most other accounts.

margin   Cash used to purchase investments with supplemental credit supplied by broker; subject to terms of a margin account agreement.

margin call   Broker's demand for additional cash or securities to maintain a minimum margin.

marginable   Securities eligible for margin according to rules established by the Federal Reserve.

marginal income tax rate   Highest tax rate paid by an investor (i.e., tax paid on last dollar earned).

mark to market   Calculate the market value of a position; in a margin account, used to ensure that minimum margin is maintained.

market capitalization   Also called *market cap* or *market value,* the total value of outstanding stock, equal to share price multiplied by number of shares **outstanding.**

market maker   Broker responsible for maintaining a liquid, orderly market in a stock.

market order   Instruction to buy or sell stock at best available price; the most common type of order.

market risk   Risk arising from the inherent volatility of financial markets.

market timer   Investor who trades actively, trying to anticipate relatively short-term price movements.

market value   See **market capitalization.**

markup   Surcharge by an over-the-counter (OTC) securities dealer.

maturity date   Date that principal gets repaid.

median   For a set with an odd number of elements, it is the middle number in terms of size; if the set has an even number of elements, it is the average of the two numbers closest to the middle.

merger   Combination of two or more corporations into a single corporate entity.

microcap   Stocks with a **market capitalization** below $300 million.

mid cap   Stocks with a **market capitalization** between $200 billion and $10 billion.

minority shareholder   Shareholder with less than a controlling interest.

MITT (Market Index Term Trust)   An exchange-traded derivative that guarantees investors a degree of principal protection along with an index-determined level of return.

mode   The most frequent value in a data set. For example, in the set {2, 2, 2, 3, 3, 4,}, the mode is 2.

model   Set of mathematical formulas or computer programs representing a part of the world; a set of computer programs designed to simulate some aspect of the financial markets.

model risk   Risk that a model misrepresents reality.

modern portfolio theory (MPT)   The standard theory for building an optimally efficient market portfolio.

money market account   A securities account invested in money market instruments.

money market instrument   Short-term debt obligations such as Treasury bills, certificates of deposit, and commercial paper.

money-weighted rate of return   A measure of investment performance that takes into account how much money the investor actually had at risk during each period in question.

mortgage-backed security (MBS)   Debt obligation backed by pools of mortgages.

mortgage pool   A collection of mortgages held as collateral for **mortgage-backed securities.**

moving average   An average recalculated in each new period by throwing out the oldest value of the previous period and adding in the latest value.

MPD (Market Participation Deposit)   Similar to MITTs, but sold over the counter by J.P. Morgan's private bank.

muni   Tax-exempt municipal securities

mutual fund   A registered investment company, especially an open-end fund.

mutual fund group   See **fund family.**

N

naked call   A call written by someone who does not own the underlying asset.

National Association of Securities Dealers Automated Quotation (Nasdaq)   The largest screen-based equity exchange in the U.S. **Market makers** maintain liquidity and orderly trading.

net asset value (NAV)   The value at which an open-end fund may be redeemed on a daily basis; also, the value at which a no-load fund may be purchased.

New York Stock Exchange (NYSE)   The largest stock market in terms of market capitalization. Part of NYSE Euronext.

no-action letter   SEC ruling that a proposed product or service will be permitted.

no-load (fund, stock)   A fund or stock that is sold without a commission or sales charge.

noise   Apparently random fluctuations in price or other data.

nominal dollars   The dollar value of an investment, without adjustment for inflation.

number cruncher   Someone who uses, builds, or tests financial models; a **quant.**

O

off-balance-sheet investments   Those investments that are not recorded as assets or liabilities on a company's balance sheet; frequently they appear as **footnotes to the financial statement.**

officers (and directors)   Corporate management and insiders.

offshore   Refers to investment companies and securities outside of a nation's regulatory domain.

OID   See **original issue discount.**

online broker   A brokerage firm that is set up for trading via remote computer terminal.

onshore   Investment company located domestically.

open-end   The most popular form of mutual fund, quoted in terms of **net asset value.**

open interest   Total number of futures or options contracts for a particular exchange, commodity, and contract month.

open-outcry market   The system of buying and selling securities on an exchange using continuous trading.

opening price   The first price at which a stock trades during the day; on the NYSE, opening and closing prices are set by a call market.

operational risk   Risk inherent in the operation of a business.

option   Right to buy or sell an underlying asset under certain conditions (e.g., at set prices, times).

ordinary income   Any income taxable at the ordinary income rate.

original issue discount (OID)   Equivalent of interest for a security (such as a Treasury bill or zero-coupon bond) that is issued at a discount to face value. Different from bonds that trade at discount or premium to par, reflecting capital gains or losses.

out-of-the-money   An option whose exercise price is unattractive compared to the market price.

outstanding   In terms of shares, those owned by investors.

over the counter (OTC)   Anything not done on an exchange.

overpriced   Overvalued.

owners' equity   From an accounting standpoint, the portion of a company's assets belonging to shareholders.

ownership interest   What a stockholder's stock represents.

P

P&L   Statement of profit and loss; part of a company's financial statement.

paper profit   An increase in unrealized capital gains.

par value   Value shown on the face of a bond.

pass-through   Tax status of investment companies that allows them to pass taxable income and capital gains to the ultimate investors, who are individually responsible for paying taxes on those earnings.

passively managed   A portfolio created to duplicate an index or other benchmark.

pay date   Date on which a dividend or other payment is received.

payment for order flow   Often-criticized practice of brokers compensating other brokers who send them orders for a given stock, which may not give the customer the best price.

performance   See **return on investment, time-weighted return.**

performance presentation standards (PPS)   Standards developed by the Association for Investment Management Research describing how investment performance should be measured, verified, and reported to customers and prospects.

PIPEs   See **Private Investments in Public Equity.**

political risk   Investment risk arising from political turmoil.

positive yield curve   The "normal" state of affairs, in which longer maturities offer greater yields.

preemptive right   Right of existing shareholders to purchase a new issue of the company's shares, at a discount, before they are offered to the general public.

preferred stock   Stock that offers some bond-like characteristics such as income and safety of principal.

premium bond   Bond trading above par because its coupon rate is higher than the prevailing rate of interest.

present value   The value of a future stream of cash flows, at some assumed discount rate.

presidential election cycle (PEC)   A four-year stock market cycle in which returns are higher *on average* and risk is lower *on average* during the second half of a president's term.

price target   The price that a Wall Street analyst forecasts for a stock.

price-weighted   An index weighted to account for the price of its components.

primary dealer   A bond dealer allowed to deal directly with the Federal Reserve Bank of New York.

primary market   The market for newly issued securities, including IPOs.

prime rate   Interest rate charged by commercial banks to top corporate customers and used (like LIBOR) as a benchmark against which other rates are calculated.

principal amount   See **face value.**

Private Investments in Public Equity (PIPE)   An alternate source of financing for public companies.

private placement   A privately issued security.

privately held corporation   A corporation owned privately; shares are not available to the public.

profit and loss (P&L) statement   Financial statement showing the result of operations for a specific time period.

promoter   Person involved in organizing and financing a public corporation.

prospectus   Legal document describing a securities offering and disclosing risk.

proxy   Someone to whom you give the right to vote your shares at a shareholder meeting.

public company   Company that issues stock to the public.

public offering   Sale of stock to the public. (Compare to **private placement.**)

put bond   Bond that can be sold back to issuer at par on a certain date or dates prior to maturity.

put-call parity   Relationship between prices of puts and calls allowing you to derive a fair price for one if you know a fair price for the other—as long as they have the same strike price and expiration date.

put option (puts)   Option giving the holder the right—but not the obligation—to sell an underlying asset at a specified price on specified date(s).

Q

quant   A mathematician who works in financial markets.

quantitative analysis   Mathematical modeling of the financial markets, used in portfolio management, especially by institutions and hedge funds.

quantitative model   See **model.**

R

raise cash   Sell securities.

real dollars   Dollars adjusted for inflation. (Compare to **nominal dollars.**)

realized capital gains   Capital gains counted after a sale; subject to capital gains tax.

recommended list   The list of stocks that a brokerage firm's analysts like.

record date   Date used to determine shareholders entitled to a dividend; also called *date of record.*

refunding   Issuance of new bonds to pay off older bonds with a higher interest rate.

registration   Process of filing required information with regulators, especially the SEC.

Regulation A   SEC regulation allowing simplified registration for small issues.

Regulation T   Federal Reserve regulation governing margin requirements.

regulatory risk   Investment risk attributable to actual or potential changes in regulations.

reinvestment   Taking cash proceeds from an investment and redeploying them in another investment.

reinvestment/rollover risk   Risk that the new investment will not be as good as the old one; especially relevant when bonds are called in a lower-interest-rate environment.

remargin   Contribute new funds to a margin account to bring it up to minimum requirements.

reorganized   Corporate restructuring, undertaken either to avoid bankruptcy or to emerge from bankruptcy without liquidation of assets.

replicate   Duplicate a portfolio or one of its characteristics, especially **performance.**

resistance level   Technical indicator.

return   Gain or loss on investment; rate of return.

return on equity (ROE)   Measure of return on a corporate shareholder's equity.

return on investment (ROI) Measure of return as proportion of original investment.

return relative Factor used in compounding multiperiod returns.

revenue Sales.

rich Overvalued according to some financial analysis, **indicator,** or **model.**

rights offering Kind of dividend in which existing shareholders are granted options.

rising bottom Bullish technical indicator.

risk Chance that your investment objectives won't be met in your time frame.

risk arbitrage Buying and selling of stock in companies involved in mergers and acquisitions.

risk-free rate Overnight rate of interest on highest-credit-quality instrument.

rocket scientist See **quant.**

rule of 72 Rule for determining how quickly money doubles at various rates of compounding.

rule 144A Type of illiquid security.

S

safe harbor Rules for determining whether an investment must be registered with SEC.

Samurai bonds Foreign bonds issued in Japan, denominated in yen.

scrip Document representing a fractional share; scrip dividends are sometimes paid instead of cash dividends by companies that need to conserve cash.

SEC Securities and Exchange Commission.

secondary market Market in which already issued securities trade.

sector a broad classification of companies, which may be further divided into subsector, industry group, and industry.

securitization a process in which a collection of assets is used to create a set of related securities that are sold to investors.

security Paper or computerized document expressing financial claims to an issuer's assets; abstractly, the claim itself, independent of the form in which it is represented.

selective Street jargon for being cautious about committing additional capital to the stock market.

self-regulatory organization (SRO)   Organizations, such as FINRA, and in prior years, NYSE and NASD, allowed to regulate their members under the supervision of the SEC.

sell discipline   Conditions under which a security would be sold.

sell side   Underwriters and brokers/dealers who sell securities to retail and institutional investors.

selling climax   Technical indicator of the end of a bear market.

senior debt   Debt that must be paid before any others are paid.

sensitivity   Measure of the degree of responsiveness of some financial variable to a small change in some market condition. In mathematical terms, a partial derivative or partial difference.

sentiment   Market psychology.

Series 7   An exam that brokers must take and pass before they can be licensed to sell securities.

share   Unit of stock.

share repurchase (stock buyback)   Corporate initiative to lower the amount of stock **issued** and **outstanding.**

shareholder   Person or corporate entity that owns stock.

short sale   Sale of securities not owned by the seller; used by investors anticipating a decline in the value of a security, or as a hedge.

short-short rule   Old rule making it difficult for mutual funds to trade actively by imposing tax penalties for too much short-term trading (no longer in effect).

simple return   Arithmetic return.

since inception   Measure of investment performance since a fund opened.

sinking fund provisions   Requirement that a certain portion of debt be called according to a schedule.

SIPC   Securities Investor Protection Corporation, a nonprofit organization set up by Act of Congress in 1970 to insure the securities and cash in the customer accounts of SEC registered broker/dealers.

SIPC insurance   Insurance of up to $500,000 in securities, including up to $100,000 in cash equivalents per **customer** against failure of a member firm.

small-cap   Stocks with a **market capitalization** between $300 million and $2 billion.

smoothed   Mathematical technique for eliminating random price fluctuations.

socially responsible investing   Taking social or moral factors into account as part of the investment process.

soft dollars   Frequently questioned practice allowing institutional investors to pay for various services by directing their commissions to a particular broker.

soybean complex   Futures on soybeans, soybean oil, and soybean meal.

SPAC   See **Special Purchase Acquisition Corporation.**

SPDRs   S&P 500 Depository Receipts, an exchange-traded index product developed and traded by the American Stock Exchange (AMEX).

S&P Goldman Sachs Commodity Index (S&P GSCI)   A broad commodity index.

Special-purchase acquisition company (SPAC)   A publicly traded company created to identify and acquire or merge with an existing private company.

special situation   A stock believed to be undervalued because of an unusual set of circumstances.

specialist   NYSE member responsible for making a market in a particular stock.

spin-off   Breaking off part of a company and making it into a separate company with its own stock.

split   See **stock split.**

spot market   Commodities market with immediate payment and delivery of goods.

spread   The difference between bid and asked price.

SRO   See **self-regulatory organization.**

stagflation   Combination of economic stagnation and inflation.

Standard & Poor's 500 Index (S&P 500 Index)   Index of large capitalization stocks.

statutory voting   Standard means of electing a corporate board of directors. (Compare to **cumulative voting.**)

stepping up of the basis   Reestablishment of the cost basis for tax purposes.

stock   Securities representing an ownership interest in a corporation's undivided assets.

stock buyback (share repurchase)   Repurchase of shares by a corporation to reduce the number of shares outstanding, thus making remaining shares more valuable.

stock certificate   A physical document showing the legal owner of some number of shares of stock.

stock dividend   Payment to shareholders from corporate earnings, usually in the form of cash or shares.

stock exchange   A market with a physical trading floor where buyers and sellers trade securities, especially equities.

stock fund   A mutual fund that invests primarily in stock.

stock loan   Lending stock to a short seller in return for some payment; brokers frequently obtain the right to lend out securities held in a margin account.

stock options   Options to purchase stock.

stock split   Change in the per-share value of a stock by issuance of new shares to shareholders, in proportion to the number of shares held. For example, a 2-for-1 split doubles the number of shares. A reverse split is used to reduce the number of shares outstanding, thus raising the price of individual shares.

stockholders' equity   See **owners' equity.**

stop order   An order triggered when stock reaches a predefined price, called the *stop price.* Similar to a **limit order,** except that the trade can occur above or below the trigger price.

story stock   Stock of a new company without real earnings, but with an exciting idea, opportunity, or technology.

straddle   Combination of put and call options with the same strike price, usually close to the current market value.

strangle   Combination of call and put options with different strike prices, each option being out of the money.

strip   Separation by brokers of a debt security into *corpus* (principal) and coupons to be sold separately as **zero-coupon bonds.**

strong buy   Highest recommendation by a Wall Street analyst for a stock.

subordinated debt   Debt that is lower in the **creditor hierarchy** than other, more senior, debt.

subscription rights   Opportunity to purchase (subscribe to) additional shares of stock at a discount from the public offering price.

subsidiary   A corporation or other business entity that is controlled by another business entity.

sucker's rally   The months immediately following the crash of 1929, when stocks gave a false start.

survivor bias   Distortion of average performance by excluding funds closed due to poor performance.

swap   A two-party transaction involving securities, currencies, commodities, or other assets in conformance to a precise set of rules called a **swap agreement.**

swap agreement   Rules governing swap transaction, standardized by International Swaps and Derivatives Association (ISDA).

swaption   Derivative combining features of both swaps and options.

T

takeover   Purchase of a controlling interest in a corporation, frequently resulting in a merger.

tax deferral vehicle   IRA, 401(k), variable annuity, or other mechanism for deferring taxes.

tax lot   A security holding that can be treated as a single unit for tax purposes; must have been purchased at the same price on the same date.

tax risk   Investment risk arising from uncertain tax status or from changes in tax code.

taxable muni   Municipal bond whose income is not exempt from federal tax.

technical analysis   Intuitive, graphic approach to understanding what the market, or a particular stock, is doing. Includes many charting techniques.

ticker   A device for transmitting lists of stock or other prices over telegraph lines. See **ticker symbol.**

ticker symbol   Abbreviations for stocks, mutual funds, and other securities; frequently used in newspaper financial tables and by electronic financial information services.

time value   Value of an option over and above its **intrinsic value,** attributable to the chance that it may gain in intrinsic value before expiration.

time-weighted rate of return   Measure of investment performance in an average period.

time-weighted return   See **time-weighted rate of return.**

top-down approach   Investment approach that begins with and emphasizes global factors in making investment decisions.

tracking error   Deviation of a portfolio from an index or other benchmark.

transformed   Applied a mathematical formula to smooth or otherwise change data for purposes of analysis.

TreasuryDirect   A web-based facility for buying Treasury securities directly from the U.S. government.

Treasury Inflation Protection Securities (TIPS)   U.S. Treasury bonds that pay interest and principal; linked to a measure of consumer inflation.

treasury stock   Shares issued but still owned by the corporation. See **outstanding shares, issued shares.**

trend is your friend   A maxim of technical analysts who urge investors not to "fight the tape."

trendline   A line drawn by technical analysts that is intended to reveal the market's trend.

triple witching Friday   Simultaneous expiration of index futures, index options, and options on index futures.

turnover   The rate at which a stock, portfolio, or market is traded; expressed as an annual percentage.

12b-1 fee   Fee charged by mutual fund distributors; used to compensate fund salespeople, although may also be used to defray marketing and advertising expenses.

U

underlying asset   The asset an option holder has the right to buy (call) or sell (put).

underpriced   Undervalued or **cheap.** (Compare to **rich.**)

underwriters   Investment bankers who help issuers sell securities to the public and make private placements.

unrealized capital gain   Increase in value of a security or portfolio that has not been converted into cash, in which case it would no longer be a **paper profit** and taxes might be due.

V

value   An investment approach based on fundamental analysis.

variable annuity   An investment product that uses insurance features to gain tax-deferred status.

virtual private network   A network that piggybacks a public network (e.g., the Internet) but uses software to simulate a private network.

VIX (Volatility Index)   A measure of the **implied volatility** of the S&P 500, considered a fear gauge. A higher value is correlated with a nervous market.

volatility   A measure of how much the price of a security moves around its mean, or average, value; more generally, the tendency of security prices to fluctuate.

volume   Number of shares or other units of a security bought and sold; the dollar value is called the *dollar volume.*

voting stock   Stock that comes with voting rights

W

Wall Street Crash of 1929   October 24–30, 1929, the days of the first great crash of the twentieth century.

warrants   Long-term equity options.

WEBS (World Equity Benchmark Shares)   Index funds based on Morgan Stanley Capital International Equity Indexes.

World Wide Web   Part of the Internet accessible through web-browsing software.

wrap account   Brokerage account that charges a management fee in lieu of commissions.

Y

Yankee bonds   A bond denominated in U.S. dollars and issued in the U.S. by a foreign issuer.

yield   One of several measures of return, particularly for fixed-income securities.

yield curve   Graph showing the relationship between yield and time to maturity.

yield to call   A measure of the return on a bond, assuming it is called on its **call date.**

yield to maturity   A measure of the return on a bond, assuming that it is held until maturity.

Z

zero-coupon bond   Bond purchased at discount, paying par at maturity.

zero-sum game   A situation ("game") in which money changes pockets but no value is created.

Index